D0866465

Anthology
of Contemporary
Latin American
Literature
1960–1984

Anthology
of Contemporary
Latin American
Literature
1960–1984

Edited by
Barry J. Luby
and
Wayne H. Finke

Rutherford • Madison • Teaneck
Fairleigh Dickinson University Press
London and Toronto: Associated University Presses

HOUSTON PUBLIC LIBRARY

R0157398535
HUM

© 1986 by Associated University Presses, Inc.

Associated University Presses
440 Forsgate Drive
Cranbury, NJ 08512

Associated University Presses
25 Sicilian Avenue
London WC1A 2QH, England

Associated University Presses
2133 Royal Windsor Drive
Unit 1
Mississauga, Ontario
Canada L5J 1K5

'NDEXED IN _BCL 3rd + R.A. 14thed_

The paper used in this publication meets the
requirements of the American National Standard
for Permanence of Paper for Printed
Library Materials Z39.48-1984.

Library of Congress Cataloging-in-Publication Data

Anthology of contemporary Latin American literature.

Includes index.
1. Spanish American literature—20th century—
Translations into English.   2. English literature—
Translations from Spanish.   I. Luby, Barry J.
II. Finke, Wayne.
PQ7087.E5A56   1986   860'.9'98   85-47789
ISBN 0-8386-3255-6 (alk. paper)

Printed in the United States of America

CONTENTS

PREFACE

This anthology of contemporary Latin American literature is an outgrowth of the Winter 1980 issue of *The Literary Review,* which was devoted to Latin American writing of the sixties and seventies.[1] In that issue our aim was to present to the English-reading public selected poetry and prose of both prominent and less well-known writers whose work seemed best to illustrate the "coming of age" of Latin American literature. All of the works selected for *The Literary Review* were appearing in English for the first time.

The issue was well received, both critically and on the part of readers of *The Review,* and we have had many requests to expand that brief collection into a broader anthology. The editors of *The Literary Review* have kindly consented to our basing this anthology on that Winter 1980 issue. Many of the works included there are reprinted here, and much of our introductory essay is incorporated into this introduction.

In this work we have been able to enlarge the collection not only in the number of works, but also, and more important, in the number of Latin American countries represented. Readers of *The Literary Review* will find two major changes in the present anthology: first, the inclusion of many Cuban writers—Robert Lima was the only Cuban represented in *The Review*—and second, a far wider range in style, particularly in the poetry.

It is unfortunate that because of space limitations José Kozer, and Severo Sarduy of Cuba were not among our *Literary Review* selections, and we hope that their inclusion here, along with many other Cuban writers, will give them the attention they deserve. Concerning the poetry, we ourselves feel that far too much emphasis was given to political poetry; while we have certainly incorporated some of the best of it into this anthology—how could we eliminate Martínez Ortega's "Words Before the End"?—we have endeavored to present the gamut of poetic style that is to be found in Latin American literature in the last two decades.

ACKNOWLEDGMENTS

Jorge Enrique ADOUM:
"Ecuador"—*Informe personal sobre el asunto* (Madrid: Joaquín Giménez-Arnau, 1973), pp. 89–90.
"Fait Divers"—ibid., pp. 93–94.

Laureano ALBAN:
"Self-Portrait"—*Autorretratos y transfiguraciones* (León: CSIC, 1982), pp. 13–15.
"It is the hour of the sea"—*El viaje interminable* (San José: Ed. Costa Rica, 1983), pp. 19–21.

Gustavo ALVAREZ GARDEAZABAL:
"Donaldo Arrieta"—*La boba y el Buda* (Bogotá: Instituto Colobiano de Cultura, 1973), pp. 13–18.

Reinaldo ARENAS:
"Epigram"—(Unpublished).
"A Story"—(Unpublished).
"Marx's Contribution"—(Unpublished).
"Processional"—(Unpublished).
"Will to Live by Manifestation"—(Unpublished).

Homero ARIDJIS:
"Chapultepec"—*Construir la muerte* (Mexico: Joaquín Mortiz, 1982), p. 34.
"Encounter"—ibid., p. 17.

Juan José ARREOLA:
"The Switchman"—*Cuentos* (Havana: Casa de las Américas, 1969), pp. 66–76.

Carlos Germán BELLI:
"Segregation #1"—*Antología de la poesía hispanoamericana*, ed. S. Baciu (Albany: SUNY, 1974), Vol. 2, p. 1006.
"Bah, Vitamin A"—*Sextinas y otros poemas* (Santiago: Ed. Universitaria, 1970), p. 23.
"Antibiotic Miscellany"—ibid., p. 29.
"Sextain of Kid and Lulu"—ibid., pp. 41–42.
"Looking at my little daughters"—ibid., pp. 53–54.

Adolfo Bioy casares:
"The First Class Passenger"—*Historias fantásticas* (Buenos Aires: Emecé, 1974), pp. 230–32.

Alfredo Bryce Echenique:
"In Paracas with Jimmy"—*Todos los cuentos* (Lima: Mosca Azul, 1979), pp. 23–33.

Cecilia Bustamante:
"Vocabulary"—*Discernimiento* (Mexico: Premiá, 1982), p. 15.
"Dawn"—*El nombre de las cosas*, 2nd ed. (San Salvador: Cuscaclan, 1978), p. 42.

Jesús Cabel:
"Last Vision of the Promised Land" (sections 3, 5, 6)—(Unpublished).

César Emilio Cantoni:
"Absent Man"—*Antología poética hispanoamericana* (La Plata: Fondo Editorial Bonairense, 1978), pp. 86–88.
"In Memoriam Dylan Thomas"—ibid., pp. 88–91.

Ernesto Cardenal:
"Psalm 36"—*Poesía escogida* (Barcelona: Barral, 1974), pp. 47–48.
"The Heavy Drops"—*Epigramas* (Barcelona: Tusquets, 1978), p. 59.
"The Rains of May"—ibid., p. 50.
"Our Poems"—ibid., p. 48.
"The National Guard"—ibid., p. 50.
"Girl"—ibid., p. 49.
"You were alone"—*Poesía de uso* (Buenos Aires: El Cid Editor, 1979), p. 60.
"I have distributed clandestine leaflets"—*Antología* (San José: EDUCA, 1972), p. 47.
"Epitaph for Joaquín Pasos"—ibid., pp. 51–52.
"Epitaph for the Tomb of Adolfo Baez Bone"—ibid., pp. 49–50.

Magolo Cardenas:
"But What If I Liked the Panchos"—*Pauta* (Revista de la Universidad Autónoma de México), vol. 7, no.5 (Jan.–Mar. 1983), pp. 29–33.

Jorge Carrera Andrade:
"Final Invocation"—*Poesía última* (New York: Las Américas, 1968), pp. 103–5.

Héctor Carreto:
"Sleeping Beauty's Request"—*La espada de San Jorge* (Mexico: Premiá, 1983), pp. 46–47.
"Vanity of Vanities"—ibid., p. 15.
"St. George's Sword"—ibid., pp. 49–50.
"St. Theresa's Confession"—ibid., p. 48.

Aida CARTAGENA PORTALATIN:
"Colita"—*Tablero* (Santo Domingo: Ed. Taller, 1978), pp. 13–17.

Carlos CASTRO SAAVEDRA:
"Unemployed"—*Obra selecta* (Manizales: A. Nariño, 1962), p. 321.

Antonio CISNEROS:
"Your Head of an Italian Archangel"—*El libro de Dios y los húngaros* (Lima: Libre-I Ed., 1978), pp. 39–44.
"Café on Martirok Utja"—ibid., p. 27.
"Sunday in St. Christina's of Budapest"—ibid., pp. 15–16.

Juan Gustavo COBO BORDA:
"Errant Dwelling"—*Roncando al sol como una foca en los Galápagos* (Bogotá: Colcultura, 1982), p. 12.
"In the Hotel of Your Soul"—ibid., p. 17.
"I Lost My Life?"—*Todos los poetas son santos e irán al cielo* (Buenos Aires: El Imaginero, 1983), p. 13.

Humberto COSTANTINI:
"Immortality"—*Cuestiones con la vida* (Buenos Aires: Ed. Katún, 1982), p. 39.
"Gardel"—ibid., p. 83.
"Algebra"—ibid., p. 108.

Pablo Antonio CUADRA:
"The Calabash Tree"—*Siete árboles contra el atardecer* (Caracas: Ed. de la Presidencia de la República, 1980), pp. 79–85.
"The Indian and the Violin"—*Nueva Estafeta*, no. 40 (Madrid: Mar. 1982), pp. 4–6.

Belkis CUZA MALE:
"Pandora's Box"—(unpublished).
"Oh, My Rimbaud"—(unpublished).
"Women Don't Die on the Front Lines"—(unpublished).
"The Nature of Life"—(unpublished).
"Order of the Day"—(unpublished).

Roque DALTON:
"Poet in Jail"—*Poesía hispanoamericana 1960–1970*, ed. Saúl Yurkievich (Mexico, n.p., 1972), pp. 167–69.
"The Art of Poetry"—*Poesía* (Havana: Casa de las Américas, 1980), p. 59.
"The Sea"—*Antología poética hispanoamericana actual* (Buenos Aires: Ed. Platense, 1973), p. 147.

Matilde DAVIU:
"Ophelia's Transfiguration"—*Maithuna* (Caracas: Monte Avila, 1978), pp. 27–42.

Gerardo DENIZ:
"Crisis"—*Gatuperio* (Mexico: Fondo de Cultura, 1978), pp. 13–15.
"Tolerance"—ibid., p. 29.
"Infancies I"—ibid., p. 61.
"It was I"—ibid., p. 109.

Rodrigo DIAZ-PEREZ:
"Edgar Allan Poe's Room"—*Antología poética hispanoamericana* (La Plata:
Fondo Editorial Bonairense, 1978), pp. 151–52.
"Cycles"—ibid., p. 154.
"Fleeting Afternoon"—ibid., p. 155.
"Memories"—ibid., pp. 155–56.

Julieta DOBLES:
"Caged Laurel"—(unpublished).
"Music in the Caress"—*Hora de lejanías* (San José: Ed. Costa Rica, 1982),
pp. 23–24.
"Thanatos in Stone"—ibid., pp. 42–45.

Roberto ECHAVARREN:
"For Tonight"—(unpublished).
"Oyster Bar"—(unpublished).

David ESCOBAR GALINDO:
"We"—*Canciones para el Album de Perséfone* (San Salvador: Ministerio de
Educación, 1982), pp. 13–14.
"Myths and Flowers"—ibid., pp. 18–19.
"Dawn"—ibid., p. 20.
"We Sprout Beneath the Soil"—ibid., p. 28.
"Oblivion"—ibid., p. 29.
"If I Walk"—ibid., p. 35.
"Suddenly Our life"—ibid., p. 41.
"In the Light"—ibid., p. 58.

Mauricio FERNANDEZ:
"Moon"—(unpublished).

Pablo Armando FERNANDEZ:
"I Hope You Awaken"—*Suite para Maruja* (Havana: priv. printing, 1978),
pp. 9–12.
"My Wife"—ibid., pp. 13–14.
"In a Low Voice"—ibid., p. 15.

Rosario FERRE:
"Catalina"—*Sin Nombre*, vol. 10, no. 2 (July–Sept. 1979), pp. 49–50.
"To the Cavalier of the Rose"—ibid., pp. 50–51.
"Epithalamium"—ibid., p. 51.

Hjalmar FLAX:
"Our Father"—*Tiempo adverso* (Barcelona: Victor Pozanco Editor, 1982), p. 95.
"In Tow"—ibid., p. 61.
"Advanced Course"—ibid., pp. 100–101.
"Love or Cult"—ibid., p. 45.
"Carpe"—ibid., p. 12.
"Departed of Spring"—ibid., p. 47.

Blanca GARNICA:
"The Letter"—*Antología de la poesía boliviana* (La Paz: Ed. los Amigos del Libro, 1977), p. 572.
"I Do Not Know"—ibid., p. 573.

Freddy GATÓN ARCE:
"Monday, October 10   I"—*Estos días de Tíbar* (Santo Domingo: Ed. La poesía sorprendida, 1983), p. 12.
"Monday, October 10   II"—ibid., p. 13.
"Sunday, July 31"—ibid., pp. 26–27.

Juan GELMAN:
"Maria the Servant Girl"—*Antología básica contemporánea de la poesía iberoamericana* (Buenos Aires: Ediciones Nereo, 1978), vol. 2, pp. 198–99.
"Medals"—*Antología consultada de la joven poesía argentina* (Buenos Aires: Fabril, 1968), p. 63.
"History"—ibid., p. 60.
"Poetic Art"—ibid., pp. 58–59.
"Nun on the Bus"—ibid., p. 59.

Mempo GIARDINELLI:
"Revolution on a Bicycle"—*La revolución en bicicleta* (Barcelona: Editorial Pomaire, 1980, pp. 95–105.

Alberto GIRRI:
"Lyric"—*Obra poética* (Buenos Aires: Corregidor, 1972), Vol. II, p. 52.
"Quartet in F Minor"—ibid., p. 38.
"Poem from Kierkegaard"—ibid., p. 91.

Margot GLANTZ:
"Genealogies"—*Las genealogías* (Mexico: Martín Casillas, 1983), pp. 15–19.

Isaac GOLDEMBERG:
"Body of Love"—(unpublished).
"Origins"—(unpublished).
"The Beehive and Its Roots"—(unpublished).

14   Acknowledgments

Alexis GOMEZ ROSA:
    "High Quality, Ltd."—(unpublished).

Jorge GUITART:
    "Buffalo"—(unpublished).
    "The Book and the Child"—(unpublished).
    "The Fire"—(unpublished).
    "Something Neither Vivid Nor Concrete"'(unpublished).

Oscar HAHN:
    "'Photograph"—*Arte de morir* (Santiago: Nascimento, 1979), p. 35.
    "Doves of Peace"—ibid., p. 19.
    "The Last Supper"—ibid., p. 41.
    "Ocular Landscape"—ibid., p. 55.
    "Canis Familiaris"—ibid., p. 59.
    "Comet"—*Mal de amor* (Santiago: Ganymedes, 1981), pp. 79–80.
    "Top Sheet"—ibid., pp. 73–74.

Javier HERAUD:
    "I Do Not Laugh at Death"—*Poemas* (Havana: Casa de las Américas,
    1967), pp. 77–81.

Francisco HERNANDEZ:
    "#8"—*Mar de fondo* (Mexico: Joaquín Mortiz, 1983), p. 70.
    "#11"—ibid., p. 73.
    "#17"—ibid., p. 79.
    "#18"—ibid., p. 80.

Francisco HINOJOSA:
    "The Green Lagoon"—(unpublished).
    "The Dandy"—(unpublished).

David HUERTA:
    "Nine Years Later"—*Versión* (Mexico: Fondo de Cultura, 1978), pp. 44–
    47.

Jorge IBARGUENGOITIA:
    "What Became of Pampa Hash?"—*La ley de Herodes y otros cuentos*
    (Mexico: Joaquín Mortiz, 1967), pp. 33–41.

Roberto JUARROZ:
    "I Do Not Hold God"—*Poesía vertical* (Caracas: Monte Avila, 1976),
    p. 296.
    "Life"—*Poesía vertical. Antología mayor* (Buenos Aires: Ediciones Carlos
    Lohlé, 1978), p. 76.
    "There Are Few Whole Deaths"—ibid., p. 172.
    "You Have No Name"—ibid., p. 28.
    "Vertical Poetry   I"—*Octava poesía vertical* (Buenos Aires: Carlos Lohlé,
    1984), p. 7.

"Vertical Poetry II"—ibid., p. 20.
"Vertical Poetry XIII"—ibid., p. 8.
"Vertical Poetry XVII"—ibid., p. 23.
"Vertical Poetry LXXII"—ibid., p. 69.

José KOZER:
"You Remember, Sylvia"—*Bajo este cien* (Mexico: Fondo de Cultura, 1983), p. 32.
"This Is the Book of Psalms"—ibid., p. 27.
"Reminiscences of Grandmother at Home"—ibid., p. 29.
"A Franz Kafka Triptych"—ibid., pp. 129–131.
"St. Francis of Assisi"—ibid., p. 136.

Pedro LASTRA:
"Later We Will Talk of Our Youth"—*Cuaderno de la doble vida* (Santiago: Ediciones del Cameleón, 1984), p. 7.
"Drawbridges"—ibid., p. 8.
"Etude"—ibid., p. 9.
"The Dissolving of Memory"—*Noticias del extranjero* (Mexico: Premiá, 1979), pp. 45–46.

Enrique LIHN:
"'The Sewer"—*A partir de Manhattan* (Santiago: Ganymedes, 1979) pp. 11–12.
"Elizabeth Rawsthorne"—ibid., pp. 13–14.
"Old Woman in the Subway"—ibid., p. 19.
"Edward Hopper"—ibid., p. 25.
"Reality and Memory"—ibid., p. 65.
"Nineteenth Century Lions"—ibid., p. 51.

Robert LIMA:
"Peripatetic"—(unpublished).
"Persona"—(unpublished).
"Lorca"—(unpublished).
"Sillustani"—(unpublished).
"Civil War: Spain"—(unpublished).
"Child Ecology"—(unpublished).

Juan LISCANO:
"III"—*Fundaciones* (Caracas: Monte Avila, 1981), p. 15.
"IV"—ibid., p. 17.
"VIII"—ibid., p. 25.
"XIII"—ibid., p. 35.
"XVII"—ibid., p. 43.

José LOPEZ-HEREDUA:
"The Retiree"—*Milagro en el Bronx y otros cuentos* (New York: Las Américas, 1984), pp. 31–39.

Jaime MANRIQUE:
"Ode to a Hummingbird"—(unpublished).

Juan Carlos MARTINEZ:
"Luis and Clara"—(unpublished).
"I am by nature"—(unpublished).
"My Country"—(unpublished).
"The Plastic Flower"—(unpublished).

Aristides MARTINEZ ORTEGA:
"Words Before the End"—*A manera de protesta* (Panama: Ed. Tareas, 1964), pp. 37–39.

Pedro MIR:
"The Hurricane Neruda"—*El huracán Neruda* (Santo Domingo: Ediciones de Taller, 1975), pp. 7–11.

Eduardo MITRE:
"You tread"—*Morada* (Caracas: Monte Avila, 1975), p. 15.
"From Dark to Light"—ibid., p. 33.
"For it is law"—ibid., p. 66.
"Twins"—ibid., p. 35.
"It was"—ibid., p. 38.
"In ter mit tenT"—ibid., p. 38.

Alvaro MUTIS:
"Caravansary"—*Caravansary* (Mexico: Fondo de Cultura, 1981), pp. 15–20.
"Invocatiion"—ibid., pp. 21–22.

Luis Rogelio NOGUERAS:
"Poetic Material"—*Imitación de la vida* (Havana: Casa de las Américas, 1981), p. 31.
"Non Omnia Morior"—ibid., p. 43.
"There is a poem"—ibid., p. 104.
"Time Maude"—ibid., p. 76.
"Love the Wild Swan"—ibid., p. 34.

Julio ORTEGA:
"Syllables and Lines" (excerpts)—*Rituales* (Lima: Mosca Azul, 1976), pp. 14, 18.

José Emilio PACHECO:
"First Degree Equation with One Variable"—*Los trabajos del mar* (Mexico: Era, 1983), p. 57.
"The '&' "—ibid., pp. 46–47.
"In Defense of Anonymity"—ibid., pp. 72–75.

Juana Rosa PITA:
"Stroke the Back"—*Manual de magia* (Barcelona: El Ambito Literario, 1979), p. 46.
"The Height of Letters"—*Las cartas y las horas* (Washington: Ed. Solar, 1977), p. 35.
"Walls Like Tears"—*Mar entre rejas* (Washington: Ed. Solar, 1977), p. 44.

Alberto Luis PONZO:
"History"—*Ocupaciones y límites* (Buenos Aires: Fundación Argentina para la Poesía, 1982), p. 74.
"Powers"—ibid., p. 74.
"Languages"—ibid., p. 75.
"Inscriptions"—ibid., p. 75.
"Tutmosis"—ibid., p. 112.
"According to a Native American"—(unpublished).
"Eleven O'Clock"—(unpublished).

Ulises PRIETO:
"I come painting dreams"—*Los mascarones de oliva* (Miami: Ediciones Universal, 1978), pp. 13–14.
"Red and Black"—ibid., p. 18.
"I'm on the Road to Varadero"—ibid., p. 63.
"Miami"—ibid., pp. 16–17.
"Before the Coastline"—ibid., p. 50.

Lilliana RAMOS:
"The Island's Economy"—*Sin Nombre*, vol. 10, no. 2 (July–Sept. 1979), pp. 57–59.
"The Golden Age"—ibid., pp. 59–61.

Julio Ramón RIBEYRO:
"The Double"—*La palabra del mudo* (Lima: Ed. Milla Batres, 1972), pp. 119–25.
"Vultures Without Feathers"—ibid., pp. 5–16.

Gonzalo ROJAS:
"Love Letter"—*Zona Franca* (Caracas), 3a época, año 5, nos. 32–33 (Nov. 1982–Feb. 1983), p. 8.
"Lost Port"—*Oscuro* (Caracas: Monte Avila, 1977), p. 177.
"The Farce"—(unpublished).
"Sunday Daimon"—(unpublished).
"Visiting Professor"—(unpublished).

Juan SANCHEZ PELAEZ:
"The Circle Opens"—*Rasgos comunes* (Caracas: Monte Avila, 1975), p. 9.
"Today"—ibid., p. 16.
"VI"—*Por cuál causa o nostalgia* (Caracas: Fundarte, 1981), p. 29.

"VIII"—ibid., p. 35.
"XIII"—ibid., p. 49.

Severo SARDUY:
  "Entering you"—*Daiquirí* (Tenerife: Poéticas, 1980), p. 6.
  "The shiny greased piston"—ibid., p. 7.
  "Neither voice preceded by echo"—ibid., p. 8.
  "Though you oiled the threshold"—ibid., p. 9.

Javier SOLOGUREN:
  "love and bodies"—(unpublished).
  "in you"—(unpublished).
  "celebration"—(unpublished).

Guillermo SUCRE:
  "Whitebodied Lady"—*En el verano cada palabra respira en el verano* (Buenos Aires: Alfa, 1976), p. 17.
  "Not Keeping Silent"—ibid., p. 67.
  "Atlantic April"—ibid., p. 83.

David UNGER:
  "The Limbo Bar"—(unpublished).
  "Hotel Canada"—(unpublished).
  "Insomnia"—(unpublished).

Armando F. VALLADARES:
  "Reality"—*El corazón con que vivo* (Miami: Ediciones Universal, 1980), pp. 135–40.

Carmen VALLE:
  "With the Psychiatrist"—*Glenn Miller y varias vidas después* (Mexico: Premiá, 1983), p. 11.
  "Hide 'n' Seek"—ibid., p. 23.
  "Days"—ibid., p. 31.
  "When We Live"—*Un poco de lo no dicho* (New York: Ed. La Ceiba, 1980), p. 10.

Aníbal YARYURA-TOBÍAS:
  "The Voyeur"—(unpublished).

Saúl YURKIEVICH:
  "Spaces"—*Hispamérica*, vol. 4, no. 10 (April, 1975), pp. 65–68.
  "Perhaps Pursuit"—(unpublished).

Raúl ZURITA:
  "Pastorale"—*Anteparaíso* (Santiago: Editores Asociados, 1982), p. 95.
  "Pastorale of Chile"—ibid., p. 103.
  "Splendor in the Wind"—ibid., p. 159.
  "Utopias"—ibid., p. 41.

INTRODUCTION

Politically conscious and active intellectuals in Latin America can generally be divided into two groups according to the extent of their knowledge of politics and political theory. The first of these groups comprises writers who are well versed in political theory, active politically, and totally aware of the reasons for their commitment. In the second category can be found writers who, though equally committed, readily acknowledge the paucity of their knowledge of political philosophy. The two groups are in no way incompatible, however, if one accepts the realities of Latin American politics: logic plays a far less significant role than in the rest of the world's politics, which themselves are none too logical. As Salvador de Madariaga stated, "The American writer is immersed in the problems of the Americas. He does not have to invent problems. He lives them. They are at the very core of his meditation."[2]

Creative intellectuals in Latin America are no different from artists in other countries; essentially, all circulate in an arena of pure intuition, of vital but not always definable energy. Julio Cortázar describes this world of intuition:

> . . . . having my imagination as a pilot and as my sail, passions, desires, love—all that vibrates around me—the street, houses, women and children, cats, crabs, and poplars; elements which create in each place in the world a perfect moment of life, fleetingly beautiful and endlessly dramatic.[3]

Cortázar, Carlos Fuentes, and Mario Vargas Llosa are really saying the same thing as Ortega y Gasset; that it is impossible for a writer to divorce himself from his circumstances. The battle, for the Latin American writer, is a moral struggle. He is fighting for the freedom of his countrymen and for social justice that would enable each man to exert some control not only over his own personal destiny but over the fate of his country as well.

To the Latin American intellectual, the intricacies of politics are part of his very essence, a cornerstone of his personality. This does not mean that the writer limits himself to the realities about him; he is not a journalist. But in the world he creates are to be found similarities, sometimes mirror images, that enable his readers to understand better the vagaries of their real-world predicament as Latin Americans.

What accounts for the fact that in Latin American literature today, whether the works openly treat of politics or seemingly have no political theme, most artists are actively engaged in the struggle for independence, while in North America and Europe political matters are left for the most part to the political scientists, the futurists, the planners? The Latin American writer may belong to no political movement, may know very little of political philosophy; yet both his works and his personal life are polemic, with personal and national independence being the overriding theme. Julio Cortázar believes this unique involvement is attributable to "the dropping of masks."[4] For centuries, Cortázar states, both the Latin Americans and their foreign oppressors clung to certain illusions—masks—that they have now abandoned. On the one hand, the foreign oppressors have dropped their pretense of being protector, teacher, benefactor in the economic, technological, and intellectual growth of Latin America and now do not hide their real intent: "the face that wishes to dominate and exploit."[5] The intellectuals, on the other hand, have ceased to believe in the myth that foreign cultural infiltration and foreign economic exploitation would promote the development of Latin America. Having set aside the myth, a strong reaction can at times be seen, as in Martinez Ortega's "Words Before the End"—one of the selections included here. There is a real anger in his scathing, sardonic "listen to me Uncle Sam... We are content with...the Army boys/sweeping over us in jeeps to the rhythm of chewing gum," and in his bitter comments on foreign aid:

> The world so aided by you cannot forget
> that you bring relief to our catastrophes with your surplus.

This same reaction is expressed, though with somewhat less biting irony, by Gonzalo Rojas in "Visiting Professor" when he describes

> those airy six foot female beauties
> of white hide whom I teach here in
> the Angloworld for good pay with the pardon
> of Socrates. . . .

Nor has it been only the intellectuals who have "dropped their masks." As Che Guevara stated, "These people have said 'That's enough,' and have begun to walk."[6] Not that the unmasking was a complete one, in the case of some intellectuals; nor was it an easy one. No longer could they remain detached. Instead they were obliged to plunge their whole being into the thick of combat. Cortázar describes this new world of the intellectual in Latin America thus:

If at one time one could be a great writer without participating in the immediate historical destiny of man, now one cannot write without that participation which is his responsibility and duty; and only those works which unite them, although they be purely imaginative, although they invent the infinite, playful gamut of which the poet and novelist are capable, only they will contain in some inexplicable way that trembling, that presence, that atmosphere which makes them recognizable and necessary, which awakens in the reader a feeling of contact and closeness.[7]

It becomes clear, then, that political involvement is in no way incompatible with the artist's role as creator. His work simply encompasses the historical and political realities of his time. A change in style may become apparent, as in the case of poetry.

In the evolution of Latin American poetry there appear to be three phases. Originally, poets tended to treat of highly personal subjects and of their own individual sentiments. The poems of Juan Sánchez Peláez included in this anthology are typical of this early phase, as is the work of Oscar Hahn of Chile, particularly his beautiful "Photograph": "Someone developed the negative of your death." In the second stage of its evolution, Latin American poetry threw off the personal, the lyric, and turned to polemical writing, and in the final step toward their "coming of age," Spanish American poets began to speak more of universal things.

Yet, as we point out below, a phenomenon peculiar to Hispanic American literature is that there really are no clear-cut "periods." We find not only poets who write in the early, highly personal and often lyrical style and at the same time who turn their pens, as John Milton put it, "to the work of the left hand"—i.e., to polemics—but also poets whose work encompasses all three phases of the development. Three of Robert Lima's poems included here—"Peripatetic," "Lorca," and "Sillustani," for example—are characteristic of the earliest phase, yet in "Long Live Death" and "Child Ecology" Lima writes of political and social matters. Similarly, in the work of Carlos Germán Belli one finds both lyric romanticism, in "Poem" and in "Why Have They Moved Me?", as well as political protest, albeit mild, in "Segregation N. 1."

The protest intensifies in Hjalmar Flax's witty and iconoclastic "Our Father"

> For thine is the country,
> the power and the dollars,
> for ever and ever,
> amen.

It reaches a fierce though optimistic peak in Ernesto Cardenal's "Psalm 36." Representative of the solely polemical stage is Ortega's "Words Before the End," where no trace can be found of the lyric, the personal, the feeling of hope; only biting satire and hatred for "Uncle Sam" remain. In "Reality,"

Armando Valladares of Cuba expresses just as intense feeling against the "Soviet-made guns" that fire at a gigantic fish (symbol of Christianity), but turns his political tale into a highly original allegory when the fish "took flight in a dazzling white dove that fluttered . . . and set off toward the infinite sky in a ray of love." Then Valladares quickly reverts to the role of polemicist; the international dignitaries who witnessed the killing of the fish participated in a kind of mock communion, their goblets filled with the blood of the fish, and they offered toasts "with the bubbling lymph."

Typical of the third stage in the evolution of Latin American poetry is the universal philosophy of Carmen Valle:

> We make ourselves
> tourists of life
> and we end paying
> the fare
> in monthly installments
> for all eternity.

A lovely haiku by Alexis Gómez is another example of the third stage:

> Little seahorse,
> In which shipwreck
> did you lose your whinny?

José Emilio Pacheco's "First Degree Equation" is still another example of this third phase. Though full of gloom—"the last voice of nature in the valley" had a choice: "two forms of asphyxiation"—the poem nevertheless treats of a global problem and expresses universal despair. Nostalgia and anguish, sentiments common to all peoples, are beautifully expressed in Pedro Lastra's "Later We Will Talk of Our Youth" and "Drawbridges," and in Roque Dalton's "The Art of Poetry":

> Anguish exists.
>
> Man uses his old disasters like a mirror.

Social awareness marks the Latin American literature of the sixties through the early eighties. Many Marxist critics err in their assumption that true social awareness, especially empathy with the oppressed masses, cannot belong to the bourgeois intellectual. They imply, wrongly, that to understand the oppressed one must actually be one of the oppressed. Not so. In Latin America, Carlos Fuentes's *Where the Air Is Clear*, Mario Vargas Llosa's "The Time of the Hero," and Gabriel García Márquez's *No One Writes to the Colonel and Other Short Stories* are proof of this. All the authors are members of the bourgeoisie, and all have managed to present cross sections of reality while guarding their own creative beauty and style. These were among the works that created a virtual revolution in the habits and tastes of the Latin American public. No longer did readers feel obliged to import their cultural fare; a whole native literature had emerged that they could devour.

Cortázar cites an example of this revolution in reading tastes and habits. His own novel, *The Book of Manuel,* was published in Buenos Aires in 1973 and had its usual outlet in the typical bourgeois bookstores. Within a week, however, the book became available on newsstands—which regularly cater to the average Latin American reader who rarely enters a bookstore.[8] Masks had been shed, barriers had been broken; the Latin American public could sense the unity in feeling and purpose among all Latins—commoner, bourgeois, intellectual—a shared pride in their own culture and a renewed impetus toward national independence.

The Latin American writer is no longer divorced from his work; readers no longer accept (or at any rate, accept far less readily than in the past) a book that merely touches or satisfies them. Now, the writer himself has become one with them in their struggle against oppression, dictatorship, fascism, and economic and cultural exploitation. Many writers in the more-underdeveloped countries, such as Paraguay and Uruguay, do not even write for themselves; they use the collective "we." Such is the case with Eduardo Galeano, who, in addition to his political essays, is best known as the editor of *Crisis,* the Buenos Aires monthly review devoted to politics, culture, and literature that is one of the best publications of its kind in Latin America today. Galeano's book *Canción de nosotros,* like *Crisis,* is concerned with identifying aspects of Latin American social and political history that define its present state of grave crisis. As David William Foster points out in his review of Galeano's book, the "nosotros" ("we") of the title refers to his fellow Uruguayans, whom he portrays in their futile and tragic attempt to survive in the current political and economic situation of Uruguay.[9] Galeano concurs, but would substitute his own country, Uruguay, in Vargas Llosa's rhetorical question: "At what moment did Peru screw itself?"[10]

Thus, the Latin American intellectual is no longer found in the context of a social elite. In light of the phenomena of mass communication, educational reforms, and the waves of European immigration to Latin America in the last fifty years, there is a tendency now for writers to spring from the middle and lower economic classes of society, and they address the masses at large. While writers of past centuries were fairly rooted to their local conditions, contemporary authors have enjoyed the advantage of extensive travel. Their creations, therefore, while immersed in local problems, have a much more universal accent; though the writer depicts social injustices, repression, and the like in his homeland, these problems are not exclusive to the nations of Spanish America. For example, the hypocrisy of Juan

Gelman's "That night men and women perfumed themselves" in "Maria the Servant Girl," included in this anthology, is certainly a universal trait. Matilde Daviú manages to create, in "Ofelia's Transfiguration," the perennial Latin American atmosphere of police state tactics and class consciousness, but she adds the universal dimension of the town's prostitute being the only one in town good enough to help the victims of police brutality and also has her Ofelia "the only one who dreams in this town of forgetfulness." "Colita," Aida Cartagena Portalatín's wry story of the little black girl who refuses to be kept inside her guardian's "music box" to perform, as she believes black girls should, also juxtaposes a Spanish American landscape to a world-wide problem.

This universality of theme is perhaps best exemplified by Juan José Arreola's masterpiece, "The Switchman." It is strange that this classic, Kafkaesque tale of the human condition had never appeared (to our knowledge) in English until *The Literary Review* introduced it. We are reprinting it here not only for its own worth as a great story, but to dispel once and for all the notion that Hispanic American literature is limited to regional themes.

The writer in Latin America today forms a part of what we can call *literatura comprometida*, that is, literature of social commitment. The continued economic hardships, social injustice, and political tyranny and instability are so much a part of Latin American life that no writer can fail to address these issues. Common to all Latin American works are

> themes of revolt and repression, absence of human and civil rights, culture of dependence, poverty and exploitation, possession and dispossession of land, venality of judges and bureaucrats, isolation and defenselessness of peasants caught between warring factions [and] tyranny of ignorance and superstition.[11]

As Kurt Levy expressed it:

> What has gradually changed in the course of these fifty years is the emphasis, taking into account stylistic nuances, structural awareness and human focus. We have seen how, thematically and ambientally, the overwhelming force of nature gave way to collective social problems which in turn yielded increasingly to the dilemma of the individual conscience whatever his milieu.[12]

Saúl Yurkievich treats magnificently of these problems of the individual in poems included here—"Spaces" and "Perhaps Pursuit."

José Revueltas notes that after World War II a North American imperialist system was created in which world powers have come to be subordinated to North American politics. The hegemony of imperialism within the capitalist field can be said to have reached its apex.[13] The Soviet Union did not wait long to set up its own imperialist sphere. This imperialism has had an impact on Latin American literature in the dichotomy that is to be found between the works emanating from the more-developed countries and those coming from the less-developed nations. While in the smaller, less-developed nations the themes of the writers tend to reflect the notion of oppression and enslavement by the ruling regime, as well as an anti-Yankee (and anti–Soviet Union) sentiment, more-developed nations—Argentina and Venezuela in particular—manifest in their literatures the pervasive themes of social relationships and economic pressures upon the individual. Adolfo Bioy Casares's "The First Class Passenger" is an interesting illustration of this point. The protagonist rues "the good old days" before the merging of first- and second-class passengers (i.e., citizens) into one common group. The Argentinian psychiatrist-writer Aníbal Yarura-Tobías is dealing also with a problem of the human condition. His slyly humorous tale of Georgi, "a charming Peeping Tom who had ejaculated over the most important window sills" of his town, is full of psychological insights that have no national boundaries. Georgi might have been in Poland or China when he thought: "What a pleasure to be there in the middle of the action without being there."

The impact of economics on the daily life of Latin American citizens accounts for its reflection in so much of the literature. Poverty, disease, social inequalities are still part of the Latin American landscape despite revolutions, military dictatorships, foreign aid, and foreign intervention. In light of this economic—and consequently political and social—morass, many Latin American writers have adopted more decisive stances—cynicism and even nihilism—as a way of putting an end to the seemingly unending conditions of poverty and subsistence living. Alvaro Mutis, in "Caravansery," tells us: "We will always go farther than our most secret hope, but in the opposite direction." And Jesús Cabel states, "Clawing at the earth is nothing new to us." Julio Ortega adds: "This world tells lies living in its wounded law."

The plight of indigenous peoples in some countries with heavy native populations (Mexico, Peru, Bolivia) is yet another concern of many Latin American writers. Carlos Fuentes in particular has portrayed Aztec myths and the *angst* of contemporary life. In Mexico today, it should be noted, more than half the population is of Indian blood. Commenting on the indigenous element in Latin American literature, Salvador de Madariaga states:

As to race, in Hispanic America there are the Indian and the Negro. But the Indian, in many cases, and the Negro always have been Hispanic Americans by virtue of three centuries of culture, with the result that it is not possible to simplify what is a very complicated matter.[14]

Two other factors in the "coming of age" of Hispanic American literature can be elaborated here. The first is the influence of immigration. Focal points or receptors of immigrants in large numbers, such as Argentina, Uruguay, Chile and Cuba, have helped to give a less Latin American and more universal perspective to much of the literature. Jewish immigration has certainly had an impact in universalizing Hispanic American writing in the works of Margo Glantz of Mexico and especially in the output of José Kozer. The second factor, ironically, is the impact of emigration—either the voluntary departure from his homeland of the Peruvian Julio Ramón Ribeyro, for example, or the enforced exile of many Latin Americans for political "offenses": Mempo Giardinelli from Argentina or Rodrigo Díaz-Pérez from Paraguay.

Turning first to Ribeyro, who has for some time lived in France, there is magnificent blending of Hispano American and French styles. In "Vultures Without Feathers," Riveyro gives us a splendid bit of local color from his native Peru, yet there is a strong Gallic flavor that evokes the naturalism of Zola. In "The Banquet," which, because it has already appeared in print in English, we have not been able to include in this collection, he depicts a very decidedly Latin American political atmosphere and spices it with the irony of Maupassant. "The Double," we feel, is a masterpiece. Here, Ribeyro abandons his Latin American past altogether and presents a splendid tale of suspense. "Each of us has a double who lives in the Antipodes," states the narrator, who then proceeds to become obsessed with finding his own double. The story is highly original—the reader has no feeling of *déjà-vu*—yet upon reading it we find that somehow Ribeyro has recalled for us Balzac's *Peau de Chagrin* and even the works of Edgar Allan Poe.

The enforced exile brought about by the Cuban revolution has had tremendous repercussions on many Cuban writers, though the impact has been a less happy one than the change in Ribeyro's style. Nostalgia and a sense of displacement and betrayal mark virtually all of the works by Cuban exiles included here. Ulises Prieto grieves for his homeland as "From the South a breeze arrives/blowing cruelly upon my wound," and he pays homage to the Miami that took the refugees in "With our bile as baggage."

It is in the poetry of José Kozer, however, that the sense of exile is brought to its height. Not only does Kozer lament that he himself was forced to leave his homeland, but he also evokes the memory of his father, and his father's father, Jews who had been forced to leave theirs. "He's Still Alive, Grown Small My Father" recalls his father's "host of charred brothers in Poland." One of Kozer's best poems, we feel, is "Remember, Sylvia," in which he tells of his father who had

> . . . to emigrate, poor Papa (from Odesssa to Vienna,
> Rome, Istanbul, Quebec, Ottawa, New York.
> He would reach Havana as a document and five passports . . .

Not all of Kozer's poems reflect a sense of exile. Indeed, many of his best are delightful dioramas of his Jewish inheritance set down in the streets of Havana. In "General Cleaning," not included here but well worth seeking out,[15] he wryly contrasts his pious mother's preparations for the Sabbath as "three sweet young Cuban women shook the ass off a song in the streets." Kozer's versatility is apparent in some of his later poems, e.g., "A Franz Kafka Triptych," which contains the magnificent line: "By having no clairvoyance he came to know the future."

Certainly not all Cuban writers reflect a sense of exile of their works. Juana Rosa Pita's "The Height of Letters," for example, contains the beautiful image of poetry resulting "from the irrational rite of filling inkwells with blood." Furthermore, many Cuban writers—Pablo Armando Fernández and Luis Nogueras, in this anthology—are still in Cuba. The impact of the Cuban Revolution, as Jorge Rodríguez Padrón points out,[16] has nevertheless produced a deep, psychological "mutation" in that nation's writers.

To sum up, the literary panorama of present-day Latin America presents a tapestry of works that tend to focus on the external realities—political, social, and economic—bearing down upon the individual, whether he lives in the larger, mechanized metropolis or in a small town or village. Because of the great distances separating the twenty-one Latin American nations and ourselves, North Americans sometimes fail to achieve a proper perspective regarding the immensity of the problems beleaguering the citizens of both the developed and underdeveloped countries to the south. Much of the vast geographical expanse that is Central and South America, as well as the Caribbean, has yet to be conquered by man and his technology.

The structure of Latin American society has changed little over the generations, in spite of the casting off of the yoke of Spanish colonialism. Henri Thiers' famous dictum, *"Plus ça change, plus c'est la même chose,"* adequately sums up the state of affairs in Latin America, where oligarchical rule continues to be the recognized pattern of government.

Another characteristic of these countries, already mentioned but worth elaborating upon, is the condition of instability, both political and economic, which appears as a chronic ailment, injurious to the health if not threatening the survival itself of the Latin American nations. Given the scarcity of goods and products, serious unemployment, great disparities of wealth and poverty, and severe inflation, one ought not be surprised at the bleak panorama of those caught in the web. The resulting dejection and frustration grind upon the citizen daily, eroding his strength and pushing him toward the lethargy of helplessness and indifference.

This is not to say that all works of social protest are bitter and full of frustration. In his story "In Paracas with Jimmy," Alfredo Bryce Echenique does indeed describe the exploitation of the workers, represented here by the narrator's father, and the wide gulf between the rich and the poor. Yet, the author tempers his social protest with a beautiful description of a boy's love and admiration for his father.

These are the realities of contemporary Latin American society, and from these realities grew the themes of the Hispanic American literature of the sixties through the early eighties.

To end this introduction, it seems appropriate to consider the roots of today's literature. In Latin America, narrative writing began with the short stories of Jorge Luis Borges in the 1940s. The novel appears later, about 1947, "with its forceful development taking place in the early fifties."[17] It was not until the 1960s, however, that Spanish American literature burst into prominence among readers in the non-Spanish-speaking world. Of course, there had long been a small but faithful public of specialists and *aficionados*, particularly for the works of Borges. The new level of awareness, however, was an entirely different matter. Many people during this period found themselves interested in Spanish America as a result of reading its literature, rather than the reverse. This reader reaction is highly significant, since many earlier works were merely romantic, picturesque, and exotic and lacked any real aesthetic originality. This new phenomenon, the surge of interest in Latin American literature, can be explained by the fact that published works show more originality in form and content than in the period prior to 1960. No longer is the literature "derived;" no longer does it feel the need to emulate foreign sources. It holds its own as an indigenous body of literature.

Quantitatively and qualitatively, then, new writers have risen to international acclaim: Carlos Fuentes, Gabriel García Márquez, Mario Vargas Llosa, to mention only a few. And rightly so, for their works have substance and merit. Three significant writers are primarily responsible for this renaissance, for the renewed enthusiasm: the novelist Miguel Angel Asturias, Jorge Luis Borges with his short stories, and the poet Pablo Neruda; all of whom have written prolifically and well. Asturias was awarded the Nobel Prize in 1967 for his works rendering in fictional form the myths and problems of his native Guatemala. Borges, always a great storyteller, confined himself mainly to short fiction but had vast influence because of his originality. Neruda, considered the greatest modern, Latin American poet, also won the Nobel Prize. His service in the diplomatic corps of Chile took him to Europe, North America, and Asia, and his experiences served to enrich his work and give it a more universal expression. These writers' careers began in the 1920s. In an in-between generation, Juan Rulfo and Julio Cortázar constitute a similar pair. Rulfo was known for mythologizing the reality of rural Mexico and the Mexicans. "Anacleto Morones" abounds in the lore of the Mexican peasant, yet the excellence of the tale lies in Rulfo's ability to add other dimensions to it. (Because the story has since been published in English, we cannot include it in this anthology; we are pleased to state, however, that *The Literary Review* was the first to offer it in English translation.) Cortázar, on the other hand, broke the longstanding stylistic pattern of Latin American literature by altogether eliminating the regionalistic factor. Ribeyro, with "The Double," is clearly his heritor.

Wide international interest in Hispanic American prose and poetry brought into print many studies of the literature of individual countries. This anthology attempts to avoid the regionalism and to look at Spanish American literature as a whole during the period of the 1960s through the early 1980s. The diversity of styles and tendencies may strike the European or North American reader, but as Federico de Onís points out:

> One of the most constant notes of American literature is the fact, repeated over the generations, of the coexistence of tendencies and schools which in Europe are chronologically successive and which would be at the same time incompatible.[18]

Concerning the criteria for selecting the authors included in this anthology, or for omitting some very prominent Latin American writers, the first criterion was to include only original translations into English. This of course accounts for the omission of Borges, for example, whose works have been completely translated. It explains also the inclusion of lesser-known works of famous writers, their well-known pieces having already been translated and included in many anthologies. We are in fact quite proud to publish even works that have not yet appeared in print in Spanish! We felt it worthwhile to provide the reader with the less-familiar works of prominent writers such as Adolfo Bioy Casares, José Arreola, and Julio Ribeyro. Indeed, in reference to the last two, we consider both "The Switchman" and "The Double" to be masterfully written stories that, might never have been widely available had the former not been included in *The Literary Review* and the latter presented in this anthology.

Although we make no claim to have included here all Latin American writers whose work ought to be accessible to readers of English, we have endeavored to present a cross-section of Latin American literature from the sixties through the early eighties and hope that readers will go on to explore for themselves a literature that has indeed "come of age."

Barry J. Luby
Wayne H. Finke

Notes

1. *The Literary Review,* Winter 1980, vol. 23, no. 2.

2. Salvador de Madariaga, *Presente y porvenir de Hispanoamérica y otros ensayos* (Buenos Aires: Ed. Sudamericana, 1959), 568.

3. Julio Cortázar, "Politics and the Intellectual in Latin America," *Books Abroad,* 50 (1976), 533.

4. Ibid., 534.

5. Cortázar, "Politics."

6. Ibid., 535.

7. Cortázar, "Politics."

8. Ibid., 536.

9. David William Foster, review of *Canción de nosotros*, *Books Abroad*, 50 (1976), 607.

10. Eduardo Galeano, *Canción de nosotros* (Buenos Aires: Ed. Sudamericana, 1975), quoted by Foster, *Canción*, 607.

11. Ramón Layera, "The Latin American Theater of Social Protest and Denunciation," in *Hispanic Literatures: Literature and Politics*, ed. J. Cruz Mendizábal (Indiana, Pennsylvania: Indiana University of Pennsylvania, 8/9 October 1976), 277.

12. Kurt Levy, "The Contemporary Hispanic-American Novel: Its Relevance to Society," *Latin American Literature*, 3, no. 5 (1974), 18.

13. José Revueltas, "América Latina: Literatura del Tercer Mundo," in *Panorama actual de la literatura latinoamericana* (Madrid: Fundamentos, 1971), 307.

14. Madariaga, *Presente y porvenir*, 509.

15. José Kozer, *The Ark Upon the Number*, trans. Ammiel Alcalay, Cross Cultural Review Chapbook 28 (Merrick, New York: Cross Cultural Communications, 1982), 9.

16. Jorge Rodríguez Padrón, "Poesía hispanoamericana: Breve introducción de urgencia." An expanded version of this essay is to appear as the prologue of an anthology of Latin American poetry entitled *Puerta Lateral*, to be published by Espasa Calpe, Colección Austral.

17. Jorge Ayora, "The Ideas of Modern and Spanish American Fiction," *Latin American Literary Review*, 2, no. 4 (Spring–Summer 1974), 89.

18. Federico de Onís, *La poesía iberoamericana* (n.d.), 155.

B. J. L.
W. H. F.

Anthology
of Contemporary
Latin American
Literature
1960–1984

JORGE ENRIQUE ADOUM (Ambato, Ecuador, 1926) is a poet and writer who directed the publication *Casa de la Cultura Ecuatoriana* and lived in Africa, India, Japan and China. Presently he works for UNESCO in Paris. His published verse includes *Bitter Ecuador (Ecuador amargo), Notebooks of the Land (Cuadernos de la tierra)* and *Personal Report on the Situation (Informe personal sobre la situación).* As a critic he has published *Essays (Ensayos).*

Ecuador

I. Geography

It is an unreal country limited by itself,
divided by an imaginary line
and yet carved out in concrete at the foot of the pyramid.
If not, how could the foreign woman be photographed
astride my homeland like on a mirror,
the line just below her sex
and on the back: "Greetings from the center of the world."
(Children, large skeleton-like eyes
surrounded, and an indian weeping
mountains of centuries behind a burro)

II. Memory

The soul cavitied, that passageway aches in
the root's nerve, and I, Pavlov's dog, in a leap
sit beside the doorway of the tin-shop
(there it was always during the day) to sniff about the street
on which I returned and they follow beating me.
When one has no homeland yet save
for that incurable sadness beneath one's pride,
the homeland is the pocket of memory from which
I extract this: throngs of indians in the drunkenness
of the mass and flailed with kicks on Sunday afternoon,
the cemetery where I accompanied so many school
mates to review principles of law: this,
pieces of an old animal, this suffices me, I reconstruct
integrally the torrid patriotic Paleolithic folkloric,
the tanners of the republic, the daily clay
where we slip pleasantly. (You too, little dinosaur

bone, your ankle by which you are tied to
me, monstrous quartering, and your other ankle
by which you are bound, for I am your exile).
And the song with which they lull the victim
so that he dies without uttering a word
and with which they torment the dog
in order to see how his member swells erect.
Willingly. Just for the experiment.

Fait Divers

rita
       (we were supposed to meet on Friday
we still wanted our presence after so many nights
when love interrupted its study like another barricade
the only September barricade)
                    is Spanish but not very much so
she makes love without incurring the Spanish folly of marrying
though this perhaps comes from her mother
(she has left me waiting   something must have happened to her
although at my age a retired dynamiter one is not superstitious
there is rather a certain objective pessimism for human beings)
and she has no phone   I never learned what happens
in the clandestine midnights of the others
what happens   rita   when I envy you because you sleep with
       yourself
(besides   all things considered   why is anything going to occur
                        on Friday the thirteenth
and not on Tuesday the eleventh*   or today exaggeratedly Monday)

                 Madame Vidal regrets to announce
                 the death of her daughter yesterday.
                 Paris, September 14.

the students say it was on account of a gas leak

she used to sleep completely nude under her Lesbian hair
facedown after having made passionate love
but now she has died profoundly on me
she must have loved more this time or perhaps too much
still this morning I dried myself with the towel she used on Friday
I think they will also soon change the sheets for me
and I will lose the only thing that remains of her direct inheritance
except those two hairs that are still in the sink

---

*In the Hispanic world Tuesday is considered the unlucky day of the week.

all has been so sudden   so short
that I still have love left over and I do not know where to deposit it
of course there is the question of Greece and Biafra and Czechoslovakia
and that of South America, Central America and North America
but what are we to do   it is something else
there are centuries in which the world matters less
centuries without rita who believed in something in spite
                    of everything.

Translated by Wayne H. Finke

LAUREANO ALBÁN (Costa Rica, 1942) is a leading poet of Costa Rica. Currently he serves as cultural ambassador of Costa Rica in the United States, with the title Alternate Delegate to the United Nations. His works include *Invisible Geography of America (Geografía invisible de América)*, 1982, and *Self-Portraits and Transfigurations (Autorretratos y transfiguraciones)*, 1983. His *Endless Voyage (Viaje sin fin)* earned him the Spanish government's Prize of Hispanic Culture.

Self-Portrait

I am not stone,
or tree or word:
hard solar thing
though weeping is celebrated in my mouth.

Misfortune terrestrial.
I am not earth but its rebellion:
questioning plenitude with claws.

This is my kingdom.
For an instant I live midst the flame
oppressed in an invitation of ashes.
My eyes double shadow;
there night doubles its silence.

I fear for yesterday.
Defenseless, its loyal wisdom
discovers death in the statues.
I have not been time.
Memory is delirious prophecy:
remainder of birds
come inopportunely to dream.

This is my place.
Between things
that rise to die at the word.
Midst fears of dazzlement.
Accompanying the fleeting
transmutation of the sun, the rock,
the distances already dust
that fall from wayfarers,
and the look children leave
like an immune ember in our hands.

I have not been death,
for it undertakes
my transparency until it returns it.
Sonorous labyrinth
where are lost
lights, ashes, streets
and cities deserted like roses.
Mortal deed against death.

I am not clay.
I have not been darkness
though its wait terrifies my memory.
Crust that time forged
stamping tears,
final mirror
where the sea sinks
irreplaceable master of oblivion.

Madrid, August 1980

It Is the Hour of the Sea

The sea is a journey
of unisonous horses of ash.
An abysmal gallop of last hooves,
like a metal striking endlessly
in the blindest zone of oblivion.

Where does its sonorous science
of storm, snail and mist end?
On what shore does its
collected cold of bell end?

Tied to ships
is a colt held
by the spur of worry,
with its shiny rump of mirages
and the dark flanks like sudden abysses.

It has the force of non-memory,
the unity of shadow,
the terrified high tide of the star,
the damp eyes of shipwreck.

And then it is only sea:
a nubile mirth

licking its myriad salt
in each hand.
Girded in the corners
of sound and night,
like a sexual touch filled with fish
that had risen whole to the beds, phosphorescence.

It is the hour of the sea.
The exact, mobile hour
of desire of the sea:
the blind mane of the wind,
the neck erect and alone
like a marker of stars,
the hooves already fog,
the arrowed pupils,
and the flues where
night becomes moist.

For the sea is born in bodies
undone by the moon,
for stones unravel
a silent dampness.
For a fluid composed of
inhabited memories, deaths and dreams
emerges from the houses at night.
For the sea is the permanent
journey of the body,
the wood and the light,
the sunken eyes.
Nocturnal gold, cruel gold,
gold only distances.
One by one things
undertake the miracle
of falling to its center.
Myriad steed
blinded by terrestrial oxides.
From one river to another you run to drink
with your transparent hooves.

You trot in secret labyrinths
where dawn is born,
you rise in the round
desire of the birds,
and you fall, no ash, not affront,
to join the journey and its memory,
power and night,
beauty and time,
ash and the stalk,

in the uncertain bubble
of the deepest,
the thinest and most rapid,
the most slender and deaf,
the fullest of names,
transparency of the world.

Translated by Wayne H. Finke

GUSTAVO ÁLVAREZ GARDEAZÁBAL (Colombia) is a writer and professor of contemporary literature who has devoted himself to the novel. For his prose he has won several awards: the City of Salamanca Prize for *The Wedding and the Buddha (Las bodas y el Buda),* 1970, and the Manacor Prize for *They Don't Bury Condors Everyday (Cóndores no entierran todos los días),* 1971.

Donaldo Arrieta

In this town there are ten of us who signed the letter. The five members of the liberal leadership, the three town councilmen, Ramona Uribe, and myself, Donaldo Arrieta. If there were more of us, the things I am thinking now would be different, but we were the only ones who dared to denounce León María. That is why I am here, lying on this sidewalk, watching how people gather around me and waiting for the moment when Ramona will come with her female parrots on her shoulder repeating that it was León María, and Filopotes her goose will approach my head and dip its bill in my blood. When they do, a cycle will have been fulfilled, a cycle that began a long time ago, when father, another Donaldo like myself, arrived at the Uribe house and remained forever a liberal. It never mattered to him to denounce things he viewed as unjust. He declared himself honest in everything till his life ended, penniless, resting in Ramona Uribe's house and waiting for my return with my law degree. I became a liberal without knowing why. When I found out it was too late to back out. It was the night they informed me of Fabricio Pulgarín's death. The same itching that is leaving my legs little by little, these legs of mine hanging over the curb, began on me and I wound up speaking with members of the leadership, which was not a clandestine affair because there had always been liberals in Colombia, but because it had to be held in that fashion for fear León María would appear, give them a couple of dirty looks and a half minute later, while they were still silent from the fright his appearance had produced, a burst of machine gun fire, and four or five guffaws would be heard, and then nothing more would be heard again. That is what they had done with the leadership don Abogardo Potes had directed since the Ibagué convention. They were only three but we buried them all there on the same day. The one they treated best was don Abogardo: they pumped five bullets into his head. Fabricio Pulgarín received only one shot, from behind; the other ricocheted on the padlock he was closing. From there it seems it had fallen on each one of our heads because that night we decided to denounce León María. We called neither the mayor nor the police. That had been the

40

error we committed when they killed don Andrés Santacoloma in his home, seated on a wicker chair, reading the newspaper. There were no bullets for him, only a few stab wounds that nobody could count and which the police in their report confused with a heart attack. We protested to the mayor and he sent us the coroner's report. From that same doctor who will come shortly to see me and wait for my heart to stop beating so he can say there was no remedy and that I too died of a heart attack. But I confide once more in the fact Ramona Uribe will leave her house with her parrots and her goose Filipotes and will come to see me as she did the day we got together to sign the letter. We sent it to the newspaper "El Tiempo," denouncing the last five crimes committed on the streets in Tulua, and explained in great detail what was seen by Nely Cuervo, the leadership secretary, when León María called her aside to ask for an address and she only succeeded in hearing the machine gun fire that finished off don Abogardo and his two companions. It is said León María remained looking at her, got in a carriage that he awaited with the three assassins, nodded to her, and she never saw him again. All that we declared fearlessly; we felt strong when Ramona Uribe said she would head the list. But our strength was short-lived. We had already mailed it via Avianca, when we buried Fabricio Pulgarín that afternoon three months ago. Father Rafael said a mass for him in San Bartolomeo's. From there six of those of us who signed the denunciation carried him to the cemetery. We were the only ones who were unable to see who fired at the coffin when we passed before the office of the Intelligence Service. But the thousand and more irate liberals who followed behind saw that through one of those windows the rotund figure of the mayor (the same mayor who would cause us to die of a heart attack) had moved around in there.

From that moment we considered ourselves condemned to death. An insulting letter from León María reached all of us, except Ramona. He visited her to ask her how it had happened. He did not show that refinement with us and it seems he would not if the rest run the same fate as myself. She warned us, the priest and even Don Télez the telegraph operator told us, but no one believed, no one will believe it even though they may see me here, my mouth open here on this sidewalk, waiting for Ramona with her goose or the coroner with his heart attack. That is why I was in the procession of the Virgin a while ago. It was a family commitment León María could not interrupt on me. There was no July 16th that some member of my family did not carry the banner with the Virgin's image. Since we had found each other at least one of father's five sons had come to carry that image it is said he had given as a gift, the day Black Arrieta, the big mamma we all had, was discovered in her bed, poisoned after eating a cheese León María sold in his gallery shop before becoming the fearful police chief. And this year it was my turn, since I had not come for six years, the six years it took me to get the law degree that father could not see but which must have pained León María to see when I passed by carrying the image of the Virgin, past his house, and instead of looking at it he looked at me.

And in the same manner that man in the gray poncho with the scar on his face kept looking at me, the one who approached me ever so deliberately as soon as I left the church. He caught up to me at the corner of don Carlos Materón Street. There must exist there traces of the bullets that did not pass through my head. Many of those people at my side are counting them from here, because they do not know what else to do after the three policemen, who were waiting, fired into the air when my companions in the procession saw me fall and grab my eyes with my hands, and went after the man in the gray poncho. They pointed their bayonets at them and the assassin was able to escape down this same street where I am waiting for Ramona Uribe to appear with her parrots repeating that León María killed me and for Filipotes to bring his bill near my mouth and anoint himself with my blood and show the other geese in my town that what killed me was a bullet wound and not a heart attack the coroner will find in my autopsy.

Translated by Wayne H. Finke

REINALDO ARENAS (Cuba, 1943) is one of the best known Cuban writers in the world today. In 1970, under the Castro régime, he was forced to spend a year in a labor camp. A friend succeeded in smuggling in eighty-seven blank pages, on which Arenas wrote his furious poem of denunciation, "EL CENTRAL." His two novels, *Hallucinations (Alucinaciones)*, 1966, and *Celestino before Dawn (Celestino antes del alba)*, 1967, have been translated into several languages. The first won the first prize for the Best Foreign Novel of the Year in France. He was expelled from Cuba in 1980 and presently resides in New York City.

Epigram

The Statute on Field Schools' rubrics condemn
        a million children
not to be children but agrarian serfs.

Repeating mindless slogans daily condemns
        a million children
marked with insignia, and shorn.

Lifting their legs ninety degrees degrades
        a million children
who martially lower them and shout Hurrah!

Spring will bring the frightening word
        to a million children
who go to pick small fruit.

Caged, underfed, and swallowing tears
        a million children
fast turn to beasts, shunning death.

Neither fairies nor fantasies nor rebelliousness
nor "freedom of expression" will ever be transcendental digressions

for a million children
who will never know
that such things exist.

Never a childhood, but only hate,
        for a million children,
and the wild plantations they hack down.

An oversize hammer in the hands
                    of a million children,
with the possibility of beauty, magic or illusion

scotched by mockery and jibbing brands
of "pansy" and most probably,
"reactionary."

In front of a screen or cloud of dust
or amid some inchoate clamor
                    a million children perenially march.

Not in vain, O Fifo, have you blitzed the island
with monstrous billboards proclaiming
                    THE CHILDREN ARE MADE FOR HAPPINESS.

Without this enlightenment
                    how would we know?

A Story

Already 35 years old, with his stomach empty,
and his dozen books only in manuscript because
given their bias
they would never be published by the State,
Roberto Fernández decided to commit suicide.
        Then the Devil appeared.
        Naturally he appeared in uniform, numberless
decorations glittering along the length of his chest.
        Man and Devil chatted for several hours.
        Fernández altered all his manuscripts. He added, subtracted,
obliterated, emended, eliminated everything which might,
according to the Devil, be "wrongly interpreted
by the present generation, which is zealously building the Future."
        His works were published at once in the de luxe collection
Unidimensional Belles-Lettres. He was awarded, *ipso facto,*
by express order of the Devil, the grand prize "Aurora Metal,"
and he was allotted—a great privilege—a spacious house.
        A few days later he died "unexpectedly."
        His exequies were in the nature of an apotheosis. Honor guards
were posted at civil and military ceremonies.
The Devil himself, who presided, climaxed
the funeral eulogies with a moving oration which was carried
around the progressive world.
        His body was cremated, along with his manuscripts—those
he had carefully corrected as well as all his originals.
        Without a doubt, the Devil is a reliable guard.

Marx's Contribution

Karl Marx
never wittingly suffered a tape recorder
to be strategically emplaced in some intimate part of his aura.
No one spied on him from across the street
while he scribbled on endless sheets of paper at his ease.
He could even afford the luxury of machinating heroically
in his own good time
against the prevailing system.
Karl Marx
never encountered the "obligatory retraction,"
and he had no reason to suspect that his best friend
might be in the pay of the police,
nor, even less, was he ever forced to become an informer.
He never heard of the queue which forms before the regular queue
and gives one the right to be in the queue
which waits to find at the head of the line that what was available
were replacements for zippers (and: "They're all gone, comrade").
I don't expect
he was subject to a law that obliged him
to cut off his hair
or shave his "anti-hygienic" beard.
His times did not require him to hide his manuscripts
from Engels' eyes.
(Then, too, the friendship between these two homologues
never proved a "moral concern" for the State.)
If ever he brought a woman to his lodgings,
he never had to hide his papers under the mattress or,
for reasons of political expediency,
was he forced to deliver a discourse
(while caressing her)
on the Tsar of Russia or the Austro-Hungarian Empire.
Karl Marx
could write what he would,
come and go from the country,
could dream, meditate, speak, scheme, work against
the party or power in his time.
Everything Karl Marx could do
lies in the grave of prehistory.
His contribution to contemporary problems has been immense.

Havana, June 1973

Processional

No doubt it would have been glorious
to have walked with you through a blue view

You exhaling heaven-knows-what unheard-of
                              (misbegotten)
harmony
somehow related to your neck or footfall.
I, turning over yellow leaves with the tip of my toe, sadly
sunk in thought (egocentrically, of course)
in the twilight.
        At nightfall, nevertheless, we'd take the train
to Morocco or Marseilles
(I'm no good at biography now)
and we might breakfast in Bordeaux or Who Knows Where.
A mist descends.
And beyond the sea can be heard the song of the siren, motorized,
as impossible now as one of Homer's songs or sirens.

                    But what's this? Route 32 is cut. Detour.
"It's re-routed because Brezhnev's coming through!,"
an adolescent guard yells at us in a fury, pathetically caparisoned
in the military gear of the epoch.
And I gaze at you dressed as you are, in the same gear.
And you look at me, tearing me apart.
And the two of us decide to walk the rest of the way,
to the accompaniment of your mellow blasphemies
                            which will culminate, I know,
in the realization that tonight you won't get over the wall
                            (reinforced with broken glass)
which abuts on the Committee for the Defense of the Revolution,
hard by the little room where
                        fearfully and in vain
I'll be waiting for you.

                                        Havana, July 1973

Will to Live by Manifestation

Now they'll eat me.
Now I can feel them working their way
                        up, they're already at my
                        fingertips.
I can hear their gnawing in my
                        testicles.

Over me
earth is still
being shoveled.

The burial party is dancing,
dancing on the mound
of mud and stone that covers me.

They tamp it all down,
their mouths filled with some blasting cant
meant to stamp out my memory.
                    They've buried me.

They've danced on me.
They've stamped down all the earth.
They're all gone, having left me
                    good and dead
                    and underground.

My time has come. Now it's up to me.

**Translated by Anthony Kerrigan
and Jeanne Cook**

HOMERO ARIDJIS (Contepec, Mexico, 1940) is one of the leading poets of his generation. He has traveled extensively and has taught in several American universities. Among his works are *The Difficult Ceremony (La difícil ceremonia)*, 1963, and *Persephone (Perséfone)*, 1967.

Encounter

We go to the pyramid
via the Street of the Dead

A girl descends
in the opposite direction
burned by the sun

goddess of flesh and bone
hardly covers other pyramids

she is lost in the ruins
backwards towards never

You and I go to the pyramid
via the Street of the Dead

Chapultapec

Strong breeze   Tall trees
rock the earth in green
The sun spinning top of fire
plunges between clouds
The dark afternoon A man
leans on the breast of a woman
Red dress A duck flies
over the poplars quacks in the distance
The man the woman naked lying
between the plants The strong breeze
On their bodies last red rays.

Translated by Wayne H. Finke

JUAN JOSÉ ARREOLA (Zapotlán el Grande, Mexico, 1918) is a self-taught writer who at an early age read Baudelaire, Whitman, and Papini enthusiastically. After traveling in France, he worked for the Mexican publishing house Fondo de Cultura Económica. His works include *Confabulary (Confabulario)*, 1966, *Women, Animals and Mechanical Fantasies (Mujeres, animales y fantasías mecánicas)*, 1972, and *Inventory (Inventario)*, 1976.

The Switchman

The stranger reached the deserted station out of breath. His heavy suitcase, which no one wished to help carry, had fatigued him greatly. He wiped his face with a handkerchief, and placing his hand to shade his eyes he observed the rails which disappeared on the horizon. Discouraged and pensive he looked at his watch: the exact time the train ought to be leaving.

Someone, who appeared out of the blue, gave him a slight slap on the shoulder. Turning around, the stranger found himself before a little old man looking vaguely like a railroad man. In his hand he carried a red lantern, but so small that it looked like a toy. Smiling he contemplated the stranger, who nervously asked:

"Excuse me, has the train already left?"

"You haven't been in this country for a long time?"

"I have to leave immediately. I'm supposed to be in T. tomorrow."

"I can see you have no idea of what's going on. What you ought to do right now is seek lodging in the travelers' inn." And he pointed out a strange grayish building which looked more like a jail.

"But I want to take the train, not stay in that hotel."

"Rent a room right away, that is, if there is one. Should there be one, rent it by the month, for it will come out cheaper for you and you'll receive better service."

"Are you crazy? I must reach T. tomorrow morning."

"Frankly, I ought to leave you to your own devices. But I'll give you some information."

"Please . . ."

"This country is famous for its railways, as you know. Up to now it hasn't been possible to organize them completely, but already great strides have been taken in regard to publishing timetables and issuing tickets. The railroad guides include, and link up, all the cities in the nation; tickets are issued even for the smallest, most remote villages. The only thing lacking is for the trains to follow the indications contained in the guides and indeed

49

stop at the appointed stations. Citizens hope for progress; in the meantime they accept irregularities in service and their patriotism prevents them from showing any sign of displeasure."

"But, is there a train that passes through this city?"

"If I said so it would be equivalent to committing an error. As you can see, the rails exist, although somewhat uncared for. In some towns they are simply drawn on the ground with two chalk marks. Given the present conditions, no train has to pass by here, but nothing prevents it from doing so. In my life I've seen many trains pass and I met some travelers who were able to get on board. If you wait long enough, perhaps I'll have the honor of helping you get on a beautiful, comfortable coach."

"Will that train take me to T.?"

"Why do you insist that it has to be precisely T.? You ought to be satisfied just to be able to get on board. Once on the train your life will take effectively some course. What does it matter if that road isn't the one to T.?"

"Well, I have a valid ticket to go to T. Logically, I ought to be transported to that place, right?"

"Anybody would say you're right. In the travelers' inn you can speak with individuals who've taken precautions by buying great quantities of tickets. As a general rule, smart travelers buy tickets for every destination in the country. There are even those who have spent a veritable fortune on tickets. . . ."

"I thought that to get to T. all I needed was a ticket. Look at it. . . ."

"The next stretch of the national railway is going to be built with the money from just one person who has spent his immense wealth on round trip tickets for an itinerary whose plans, which include extensive tunnels and bridges, haven't even been approved by the company engineers."

"But the train for T., is it already in service?"

"Not only that one. In reality there are many trains in the country and travelers can use them with relative frequency, but you have to take into consideration that it is not a question of a service one can depend on. In other words, when you get on a train, nobody expects to be transported to the place he desires."

"How is that?"

"In its desire to serve citizens, the company is forced to take deperate measures. It makes trains circulate through impenetrable areas. Those expeditionary trains sometimes take several years for their trip, and passengers' lives undergo some important changes. In such cases deaths are not a rarity, but the company, which has thought of everything, adds to those trains an illuminated chapel and a cemetery car. It's a matter of pride for the conductors to deposit a traveler's body, luxuriously embalmed, on the platform of the station indicated on his ticket. Sometimes these forced trains cover stretches where one of the rails is lacking. One whole side of the coaches trembles lamentably from the blows of the wheels striking the ties. First class passengers (this is another of the company's considerations) are placed on the side where the rail is located. Passengers in second class endure the bumps with resignation. But there are other sectors where both rails are lacking; there all travelers suffer equally, until the train winds up a total wreck."

"Good God!"

"Why, look. The village of F. came about because of one of those accidents. The train ended up in rough terrain that couldn't be traversed. The wheels made smooth by the sand, were worn down to the axles. The passengers spent so much time together, that from the forced trivial conversations there arose close friendships. Some of these were soon transformed into idylls, and the result was F., a progressive town filled with mischievous kids who play with the rusty remains of the train."

"My God! I'm not ready for such adventures!"

"You have to be brave; you might even become a hero. Don't think occasions are lacking for travelers to demonstrate the bravery and capacity for sacrifice. On one occasion two hundred anonymous passengers wrote one of the most glorious pages in our railway annals. It happened that on a test run the engineer saw in time a serious omission on the part of the line's builders. On that route there was lacking a bridge that was supposed to span a wide abyss. Well, the engineer, instead of putting the train in reverse, harangued the passengers and got them to make the necessary effort to go on. Under his forceful direction the train was dismantled piece by piece, carried on shoulders across the abyss, which by the way held another secret: there was a deep river at its base. The results of this feat were so satisfactory that the railroad management abandoned forever building the bridge, instead choosing to offer an attractive discount on the tariff for passengers who are brave enough to face this extra bother."

"But I have to reach T. tomorrow."

"OK. I'm glad to see you're not giving up on your plan. It's easy to see you're a man of your convictions. But get a room for now in the inn and take the first train that passes. At least try, for there'll be a thousand persons who will do their best to keep you from your goal. When a train reaches the station, travelers, exasperated on account of the excessively long wait, pour out of the inn and literally invade the station. Frequently they cause accidents with their incredible lack of courtesy and prudence. Instead of getting on board in an orderly fashion, they trample each other. At least they prevent each other from getting on, and the train pulls out leaving them behind, all a-fighting on the station platform. The travelers, exhausted and furious, curse their lack of education and devote their time to insulting each other and getting in a few blows."

"And don't the police intervene?"

"They have tried to install a police corps at each station, but the unforeseen arrival of trains makes such a service useless and extremely expensive.

Besides, members of the force demonstrated very quickly they could be bought off, by deciding to protect the exclusive exit of wealthy passengers who gave them everything on their person in exchange for that service. Then a resolution was passed for the establishment of special schools where future travelers receive lessons in civility and adequate training which prepares them to be able to spend their lives on the trains. There they are taught the correct manner to get aboard a train, even though it is in motion and speeding. They are also furnished with a type of armor to prevent the other passengers' breaking their ribs."

"But once on board, is a person safe from new difficulties?"

"Relatively. I would only recommend you take note of the stations. It could happen that you think you'd arrived at T., and it would only be an illusion. In order to regulate life on board the overcrowded cars, the company finds it necessary to resort to certain measures. There are stations which are a pure illusion; they have been built in the middle of the forest and bear the name of some important city. With a little bit of care one can spot the trick. They are like theatrical props, and the figures that appear against them are filled with sawdust. Those mannikins easily reveal the ravages of inclement weather, but at times they are a perfect image of reality: on their faces they bear signs of an infinite weariness."

"It's a good thing T. is not far from here."

"But for the time being we lack direct trains. However, it could well happen that you reach T. tomorrow, as you wish. The railroad's organization, although deficient, doesn't exclude the possibility of a direct trip. Why, just look; there are individuals who haven't even realized what is happening. They buy a ticket to go to T. A train passes, they get on, and the next day they hear the conductor announce: 'T., we've arrived at T.' Without taking any precaution at all, the travelers get off and indeed find themselves in T."

"Would it be possible for me to do something to obtain that result?"

"Of course you could. What isn't known is whether it would do you any good. Anyway, try it. Get on the train with the positive idea that you'll reach T. Don't chat with any of the other passengers. They could disillusion you with their stories of travel, and it could even turn out that they would squeal on you."

"What are you saying?"

"By virtue of the present state of affairs, trains are filled with spies. These persons, in the majority volunteers, devote their lives to fomenting the company's constructive spirit. At times one doesn't realize what he's saying and talks just for the sake of talking. But they comprehend every sense a sentence can have, however simple it may be. From the most innocent comment they can draw a guilty opinion. If you should commit the slightest imprudence, you would be seized just like that, and would spend the rest of your days in a jail coach if they didn't force you to get off at a false station, lost in the middle of nowhere. Travel full of faith, eat the least possible amount of food, and don't set foot on the platform before you see a familiar face in T."

"But I don't know anyone in T."

"In that case double your precautions. You will have, I guarantee you, many temptations on the way. If you look out the windows you run the risk of being deceived by an illusion. Windows are provided with ingenious methods of creating all types of illusions in the passengers' spirits. It is not necessary to be weak to fall into the trap. Certain mechanisms, operated from the locomotive, make one believe the train is in motion, because of the noises and movements. However, the train remains stopped for weeks on end, while passengers see captivating landscapes pass by the windows."

"And what is the purpose of all that?"

"The company does all that with the sane purpose of reducing the passengers' anxiety and eliminating insofar as possible the sensations of moving. It is hoped they'll surrender completely to chance, in the hands of an all-powerful company, and they won't care to know where they're going or from where they're coming."

"And you, have *you* traveled much on the trains?"

"I, sir, am only a switchman. To tell the truth I'm a retired switchman, and only show up here from time to time to remember the good old days. I've never traveled, nor do I have any desire to do so. But travelers tell me stories. I know that the trains have given rise to many other towns besides the village of F., the one I told you about. It sometimes happens the train crew receives mysterious orders. They invite the passengers to get out of the coaches, generally with the pretext that they should admire the natural beauty of a given place. They are told of grottos, waterfalls or famous ruins: 'Fifteen minutes for admiring such and such a cave,' the conductor announces amicably. Once they're a sufficient distance from the train, the engineer pulls away at full steam."

"And the travelers?"

"They wander around confused for some time but they end up banding together and establishing a colony. These inopportune stops are made in adequate sites, quite far from all civilization but with sufficient natural resources. Select lots of young people are abandoned there, especially with lots of women. Wouldn't you like to end your days in some unknown picturesque place in the company of a nice young girl?"

The little old man winked, watching the traveler with a roguish glint, smiling, filled with goodness. At that moment a distant whistle was heard. The switchman gave a leap, full of fear, and began to make ridiculous, disorderly signals with his lantern.

"Is it the train?" inquired the stranger.

The old man began to run along the track, in a crazy fashion. When he was a certain distance away, he turned around and shouted:

"Good luck. Tomorrow you'll reach your famous station. What did you say your name was?"

"X!" responded the traveler.

At that moment the little old man disappeared into the clear morning. But the red glow of his lantern continued running and jumping between the rails, carelessly, toward the train.

In the background the locomotive approached like a noisy arrival.

Translated by Wayne H. Finke

CARLOS GERMÁN BELLI (Lima, Peru, 1927) is one of the most original poets of Peru. He has traveled extensively and teaches at the University of San Marcos in Lima. His poetry is characterized by its simplicity and directness, concentrating on aspects of daily life. Among his works are *The Foot on the Neck (El pie sobre el cuello)*, 1964, *Down the Mountain (Por el monte abajo)*, 1966, and *Sextains and Other Poems (Sextinas y otros poemas)*, 1970.

Segregation N. 1

(In the style of a naive and cultured poet)
I, mamma, my two brothers
and many little Peruvians
open a deep, deep hole
where we take refuge,
because above everything has a master,
everything is locked up,
firmly sealed,
because above everything is reserved:
the tree's shade, flowers,
fruits, the roof, wheels,
water, pencils,
and we choose to immerse ourselves
in the depths of the earth,
lower than ever,
far, very far from the leaders,
today Sunday,
far, very far from the owners,
among the animals' feet,
because up there
there are some who control everything,
who write, sing and dance,
who speak elegantly,
and we, blushed with shame,
we only want to disappear
in tiny little pieces.

Someday Love

Someday love
will I finally attain,
such as it is between my dead elders:

55

not within their eyes, but outside,
invisible, but perennial,
if not of fire, of air.

Bah! Vitamin A

Bah! Vitamin A, what for now,
neither B nor C, the devil take them all,
once and for all forever amen,
if I didn't swallow yours, A, B, C
on the very day, mamma, yesterday,
when even beyond the last Z,
you prepared in bulk everywhere,
without intending to reserve for yourself
part of B or C
nor that the only stepdaughter of your father
swallow pill by pill,
like an absolute owner of the pharmacy;
that now, liberal, she also swallows
from A to Z like then,
this, executor of the opposite fate,
that yesterday was the day of my vitamins,
but no longer today, tomorrow or ever.

Antibiotic Miscellany

From this antibiotic tablet
when even a fleeting effect finally,
if in the arcane horizons it turns
like the moon in the sky,
for just here,
while in secret
the pathogenic troglodyte squeezes
the grapes of his corporeal bunch,
how forcibly,
more than north wind with yellow leaves.
Let the effects come
fast like the hare,
before day changes to black night,
and let us begin to live
in an atrocious little spot,
floating here and there fiercely
between the molecules
of the great antibiotic tablet,

prescribed in vain day and night
not to eternalize
these we are today one hundred thousand pathogens.

Sextain of Kid and Lulu

Kid the Lilliputian will no longer eat
leftovers for the first time in centuries,
when he placates his cavernous hunger
with the spiced back of his Lulu la Belle
until death in a stew,
whom he worshipped even before life.

The roundest preys of life,
that sated others like leftovers
they left carelessly after death,
Kid having been fasting for centuries
not a piece will he leave of Lulu in a stew,
as placating completely his rabid hunger.

Such hunger is the most horrible of all,
and thus no more hell was his life,
on seeing Lulu yesterday tasty in a stew
for the happy one who never ate leftovers,
but the best morsel of each century,
departing contented towards death.

So coming to the cavern of death,
pained by the thirst of love and hunger,
as the greatest pain is of the centuries,
for such hunger is sated quickly in life,
when the heavens no longer serve leftovers,
but rather the manna of Lulu in a stew.

Thus body and soul both in a stew,
of his lady carrying them to death,
will be a prize for just eating leftovers
pallid from hunger here on earth,
and will not have death but great life,
eating forever and ever.

The body of Lulu peerless in centuries
will be a delicacy of gods whose stew
will recall terrestrial life,
even in the breast of black death,

as if on earth only exists hunger,
the dream of changing the leftovers is pleasant.

No longer leftovers for Kid in life,
nor captive of hunger, no, in death,
for he will eat Lulu in a stew for centuries.

Looking at My Little Daughters, with Their Friend "Daqui" the Dog

Well, the thing was not easy:
whether being a dog or human,
rather offspring of cattle or cat,
or perhaps even of another creature,
horizontally everything
between a snout and a tail;
for luckily
the girl was not of a dog
or calf
or cat,
in the good or bad sense,
and her A, her B, her C, etc.,
and even her own Z,
with what naturalness
of "pe" to "pa"
in the mouth,
and though she worships her dog,
cat or that calf,
in such a trice
in centuries that not even once
will be seen,
and more so between A and Z,
from the precise moment,
so much less bowwow, meow, moo.
But, oh, God!
if perhaps life is
so-so,
though it were a pleasant trip,
between A and Z,
what a lucky
quadrupede
more than man
can be
just with bowwow, meow, moo.

Translated by Wayne H. Finke

ADOLFO BIOY CASARES (Buenos Aires, Argentina, 1914) is one of the leading prose writers of his country, along with Jorge Luis Borges, with whom he has collaborated on numerous occasions. His best-known works are *The Invention of Morel (La invención de Morel)*, 1940, and *Faust's Vespers (Las vísperas de Fausto)*, 1949.

The First Class Passenger

Life passed monotonously in that tropical city, a modest trading center to which occasional buyers from tobacco companies were sent. When a ship cast anchor in the port, our consul celebrated the event with a banquet in the Moorish room of the Hotel Palmas. The guest of honor was always the captain, who received the invitation through a Negro messenger of the consulate along with an expressed wish that he extend it to a group of officials and passengers personally selected by him. Even though the table was covered with exotic dishes, the humidity seemed to render the most delicately prepared products of culinary art foul-tasting or even suspicious to such an extent that the only appetizing thing left was the fruit; rather, the fruit and the alcohol according to the observations of passengers who do not forget a prestigious white wine or the recreation that it presumably sparked. It was in the course of one of those luncheons that our consul heard from the very lips of the female tourist—a rich elderly woman of fine character and worldly appearance, attired in a comfortable English outfit— the following explanation or story:

I travel in first class, but I recognize without the slightest argument that today all advantages favor the second class passenger. The cost of the trip is the best example. The meals—no one can deny it—come out of the same kitchen, are prepared by the same chefs for both first and second class, but undoubtedly the crew's preference is focused on the popular classes, the freshest and most exquisite delicacies are intended for the second class dining room. As far as the reported preference for popular classes is concerned, believe me, it is totally unnatural; writers and journalists implant it, individuals whom everyone listens to without confidence or respect become stubbornly convincing in the long run. Since second class is always full, causing first class to remain practically empty, you hardly ever find a steward in first class, and as a result the service is that much better in second class.

Believe me, I assure you that I expect nothing from life; in any case I enjoy animation, young and beautiful people. And now I'll tell you a secret. Even though we categorically deny it, beauty and youth are synonymous;

old women like myself can't help become excited if a young boy comes in to play. All young people, in order to return to the class question, travel in second class. First class dances, when they are held, seem like meetings of resurrected corpses dressed in their best clothes and jewels to pass dutifully another evening. It would be more logical if at exactly midnight everyone, already half-encrusted with dust, returned to his grave. Of course we can attend second class functions, although for that it would be necessary to put aside our feelings since those second class occupants below regard us as a group of crowned royalty stooping to visit poorer sections. Second class passengers appear in first class whenever they feel like it, and no one, no authority erects a hateful barrier that society unanimously discarded a short while ago. Their visits are well received by us first class passengers though we slightly moderate our effusive attentions so that the occasional guests do not discover and become indignant at our immediate recognition of their second class status—a class which during the length of the voyage exhibits a most authentic pride. We become less pleased with their visits when it's a matter of raids or invasions, true Indian attacks that generally occur just before dawn when the invaders display an obstinate tendency to seek out some passenger, any one of us who did not securely fasten the lock in his cabin or who dallied too long at the bar, in the library or in the music room. I swear, sir, that those boys grab one without the least consideration, carry him to the bow or promenade and throw him overboard into the immense blackness of a sea full of the horrifying monsters of our imagination, illuminated by the unaffected moon of a famous poet. Every morning we first class passengers look at each other with eyes clearly saying, "So your turn hasn't come yet." Dignity, but at the same time prudence, prevents us from speaking of the vanished; since according to certain stories, perhaps unfounded—there is a terrifying pleasure in becoming scared, in supposing the enemy's organization is perfect—that those in second class probably maintained a network of spies in our midst. As I told you a few minutes ago, our class lost all its advantages including snobbishness (which, similar to gold preserves its value), but I, through some quirk probably incurable in persons of my age, cannot reconcile myself to become a second class passenger.

Translated by John Chando

Alfredo Bryce Echenique (Peru, 1939) teaches Latin American literature at the University of Vincennes. He studied at the University of San Marcos, Lima, and at the Sorbonne. He is the author of *A World for Julius* (*Un mundo para Julio*) and *So Many Times Pedro* (*Tantas veces Pedro*), as well as of books of short stories, *Closed Garden* (*Huerto cerrado*) and *Happiness, Ha, Ha* (*Felicidad, ja, ja*).

In Paracas with Jimmy

I can really see him now; it's as if I saw him sitting there in the big dining room in the summer resort, his back to the sea with its stingrays, maybe even sharks. I was sitting across from him, at the same table, yet I seem to be watching him from the doorway of that room everyone had already left, only he and I were still there, we had been the last to arrive, had just made it for lunch.

This time he had brought me along; they had sent him down just for the weekend, Paracas wasn't very far: I'd be back in time for school on Monday. Mother hadn't been able to come, so he had brought me along instead. He always took me when she couldn't go with him and I could get back in time for school. I'd listen when he told mother it was a pity she couldn't come, the Company was putting him up in a luxury hotel room for two. "I'll take him along," he said, meaning me. I think he liked to have me with him on those trips.

And how I loved them! This time it was to Paracas where I'd never been, and when my father started to pack his suitcase on Friday evening I knew I wouldn't get much sleep that night and would wake up before the alarm went off.

We left very early that Saturday morning but had to lose a lot of time at the office, before we got on to the southern highway. Apparently my father still had things to look into, maybe receive last minute instructions from his boss. I'm not sure, I stayed out in the car waiting and started to worry we'd arrive much later than we had planned.

Once we hit the highway, there were other worries for me. My father drove as slowly as ever, more slowly than mother had begged him to. One after the other, cars kept passing and leaving us behind, and I never looked at him, so as not to let him see how much it bothered me, how ashamed it really made me feel. Still there was nothing I could do, the old Pontiac, poor thing, was ancient, very bulky, black, enormous, and lumbered on, rocking like a barge on the newly-paved highway.

When we'd gone about halfway, my father decided to switch on the

61

radio. I don't know what came over him; anyway, he always did the same thing, but he tried only one station, they were playing a *guaracha*,* and he turned it off right away, without saying a word. I'd have liked to hear a little music but didn't protest. I believe that's why he liked to have me on his trips, I wasn't a kid who asked a lot of questions, I liked to be easygoing and I was conscious of it. But, one thing, I was a very sharp observer.

And that's why I watched him out the corner of my eye, and now I still see him driving, pulling up his trouser legs at the knees, letting his white, spotless socks show, and they're better than mine because I'm still just a kid; white and spotless because we're on our way to Paracas, luxury hotel, summer resort, big bank rolls and all that kind of thing. His jacket is the same for all trips outside of Lima, very light gray, sporty; it's American-made and will last him all his life. The trousers are gray too, slightly darker than the jacket, and his shirt is the newest old shirt in the world. No shirt is ever going to last me like my father's shirts last him.

And the beret, it's Basque; the real thing, he explains. It's for his travels, for the wind, for his bald head. Because my father is bald, bald as an egg, and when I look at him now, he's not a tall man anymore. I've discovered that my father is not a tall man, he's on the short side. Short and very thin. Short, bald, thin but I hadn't come to see him like that yet, and all I know now is he's the finest man on earth, easygoing like me, and really scared of his bosses, who are so fond of him because he has never been late for work in the last seven million years or out sick or failed to show up at the office, bosses who I've seen slapping him on the back and are forever congratulating him at the church door on Sundays; but they've never said hello to me, and my father is forever reassuring my mother at the church door on Sundays that his bosses' wives are absent-minded or haven't seen her, because they don't say hello to her either, and yet they didn't forget to send him greetings and good wishes when he rounded out another million years without getting sick or being late at the office, that time when he brought home the photos where I'm sure one boss had just slapped him on the back and another had already left the cocktail party but they had been there, my father said to you, showing you the first photo again.

But all this is now that I'm seeing him, not then, watching him as we got to Paracas in the Pontiac. The Pontiac had kind of slipped to the back of my mind but the hotel's white walls made me see it there: black, very ancient, poor thing, and so bulky. "Where will all those people end up?" he asked me, and I'm sure my father was scared to death, seeing those great big hearses, I don't mean because they were big but because they looked so fancy. If he ran into one of them, he would have to deal with whoever owned it, because my father was a real gentleman, when its owner, summer vacationing in Paracas with his friends, turned up and would maybe

---

*A typical dance

know my father's bosses and had heard of him, "It's nothing to worry about, Juanito," (that was and is my father's name), and they'd slap him all over the back, then there would be predinner drinks, and they wouldn't say hello to me but I'd act naturally just so he wouldn't notice they hadn't said hello to me. It was a good thing my mother hadn't been along.

But nothing happened. We found a very roomy space for the black Pontiac and there, when I got out, it sure looked old to me. We were at our Paracas hotel, four-star hotel and all. The boy who came over to the car for the suitcase was the first person we greeted. He led us to the reception desk and my father signed in and asked if we could still have "some lunch" (I remember it's what he said). The man at the desk, very distinguished-looking, much taller than my father, said okay: "Yes of course, sir. The boy will take you to your 'bungalow' so you can wash your hands, if you'd like to. You have enough time, sir, the dining room will close in a few minutes but your 'bungalow' isn't very far away." I don't know about my father, but I understood the 'bungalow' bit very well because I was attending an English school which is something I must not forget the rest of my life; every time my dad blows up once in a thousand years, and later treats us to a movie, he shouts that he even works when he's sick and has never been late in seven million years so as to give his kids only the very best, same as his bosses' kids.

The boy who took us to the 'bungalow' didn't smile much when my father tipped him but I knew that when you traveled on the Company's money you couldn't splurge, because the poor bosses would never make a dime and the Company would fold up, in the mind of my respectful father who was washing his hands while I opened the suitcase and, all excited, pulled out my swimming trunks. That's when I found out, he told me, I shouldn't go near the sea because it was infested with stingrays, and maybe even sharks. I rushed over to wash my hands, because they're going to close the dining room in a few minutes, and I left my swimming trunks lying on the bed. We shut the 'bungalow' door and went to the dining room. My father was also observant, but less than me; he pointed out the swimming pool, maybe it was because of my trunks. Paracas was beautiful, a kind of oasis, a spa; sand, palm trees, flowers, side paths and roads where girls I didn't have the nerve to look at, only a few of them now, the last ones, still hanging on, dawdled on their way to sleep the siesta of those who've already become used to the luxury hotel. Timid but curious, my father and I went into the dining room.

And it's there, sitting with his back to the sea, the stingrays and the sharks, it's there I am seeing him, as if I were in the dining room doorway, and I am really seeing myself too, at the same table, across from him, waiting for the waiter who had just about answered our greeting and had gone off for the menu (my father had asked for the bill of fare and the man had said he was going for the menu) and who according to Dad should have changed the tablecloth but it was better not to say anything because it was a luxury hotel and we had arrived for lunch at the last minute. I almost greeted the waiter again when he came back and handed the menu to my father who, in way over his head, finally ordered corvina à la something or other because the waiter had been waiting for ages. He left with the order and, smiling at me, my father arranged the menu on the table so I could read the names of some of the dishes, actually a bunch of French names, and I thought, relieved, that something terrible could have happened, like the time in a modern-looking restaurant with a menu that looked like it was for Americans, when my father passed me the menu to do the ordering and started telling the waiter he didn't know any English but he was putting his boy through an English school, and his other children too, forget the money, and the waiter, who couldn't have cared less, kept shifting from leg to leg because he wanted to get away.

Then my father chalked up a real victory. While the waiter was on his way with the corvina à la something or other, my father started talking about us splurging because the place called for it and it wouldn't break the Company if he asked for a small bottle of white wine to go with the corvinas. He said he'd be meeting with the big farmers that evening at seven and they would buy the tractors he had been asked to sell; he had never failed the Company. He was going on about this when the waiter appeared, doing his best to carry the dishes in the most impossible way, it looked like a circus act, and my father looking at him as if he were ready to start applauding, but thank God he came to his senses and put on a pretty stiff but dignified pose while the waiter did his trick of nearly spilling the dishes into our faces, he was really setting them down on the table elegantly and we weren't used to that fancy treatment. "A white such and such," my father said. I almost hugged him for the word he had just pronounced in French, the name of the wine, when he hadn't even checked it on the wine list, no, none of that; he had ordered it just like that, triumphant, a connoisseur, and the waiter could only write it down and go fetch it.

Everything was going smoothly. They had brought us the wine and now I remember that moment of perfect harmony: my father sitting with his back to the sea, not that the dining room was over the beach, but the wall holding up those picture windows kept me from seeing the swimming pool and what I am looking at now is my father's head, his face, his shoulders, the sea beyond, blue on that sunny day, the palm trees scattered here and there, my father's fine slender hand around the cool bottle of wine serving me half a glass, filling his own, "drink slowly, son," already a bit sunburned, submissive, lonely for my mother, the best in the world, and me there, almost letting the juice the corvina was swimming in run all over me, and then I saw Jimmy. I let it run all over me then. It never dawned on me why I was so scared to see him; I would soon know.

He was smiling at me from the dining room doorway and I said hi, glancing at my father to explain who he was, that he was in my class and so on, but when my father heard his last name he turned to him with a big grin on his face, he said for me to call him over and as he crossed the room, told me he knew his father, a friend of his bosses, one of the Company directors, with lots of land in that part of the country. . . .

"Jimmy, Dad." And they shook hands.

"Sit down, boy," my father said, and it was only then he said hello to me.

He was absolutely beautiful; Jimmy's was an extraordinary beauty: blond with curly gold hair, blue almond-shaped eyes and bronze skin, bronze all year round, winter and summer, maybe because he was always coming to Paracas. As soon as he sat down I noticed something strange: the same waiter who looked down his nose at my father and me came over, all smiles now, fawning, scraping and bowing, and he greeted Jimmy in a servile way but Jimmy merely smirked. And the waiter wouldn't go away, just stayed put, stood there waiting for orders, dying for them, and I almost asked Jimmy to tell him to drop dead. Of the four of us there, Jimmy was the only cool one.

And that's where the whole thing got started. I'm watching my father offer Jimmy a little wine. That's when I begin to feel scared.

"No, thanks," Jimmy said. "I had wine for lunch." And, without even wasting a glance on him, he asked the waiter for a whiskey.

I checked my father: eyes nailed to his plate, smiling, he stuffed down a mouthful of corvina that might have been loaded with millions of bones. My father didn't stop Jimmy from ordering that whiskey, and here was the waiter on his way now, almost pirouetting with the glass on a silver tray, it was something to watch the wide grin on the son of a bitch's face. And then Jimmy pulled out a pack of Chesterfields, laid it on the table, lit one up, and blew all the smoke on the top of my father's bald head, of course he didn't do it intentionally, he just did it, and then he went on being so beautiful, smiling, looking at the sea, but neither my father nor I wanted any dessert.

"How long have you been smoking?" my father asked in a quivery voice.

"I don't know, can't remember," Jimmy said, offering me a cigarette.

"No, no, Jimmy, no . . ."

"Go ahead and smoke, sonny; don't refuse your friend."

I can see my father saying those words and then picking up a napkin he hadn't dropped, almost picking up the foot of the waiter who was still standing there. Jimmy and I smoked, while my father told us he had never been tempted to smoke, and then went on about a bronchial condition he had had at some time or other but Jimmy started talking about cars, while I checked the clothes he was wearing, it all looked like silk, and my father's shirt began to age pathetically, not even his American jacket would last him all his life.

"Do you drive, Jimmy?" my father asked.

"I've been doing it for ever so long. Now I have my sister's car; I smashed mine up the other day but Dad is expecting another one. We have several cars at the ranch."

And I was scared stiff, thinking about the Pontiac; maybe Jimmy would find out it was my father's, maybe he'd laugh at it, it would look even older, bulkier, uglier to him than it did to me. "Why had we come there?" I was remembering when he'd bought the car, my father convincing Mom, "a small sacrifice," and also the Saturday afternoons when we washed it, it was a family ritual, all of us kids with cans of water, my father with the hose, my mother on the porch, all of us dying to get in and take the wheel, and my father acting the boss: "When you boys grow up, when you have a driver's license," and then in a sentimental tone: "It's cost me years of hard work."

"Do you have a license, Jimmy?"

"No, it makes no difference; everybody here knows me."

And that's when my father asked him how old he was and pretended to believe him when he said he was sixteen, and so did I; I almost called him a liar, but what for, everybody knew Jimmy was in my class and I wasn't fourteen yet.

"Manolo's coming with me," Jimmy said, "we'll go for a drive in my sister's car."

And my father gave in again, smiled once more and asked Jimmy to say hello to his father.

"It's almost four," he said, "I'm going to get some rest because I have a business meeting at seven." He said good-bye to Jimmy and left without telling me what time I should be back and I almost told him not to worry, we weren't going to crack up.

Jimmy didn't ask which car was mine and I didn't have to tell him it was the black Pontiac, the only one there, my father's car. Now I would like to tell him and when he laughed sarcastically I'd spit in his face, even if all those waiters who had greeted him on our way out, all those who didn't care about me, even if they all jumped me and tried to kill me for having messed up that face gorgeous like a little gold coin, those hands, like the hands of someone in love for the first time, opening the door of a car owned by my father's boss.

Traveling at one million miles per hour, we were in Pisco in no time at all and there Jimmy almost ran over a woman in the Plaza de Armas; traveling at God knows how many million miles per hour, with a special fourth speed, we were soon at one of their ranches and there Jimmy had a Coke, pinched one of his cousins in the cheek of her ass and didn't introduce me to his sisters; at I don't know how many thousands of millions of miles per hour, we were on our way to Ica and near there Jimmy showed me the spot where he had wrecked his car, shitty car, he said, it was no damn good.

It was 9:00 P.M. when we got back to Paracas. I don't remember how but

Jimmy took me to a lounge where my father was drinking with a whole bunch of men. He sat there, looking pleased, I had known he would do a good job. All those men knew Jimmy. They were landowners from the area and they had just bought the Company's tractors. Some touched Jimmy's hair and others were busy with the whiskey my father was treating them to in the Company's name. Just then my father started to tell a joke, but Jimmy interrupted him to say he was inviting me to dinner. "Fine, fine," my father said. "Go right ahead."

And that night I drank the first whiskeys in my life, the first full glass of wine in my life, at a spotless table, with a smiling waiter dancing attendance on us. Everyone was elegantly dressed in that dinning room filled with lights and the laughter of lovely women, with big red-faced men who slid their hands over Jimmy's gold ringlets when they walked past on their way to their tables. That's when I seemed to hear the end of the joke my father had been telling, I scowled in his direction, and I kind of locked him into his little lounge with those redneck farmers who had come to buy their first tractor. Then, and this is something really strange, I slipped far out to sea and there I started to watch myself in a festive dining room while a waiter, on his knees, served me a glass of champagne under Jimmy's almond-eyed blue stare.

At first, I didn't quite get him, I really didn't know what he was talking about or what he meant with all his talk about underwear. I was still watching him sign the bill, scrawling his name over a monstrously high figure and then inviting me to go for a walk along the beach. "Come on," he'd said and I was keeping up with him on the dark boardwalk without quite getting all his talk about underwear. But Jimmy wouldn't let up, asking me again what kind of shorts I wore and adding that his were like this, like that, till we sat down on some steps facing the sand and the sea. Waves were crashing real close to us and now Jimmy was talking about genital organs, only about male organs, and me sitting next to him, listening, not knowing what to say back, trying to make out the stingrays and the sharks my father always talked about, and suddenly racing toward them because Jimmy had just put his hand on my leg, "What's yours like, Manolo?" he said and I ran like a bat out of hell.

I'm watching Jimmy move away, very cool, heading back toward the glow of the dining room and disappearing after a few minutes. From the sea's edge, standing there with wet feet, I looked at the hotel studded with lights and at the row of bungalows, one of them mine. I thought of running back there but then convinced myself it would be silly, nothing more would happen that night. The awful thing would be if Jimmy stayed around all of the next day but right now, forget it, I'd just turn back and go to bed.

I was coming close to the bungalow when I heard a strange laugh. My father was with someone. An enormous blond man was roughing up my father's arm, congratulating him, saying something about doing a great job

and wham! slapped him on the back. "Good-night, Juanito," he said.
"Good-night, don Jaime," and he caught sight of me just then.

"Look, there he is. Where's Jimmy, Manolo?"

"He left awhile ago, Dad."

"Say hello to Jimmy's father."

"How are you, kid? So Jimmy took off awhile ago, well, he'll show up. I
was congratulating your father; I hope you'll take after him. I walked him
over to his bungalow."

"It was very nice of don Jaime."

"Well, good-night, Juanito." And he went off, enormous.

We shut the bungalow door behind us. We were both a little tight, he
more than me, and ready for bed. My trunks were still there and my father
said that tomorrow morning I could go for a swim. Then he asked me if I'd
had a nice day and whether Jimmy was a school pal and was I going to see
him tomorrow. And to all this I said: "Yes, Dad, yes, Dad," till he switched
the light off and got into bed. Lying in my bed, I racked my brain for a
stomach ache or something so I could stay in bed the next day, and thought
he had already fallen asleep. But no. In the dark, my father told me the
Company's name had come through with flying colors, he had done a good
job, my father was happy. Later, he talked to me again. He said it had been
very nice of don Jaime to walk him to the "bungalow" door, he was a real
gentleman. And a couple of hours later, he asked me: "Manolo, what does
'bungalow' mean in Spanish?"

Translated by Hardie St. Martin

CECILIA BUSTAMANTE (Peru, 1932) is a writer and poet who received the National Poetry Prize in 1965 for her work *New Poems and Audience (Nuevos poemas y audiencia)*. Her other collections of verse include *The Name of Things (El nombre de las cosas)*, 1970, and *Discernment (Discernimiento)*, 1981. Her poetry has appeared in translation in English, French and German.

Vocabulary

The word melancholy
is literary obsolete
in spite of

Solitude
misused, meaningless,
no one cares about
anyone's solitude.
You howl
like a dog at the moon.

Turbid, slow
melancholy,
distorting sadness.
Nay.

In the shade of the flowering
mushroom cloud
we radiate, irradiate
streams of fire.
Aye.

Melancholy,
melancholy,
sadness, solitude,
mention them nevermore—
dare not utter
those words
or their death will contaminate us—
melancholy, sadness,
solitude, solitude.

Dawn

Bound into that bed
death
struck two deaths.
After dawn opened
black whirls
contours
at a certain height and depth
unbinding
muffling
the wail
at the window
open
closed
luminous
dark
and latched.
It's just a word.
Breaking day
at a certain height
grows cold—oblique
at the flank of love.

Translated by Maureen Ahern & Cecilia Bustamante

Jesús Cabel (Lima, Peru, 1947) is a writer and critic whose work "Crossing Hell" ("Cruzando el infierno") won the National Poetry Prize in 1975. As a critic he has published *Bibliography of Peruvian Poetry 1967–1979*. His "Chronicles of a Condemned Man" ("Crónicas de un condenado") is an unpublished book of verse, from which the present selection is taken.

Last Vision Of The Promised Land At Water Level In A Pool Of Anguish Which Is A Tangle of Shadows Where Stagnant Days Plunder The Sun And Man Of These Woods (Excerpts)

3

That tree trunk stretching up like a mast defying History
    of that shack ten or twelve feet above water
    faded in the memory of profane rites
    high priest of crime
I keep those walls of rotted wood
    perhaps because of the rain which is another flow let loose from
      above
    that incessantly beats the weak tin roofs
    perforated halfway through the silence
    when terror frightens off hunger's corpse
and I affirm that it is a sonata of the 21st century
    but those little notes pitter patter on the tangled hair
    form the rise of the colorless and/or contaminated surf
    and carry their own voice filling us with fear
you believed in the desert when you saw the streets of Venice
    not straight as the flight of sleepwalking moths
    nor with parabolic lines beating the bay windows
    and to touch this door which slides towards time
    because it was flooded with worthless kisses that didn't even
                leave their colored imprint
    that would sustain the beautiful theory of love
    is to find the futility of the heavens at the bare feet
    of an eccentric who defecates determined to demonstrate
    that this city is a tomb where birds suffocate
    before the dragon fly stirs with new life
stooge in the seething morning
    this is the compass and nobody believes in paradise anymore

5

Obituary nor the one of the boy with his whole skeleton
on the opaque wood that cannot prolong its roots nor the aroma
 that comes from below and the candles no longer light the peace
 nor the kiss that carried the strength of other less golden times
 charged with electric impulses and the flower
 wrapped in a thousand colors looked like that fragility
 which freed his senses
 and waved his arms in time with the rain
 he was the old windmill that defended dreams and the vigil
raised its shoulders drunk as the best of wine tasters
who gives in to the trick of happiness
 a drink is always a drink and never enough
 the way you were you shouted it out at the top of your lungs
 hear him well you demon moths
until I found you my little one with startled eyes
 it seems as though a tree had killed your gracefulness
 from swinging you from branch to branch
 and you were trapped in poverty
 it was a slum with four savage paws to defend itself
 against the river's flood and canoes ride the new air
 gulping down the fish that doze beneath your buttocks
now you are still
 terribly motionless and other hands play the little
 abandoned drum
 they play cards and throw a pair of dice
 in the face of the skeptic
 thus they manage with their dead when dawn breaks
 and they decide to put him six feet deep
 he will fertilize sweet greens
 whenever the summer fruit is as beautiful
 as this woman won over in the markets

6

Observe that scene of infant murmurs
the deformed little bodies
 broken wings fighting for a kiss
 in the garbage dumps which are another kind of mountain in the
  morning
 and the image of man like rusted ruins
 since even the trees most skilled in resisting the frenzy
 of the wind whose weakness is in sheltering birds and names
 have been chopped off at the neck with no other meaning
 than survival
 clawing at the earth is nothing new for us

swallowing stones or fermenting memories
those that once inaugurated the beauty of winter
is a fact unrecorded by statistics or any other science
we have talked of freedoms and exotic drinks
  oh drinkers of forests and cliffs
  and we found salt on our lips and in our hearts a limitless
bitterness which strips us of words
  we mistook the beginning and death holds vigil in this house
  its roots emerge from the tepid loneliness of the river

Translated by Diane J. Forbes

César Emilio Cantoni (La Plata, Argentina, 1951) is a poet of the current generation and is a member of the "Latencia" Literary Group. His works appeared in the *Buenos Aires Poetical Anthology*, 1977.

Absent Man

But man does not exist.
—Vincente Aleixandre

Man, who never existed,
was scarcely a child, a sleepless bearded being,
an animal whose precious pelt
gleamed in the dark,
whose sonorous skin shone
like the green pure light of leaves;
he was only a handful of impulses,
an unkempt and instinctive guest
and he already dreamed of changing the world.

This was man:
a communer of universes,
a solitary pastor of skies and clouds,
an infancy orphan of words yet,
when he decided to embrace the horizon with his arms,
extend the domains of his kingdom,
and go beyond days and nights.

And from that nameless age,
spurred on by the proud impulse of his blood,
he stood erect like a colt that had offered
its foreshortened figure to the heavens.
He defeated the rains,
he apposed lands,
he built roads upon the sea,
he engendered ports,
he lit cities,
he extracted light from lightning,
    gold from the mountain,
    fuel from the soil . . .
He surrounded himself with projects and portents,
and thus he grew, almost imperceptibly,
intrepid and challenging,
as he raised his Babel.

Yet, the vast crossing completed,
man, who was never necessary,
was nowhere.
He indeed journeyed miles of disaffection,
desperately excessive and alone, treading
upon the dust of the days,
walking under suns of stone
until he fulfilled his dark vocation of a fossil.
But he was not a shadow, eddy, timber,
he was neither promise nor destiny.
Only a glimpse of his being was insinuated in the beginning
when his bare foot
still fit the measure of the earth.
For it is that man, lost in the mist
of time, kept his heart in a box,
cast it scornfully onto the pyre of oblivion,
like a disused lapel or collar,
so that torn from his breast
it had no sky to extend its wings
nor blood to live dreams.

Now do you understand the reason of my speech?
A heart without light is a dry branch.
Without tears man does not exist.

In Memoriam Dylan Thomas

I

Now that the holocaust has been consumated
and your dreams, sustained by their bitter, troubled vigil,
live in alliance with the winds of Wales,
fully liberated;
now that time has closed upon your life
"like a fleeting tomb," and "the worm that devours the living"*
has perforated your tunic;
now as you traverse "the woods of brambles"
where "the dead grow for their delight":
is it possible to initiate this dialog between strangers,
between two who know each other not
and whom only the unburied page draws together?
Perhaps it is more difficult to realize
that birth and death are a trick of destiny.

---

*Words and phrases in quotation marks are those of Dylan Thomas in his poems.

II

You will say: "Leave this sleepy one alone in the place where he lies,"
but the shadowy thunder that shrouds
the silent flesh of so many crawling on their knees
over the mud, sinking, with "blindness to the bone,"
forces me to resume the pulse of your memory,
the secret rhythm of your thought escaping
from "the trap of the cadaver,"
building through words
propitious signs to dispirit
the premeditated deluge of *our* ungrateful time.
And maybe because "light irrupts where no sun shines"
it is still possible to believe that dignity
is hatched among "mad men."

III

Your dialog was also established between the womb and the shroud,
and when you took your drunkenness out
through the bars of Greenwich Village,
it was only the anguish of man that swam
freely on your breath, your alcoholic kisses,
the orgiastic embrace with the spirits of wine.
For once "humanity spit from a sorrow"
to the climes of the world, how can one raffle off orphanhood,
abandonment, the cruel light
with which the colors of the day are stirred?
Perhaps if "the gentle touch of love tickled" us
it would be possible to forget the scissors of time.
I say, therefore: "Let us exorcise death
in the woman filled with summer" and let us toast
on our finiteness to the intricate domains of ecstasy.

IV

I am not your friend, it is true, nor shall I try like others
to bury your friendship "with brief winks of the eye";
yet we carry the same sorrow tied to our bowels
and we are joined by the same dryness in our mouths for singing
of the vain vestments that dazzle the imprudent.
And although "I have yearned to go away" as you too,
in the same way my feet remained stuck to the earth,
awaiting, perhaps, "some life,"
that minimum light that, overflowing
the banks of darkness, we believe will arise in the end.

V

But, Dylan, will it be possible to attain the season of life,
that day when the cemeteries will return their dead,
and cities will be established on the sea,
and kings will redeem themselves washing in their peoples' wound?
The time will arrive, indeed,
when peace will embrace our poor bones,
and then, "death will have no dominion."

VI

And now that your ceiling is a cold white stone, and worms
have built subterranean paths in the "bag of your body,"
now that death has sealed your breath forever
and your unchained heart lies asleep among shadows;
now that "time is a foolish fantasy" for you
and your ears are deaf to any music other
than the somber tunes of silence;
now your lips smile and your eyes sparkle
and no harm can lie with you nor touch you.
You have said it: "After first death there is no other."

Translated by Wayne H. Finke

ERNESTO CARDENAL (Granada, Nicaragua, 1925) is one of the outstanding poets of his century. After taking part in revolutionary activities, he came to the United States and studied with Thomas Merton. Following his ordination in Colombia he established a community in Nicaragua. His *Zero Hour (Hora cero)*, 1960, and *Psalms (Salmos)*, 1964, have firmly established him as a poet of international renown.

Psalm 36

Do not become impatient if you see them make many millions.
Their commercial stocks
                                        are like the hay of the fields.
Do not envy millionaires or movie stars
or those who appear across eight columns in the papers
or those living in luxury hotels
and eating in luxury restaurants
for soon their names will not appear in any paper
nor will even scholars know their names.
For soon they will be cut down like the hay in the fields.
Let not their inventions
        and technical progress make you impatient.
The leader you see now, soon you shall see him not
you will seek him in his palace
        but you will find him not.
Timid men will be the new leaders
                                        (the "pacifists").

They are enlarging the concentration camps
they are inventing new tortures
new systems of "investigation."
At night they do not sleep, making plans
how to crush us more
                                        how to exploit us more
but the Lord laughs at them
for he sees they will soon fall from power.

The arms they manufacture will be turned against them.
Their political systems will be erased from the earth
and their political parties will cease to exist.
Their technicians' plans will serve for naught.

The great powers
                        are like the flower in the fields.

Imperialisms
                are like smoke.

They spy on us all day long.
They have the sentences already prepared.
But the Lord will not turn us in to their police.
He will not permit us to be condemned on Judgment Day.
I saw the dictator's portrait everywhere
        —it spread like a vigorous tree—
and I passed by again
                                and it was no longer there.
I looked for it but could not find it.
I looked for it but there was no longer any portrait,
and his name could not be pronounced.

The Heavy Drops . . .

The heavy drops seem like
footsteps going up a stairs
and wind beating the door
a woman about to enter.

The Rains of May . . .

The rains of May have already arrived,
the red malinches* have bloomed anew
and the Diriá road is joyous, full of puddles:
                but you are no longer with me.

Our Poems . . .

Our poems cannot be published yet.
They circulate by hand, in manuscript,
or mimeographed. But one day
the name of the dictator (against whom
they were written) will be forgotten,
and they will continue to be read.

The National Guard . . .

The National Guard is seeking a man.
A man hopes to reach the border tonight.

---

*Central American shrub with showy flowers

The name of this man is not known.
There are many men buried deeper in a ditch.
The number and names of these men are not known.
Neither the place nor number of ditches is known.
The National Guard is seeking a man.
A man hopes to leave Nicaragua tonight.

Girls . . .

Girls, when one day you read these verses, filled with
                              emotion,
and you dream of a poet;
know well that I wrote them for one like you
and it was in vain.

You Were Alone . . .

You were alone midst the crowds
alone as are the moon
and the sun in the sky.

Yesterday you were in the stadium
midst thousands of people
and I spied you as soon as I entered
just as if you had been alone
in an empty stadium.

I have handed out clandestine leaflets

I have handed out clandestine leaflets,
shouting "Long live liberty!" right in the street
challenging the armed guards.
I took part in the April rebellion:
but I pale when I pass by your house
and just your glance makes me tremble.

Epitaph for Joaquín Pasos

He used to walk through these streets, without work, without a job,
without a peso.
Only poets, whores and the persecuted knew his verses.
He was never abroad.

He was in jail.
Now he is dead.
He has no monument.
                    But
remember him when you have concrete bridges,
great turbines, tractors, silvery silos,
good governments.
For he purified in his poems his people's language
in which one day they will write business treatises,
the Constitution, love letters and decrees.

Epitaph for the Tomb of Adolfo Baez Bone

They killed you and they did not tell us where they buried your body,
but since then all of the national territory is your
                    grave;
or rather: in each palm of the national territory where your body
                    is not found, you were re-born.
They believed they were killing you with an order of "Fire!"
they believed they were burying you
and what they were doing was burying a seed.

Translated by Wayne H. Finke

Magolo Cárdenas (Saltillo, Mexico, 1950) has published short stories in many literary magazines. She has coauthored with Arnaldo Coen and Juan García Ponce a book titled *So From Within* (*Tan desde adentro*) and has recently published *Celestino and the Train* (*Celestino y el tren*), a children's story.

But What if I Liked the Panchos, Not the Beatles

You know what, Pilar? Sometimes I think that when we were teenagers we were a lot alike, that we both suffered through the same things and we took life seriously in the same way, convinced that we stopped being little girls in one fell swoop.

To me, everything was extreme. There was no middle ground, no going halfway; everything was cut with one slice of the knife, even time, I don't know. The world then was a well-defined stage and the characters didn't even turn a page. On the other hand, the audience stared endlessly at a dressing room, an entrance and a huge character that was too big for either of us (my hands couldn't quite cover the others, the woman ones, the adult ones. The thighs, the hips and the breasts weren't my size and I swam in them). I think that day the lights came up and I didn't have any choice but to stage my play. I don't think I had ever been so alone, had ever felt so small. I got lost in the curtain and I thought the butterflies in my stomach would never stop. You'll see.

I walked towards the small town's dance hall. I was looking at the lines on the sidewalk—*step on a crack, break your mother's back*. My mom had let me off at the corner because I would have died if my friends had seen me being brought to the dance by my mother. I would have hated it if my brothers looked at my friends from the car window, curious, rude. I lived outside the city and back then my mother had to take me everywhere. I wasn't one of the girls who lived downtown or one of the older ones who could go anywhere by themselves.

The girls from my school class would have been to lots of dances already. The girls from my class, just before getting there, would primp and fix their hair. There would be somebody, Trixie García, it would have to be Trixie García, who would have the nerve to hide behind a car in order to lift up her skirt and adjust her garters one last time. *But stockings fall down on me.*

Trixie's lifted skirt and her snow-white thighs reflected in the chrome fender of the car. I saw the whole scene clearly. Step on a crack, break your mother's back.

I was almost up to the door of the dance hall. *If I count to fifteen without speeding up my steps and I haven't reached the pillar, it means I'll be a wallflower all afternoon.* Be a wallflower, sit the bench all afternoon. That's the way the girls in high school said it. A wallflower . . . how embarrassing. *Thirteen fourteen fifteen.* I missed getting to the pillar by about two steps.

You had to go up a long red stairway before reaching the inside ballroom door. With the straight skirt I had on I couldn't go up the steps two at a time. As I went up the stairway the huge sky-blue columns tipped in golden leaves at the ceiling came into view. "They must guard the place," I thought, "they must be here to guard the place."

In the middle of the ceiling there was an immense cluster of gilded leaves and grapes in plaster bas-relief from which hung a prism chandelier, half-lit. Nevertheless, the room was white, bright white and shining. Because all around there were lights like in a hospital, fluorescent lights.

I got to the last step. It was a huge ballroom furnished with metal folding chairs from the Carta Blanca beer company. The chairs were lined up along the walls and looked scared, as if on trial, just like me. A big tropical mural—sort of crooked modern style guitars, maracas, and rumba dancers with full sleeves and ruffled skirts—watched me enter. Purple, turquoise blue and brash palm green. *Well, look at that! Where could they be from? Landscapes just like the covers of Papa's old records, the cha-cha and rumba records ("rumba, Grandma, rumba").*

From the doorway I saw Betty. She was looking slowly and nonchalantly, very nonchalantly conscious of her nonchalance, at an album cover. She didn't have anybody to dance with, that was all. The poor thing, like me, was also one of "the younger girls." I headed straight towards her.

"Look," she said, "a Beatles' record."

"And what does that mean?" I asked frankly.

"What do you mean what does that mean? The *Beatles*," she answered.

I didn't dare ask any more. The Beatles on the album cover had long hair. They, on the other hand, the ones who had split into little groups on the other side of the room, didn't have long hair. They had, rather, a sort of map painted on their head, a very distinct map. Two sideburn peninsulas, a gulf behind the ears, open sea at the neck and a mountainous zone of a pompadour at the forehead. They wore pointy cowboy boots, some with gold at the toe. Their belt buckles had two horns on them, two horns on a greenish-blue background. They, the ones on the other side, spoke uninhibitedly, boldly, showing off their confidence and ease. They shouted it out, raised it to the ceiling and held it caressingly there, impassable shield, smooth polished stone. They wore really tight pants, and they couldn't keep their eyes in one place. Grown up bodies, columns reaching almost to the ceiling, feeling so tall. They smoked cigarettes blatantly. They pulled at each other, they sort of pulled each other back and forth. They, the ones on the other side, had sent out deep roots which grew down from their legs. From the waist up they sent out branches, arms lost in vague gestures. Over here, near us, the girls from my class at school whispered to each other, spoke softly and giggled shyly.

Betty said let's go get a Coke. The bar was at the back of the ballroom, an awkward and pretentious piece of furniture. Behind it there was a huge mirror which tried to pass itself off—in reflection and scattered gilding—as marble.

I left my purse there—I had no idea what you were supposed to put in one (my mother's lipstick the color of ladies' lips which I wouldn't dare to use even as a joke because it was so out of style, two Kleenex and my collection of four key rings without keys. What else do you keep in an evening bag? How do ladies find so much stuff to put in them? Having an evening bag full of things was for grown-ups.) Of course the other girls from my class would have their evening bags full of important things: keys, their boyfriends' pictures and cigarette butts in their wallets, compacts and eyeshadow. *He who feels sorry for himself does not love God,* I said to myself.

We were walking hand in hand. Betty and I were walking hand in hand, accomplices in a mute, lump-in-the-throat timidity. As we walked we could feel them looking at us, stares that slid down the back, paused, sticky, parasitic, then continued on, trickling down the legs, crawled up to the hair, hid there, lurking, and then came out suddenly at the nape of the neck—"It's giving me goosebumps. Look Betty, it's giving me goose-bumps"—fell heavy against the hips, noisy, restless, scrutinized through the brassiere.

an wen ai touch yu ai fil japi insaaaaaid

As soon as we were in the mirror's sight, we were reflected in a hundred little pieces, its golden veins suddenly spreading over our hips, our breasts, our legs. Getting to the bar was like reaching for security. The fluorescent lights revealed our presence at once in front of the mirror. "They're hospital lights," I thought. "They show everything. Just like the ones at the doctor's." Naked in front of those lights, as naked as in the doctor's office. Open, exposed, a wound that never heals. I looked at myself in that mirror sort of out of the corner of my eye. At home they had told me that French curls wouldn't look good on me. "I told you so. I insisted that you should get something simpler," I heard my mother's voice saying. It was a stupid, ugly hairdo; it made my head look twice the size it really was. I wanted to get a comb and take it all down right there in front of the bar mirror, but it was like an impenetrable helmet that would only come apart with plenty of soap and water.

An jelp mi onderstan

"I'm really not this ugly," I would have liked to tell them. "I'm really not this ugly; I'm usually not so ugly."

My dress was pinching me at the waist. My stockings and garters were pulling at my skin. From head to toe I was one taut band, skin that stayed tight and pulled even if I bent my knees, skin stretched tight from one end of me to the other.

I would have liked to turn time back to the previous morning so I could not go to the hairdresser's, and not put on "smoky temptation" colored stockings. I would have liked to change everything, change the dress that earlier had seemed like one from a Corín Tellado story, worn by a sensitive woman who falls in love in silence, who cries in silence.

Now I was so small, so minute. *Nothing about me counts, not what I am or what I think. I don't want it to count. I don't want them to pay any attention to it.* The day before I had imagined myself as solid as the Rock of Gibraltar; the image disappeared the moment I entered the dance hall. I wanted to completely erase the whole story I had imagined about that moment, but the dress, the hairdo and the stockings were my betrayers. They gave me away in an instant. On them were written, indelibly, irreversibly, my fantasies.

Now I noticed that the straight skirt I was wearing really emphasized my hips. The darts in my blouse were way too big, and no matter how much toilet paper I stuffed in my bra, it didn't help. "I'm not this ugly, really. I'm usually not so ugly."

JELP! ai nid sombadi JELP!
jelp me if yu plis aim filing daun

I had to invent some way to get out of there. I left Betty alone with the very original excuse that I felt a little queasy and was going to go splash some water on my face.

The men's room door had a derby hat, gloves and a cane painted on it. The ladies' room door had a gold fan. I pushed the door open hard and took a deep breath. No one could look at me inside there.

di guorld is triting mi bad
miseri, uooooo, miseri

I hadn't realized that I wanted to cry, that I wanted to go home, play baseball and chew gum. Ride my bike, ride my bike. I remembered my secret bike route and the favorite hill I rode down. I remembered the expanse of mountains, stretched out in the sun. I opened my whole body, set it free like a kite to the sky. I remembered the laughter, the guffaws ("listen I'm really not this ugly. Normally, really, I'm not so ugly"), and the wind ripped through the thin paper kite and it dropped to the ground. Now I was torn, ragged, folded away in the closet, dark.

> *bot evry naw an den ai fil so insequiur*
> *JELP mi if yu can aim filing doun*

The green vinyl chairs of the ladies' room lounge were built into the wall and had a canopy over the top. I lay down there to look, unconsciously, at the armchair carved with Aztec figures and at the plastic flowers. Betty came in:

"Hey, come on! They're starting to ask people to dance. They're playing the Beatles."

> *lov, lov mi du, yu nou ai lov you,*
> *ai olgueys bi tru, so pliiiiis*

Beatles' music. My idea of love songs were ones sung by the Dandys, the Panchos, or the Three Aces, music from "the romantic hour." It was impossible to understand anything by the Beatles.

> *guen ai was yonger so moch yonger den tudey*
> *ai never nided anibadis jelp in ani guey*
> *JELP!*

I liked the Panchos, my dress was out of Corín Tellado, I had toilet paper stuffed in my bra, I got my shoes on sale and my stockings were brand new. I had never heard the Beatles, I had never heard them. *Nothing about me counts, not what I am or what I think. I don't want it to count, I don't want them to play any attention to it.*

When my mom came to pick me up, I told her that everything had been fine and that they had played Beatles' music. It made me feel so upset and mad when she asked about them that I answered angrily:

"Oh, Mom, the *Beatles!*"

Translated by Diane J. Forbes

JORGE CARRERA ANDRADE (Quito, Ecuador, 1903), a diplomat, is one of the pillars of Ecuatorian poetry. Over the decades his verse has evolved towards the expression of the universal, with Latin American man as its basis. His publications include *Planetary Man (Hombre planetario)*, 1936, and *Ultimate Poetry (Poesía última)*, 1968.

Final Invocation to the Word

Word:
may you be
a shell-less
almond

Or pome
of essence,
a coin
of gold.

Little cell
of the bee:
enclose
life.

Bee:
prepare
eternal
delights.

Be a lark
of the dawn,
not a mummy
or a stone slab.

Be not
a phantom
or jail
of mist.

Be a mirror:
reflect
earth
and heaven

Or hunting
horn:
raise
the deer
of the soul,

the things
of the purest
world
without shadow.

Be a sheath
of sure
arrows,
word,
a painting
with depth
not an adornment
of froth.

Be tight
of form,
a wedding
ring.

Exact
measure
of the world:
word.

Translated by Wayne H. Finke

HÉCTOR CARRETO (Mexico City, Mexico, 1953) is the author of three books of poetry: *Far from the Ships (Lejos de las naves)*, *Still Life (Naturaleza muerta)*, which received the coveted Efraín Huerta Prize, and *Saint George's Sword (La espada de San Jorge)*.

Sleeping Beauty's Request

Lord:
      tomorrow I'll be fifteen;
I must be the queen
                  in an ivory tower
and I want a magic wand
to give me three little chicks as a gift.
I also want a nightingale to sing
         to me at night.
For that I need a man,
not a German shepherd
or a great dane,
        but a prince
           who has
a white mustang and
        a shiny erect sword
that opens a way through the woods
      and scratches the curtain
            of my bedroom.

Lord:
I am the ring awaiting
         a powerful finger
and that finger is you
        Lord
Why do you blush?
Go on,
take off my heels
and water a little saliva
on my burning lips.

Vanity of Vanities

Farrah Fawcett-Majors, with her golden curls,
Bo Derek with her blond African tresses,
Linda Carter, Wonder Woman

and all the goddesses of Hollywood
are highly indignant
for Hector, the poet,
prefers to sing to you, oh sweet Lesbia,
modest bank secretary.

Saint George's Sword

Blessèd Saint George
of the high peak:
    again this old woman
who never never
tasted meat
either by day
    or by night
prays to you.

Mutton was never
    on my plate
nor ox tail in my soup.
Never did the pig's snout
pass through my lips
nor ever ever did any bird
land on the island of Never Never.

I was always vaccinated
      and I lived in a glass case
wrapped in alcohol
    and cotton.
Thus I never caressed
      the deer's hide
nor did I feel on my back
the cat's chilling scratch.

But at night I dream myself a mare
ridden by wild rider
that plunges his sword in me
or are they knives
that desire sticks in me?

But the tea has grown cold
and the last train has passed.

That is why, dear George,
I yearn to be wounded
      by your sword of fire.
It makes no difference that blood stains

the whiteness of satin.
My only desire is to be the pork
that sates your eyeteeth.

Saint Teresa's Confession

Christ, my husband,
I confess my error to you:
it was that very dark night
     do you remember?
I was very hot
          and I went off towards the fountain.
There before my eyes
          appeared the devil
more like the minotaur Hector than a fallen angel.

And right there he stripped me
like one peals a fruit.
And he bit me.
     Ay!
          he bit me all over my body;
I felt delightful relief
in refreshing those thirsty lips
          I swear to you.
But do not get mad
     my belovèd:
I bring to you intact
     my soul
          my shell
          and my pit.

Translated by Wayne H. Finke

Aida Cartagena Portalatín (Moca, Dominican Republic) is a prolific writer and scholar whose publications include *Vespers of Dream (Vísperas del sueño)* and the novel *Ladder for Electra (Escalera para Electra)*.

"Colita"

Mommy used to call me "Colita," Colita García. But Mrs. Sarah registered me in public school as "Dawn." "There will be no such thing as 'Colita,' " she screamed. I continued to feel myself as 'Colita' even when I was 'Dawn' to others. I'll never forgive her for her teasing laugh as she chews the name Dawn when she calls me, discriminating me, especially since she has never even seen the dawn. No. Noo. And noo! I am not going to stay here with her, in her house, even though she pays my studies, tells everyone that I am a talent. Nevertheless, I'm fed up with her and the nuns at the school, Sister Tantina, long and skinny like Twiggy from T.V., and mother superior, wise but with the looks of Aldonza, Sancho Panza's wife, and go on with those theorems, and so on with that about the triangle and rectangle and what are parallel lines, and screw Colita-Aurora with punishments and telephone calls so that Mrs. Sarah attacks me like a machinegun. No. Noo. And Nooo, No!

I said no. I don't like Mrs. Sarah nor do I care about her beautiful house, nor am I going to get old inside her four walls like a tree destined for charcoal. No, I am not going to stay with her like a tree burning under a dog day sun.

No, I'm not going to remain sad, head bowed, like the leaves beaten by the thunder-rain storms, within these walls surrounded by an evergreen lawn and some fruit trees. Nor do I accept that about Dawn is an intelligent little black girl, nor that about blacks amuse me, nor that about blacks and their jazz and rhythm. Or that the blacks make the world happy and go to the store and bring me Donna Summer's latest record, and that blacks ought to be good for something, that it's good they amuse whites. No, Noo.

I like that unending music of Donna Summer, scratching, howling without stopping, falling like a vibrant exciting cascade. But it's for sure that Mrs. Sarah is not going to keep me forever inside her exciting music box, that the jazz, the boogaloo, that the ragtime or the beduim etc. That stuff is not for that old bag. She thought I wasn't going to leave. I'd love for her to see how fast I'm walking to the bus stop, dragging this heavy bundle with my clothes and books. Here, driver, I'm getting out in Haina.

I walk around a bit, smelling the air of the sugar refineries. I sit in Candita's restaurant where I have a very cold 7-Up. Hungry, that's what I am, and I move on to the Dwarf's where I drink a Pepsi and eat two rolls. I leave quickly. Donna Summer's music fills the shack and extends itself through the whole neighborhood. How I remember that little unending cascade, meowing. Her music and her singing extends throughout the shack, through the neighborhood, it is the same tune that excites and shakes Mrs. Sarah. The hell with everything, but here I am, exactly 14 kilometers from the capital. It is 7 P.M., I enter the church and hide behind the alter of St. Isidor, the farmer who takes away the rain and brings the sunshine. Let the saint hide me, that I shouldn't be found. Saint, Saint, Saint, the streets are full of job-seekers and beggars. La la la la ya ya ya ya yaaa.

Next to a wall of The Dwarf Restaurant a girl is rocking. Donna's voice gets louder as a lottery vendor puts up the volume on his radio. Donna's voice again fills the bar, the neighborhood, the town. I try to gather my hair. If I was born with it that way, so it'll stay. What is really absurd is that they discriminate and make fun of my intelligence because I am almost a high school graduate. No, Noo, No, No! It infuriates me to see how so many millions of whites are enjoying Donna Summer, the little black girl who sings excitingly. They got to a frenzied pitch over the music of Armstrong, later that of Makeba. Jazz and all that rhythm that's born so happily. Congratulations! No, if I were Donna Summer I would recall all the records from the stores' cabinets, hotels, motels and the high class houses.

I take off as a housekeeper, convinced by the mister's wife of the sugar technical department. Here in New York, eleventh floor, I cook, wash, iron, shop, stand for the nonsense of the grocery keeper, that Italian son of a bitch, who pulls my hair and calls me "ugly black girl," asking where I'm from and this and that. Or the gringo Mrs., "Colita, why do you take so long?" I explain to her that the son of a bitch holds me back, or that I stopped to see Giordano slash Manfredi with a knife and all because of some stiff in the neighborhood who both think should be taken to his respective funeral parlor, and the police very calmly declare that now the stiff is Giordano's.

I am going to have to organize myself mentally in a sequence of classified ads by Denis W. published by any newspaper of the world. They put it into my head that this was the Free World and yet here I found that the Ohio chick exploits me like a slave. I don't understand that about the Free World and exploitation, and that Colita, how ignorant you are since you know nothing of monopolies, where I go to buy a bra at the Woolworth's chain with three hundred stores of sales and production, and the coming and going of policemen here, and there, "fresh," I scream to one of them who grabs one of my—(understand?). I'm tired of seeing you having shots of tequila behind the counter at the old Mexican's place, and this place full of cops, and the I.T.T.'s and from here they place tracks for the CIA all over the world; daily violence, torture, how they beat one up, an unemployed classless guy, with the looks of a drug addict on a simple hunch and the classless one allows them to beat him. This is not being manly, Dominican-style. The cop becomes a tough guy like in the westerns. If this is the Free World, overexploited, overdone, I'm going to leave; and no, noo and no! I'm leaving and will return to Mrs. Sarah, with her continuous music, the Donna Summer music, with the same calamities, screaming at me at each instant "disparatas." And she screams and howls in anger when I read in the newspaper the injustices that are committed against the blacks in South Africa. Not satisfied with the lynchings of SWETO and Johannesburg, Steve Biko was mutilated in a cell in Pretoria.

Mrs. Sarah grabs me by the hair, she screams in an extraordinary way: "nonsense, nonsense," she drags me to the record player where she raises the volume as far as it will go. I can't even hear myself cry now. Donna Summer, my dear little black girl, fill with your voice and excite with your rhythm Mrs. Sarah's house.

Translated by Catherine Rovira

CARLOS CASTRO SAAVEDRA (Medellín, Colombia, 1924) is a poet of social motives and is considered one of the most popular poets of Colombia. He was awarded the International Peace Prize in Beijing for his "Prayer from America" ("Plegaria desde América"). His *Complete Works* appeared in 1970.

Unemployed

There is a man who goes to wear out his feet in the city;
who leaves the house and doesn't know
where to go with his unemployed bones
and with his everyday eyes worn out
by the old newspapers he finds in the offices.

Captain defeated by an exercise of streets,
prisoner in the cages of the bars,
harvester of drinks and of faces,
of palid cigarettes and blank papers;
witness of small accidents
where cups lose their handles
and witness to the humid, muddy cancer
eating at the bitter leather of his shoes.

Out of work
just like those dogs
who silently urinate on the corners of the world.

Sometimes his sad empty head
thinks hungry and intelligent thoughts;
So much wheat in the world, so much wheat,
and no bread, not one bite, to occupy my mouth,
so many jobs, so many dictatorships,
and not even a rifle to occupy my hands.

Translated by Edward J. Sullivan

ANTONIO CISNEROS (Lima, Peru, 1942) teaches at the University of San Marcos in Lima. His poetry has been translated into many languages and he is the author of *Exile (Destierro)*, which received the National Poetry Prize, and *The Book of God and the Hungarians (El libro de Dios y los húngaros)*.

Your Head of an Italian Archangel

I   [Jutka]

Your head of an Italian archangel does not suit
      those eyes reaching beyond the Urals
      on horseback.
But you are fair like a fruit out of season.
(And you say that your mother bears the face
      of the old females of the Huns).
You love strong and plentiful wine—the sea
      of Spain, you say—and you curse
the lights of a patrol car at midnight. And
      you have no identification papers.

II   [from her father to Jutka]

"The labyrinth, Jutka, the labyrinth. Rebellious
      without rime or reason. You know not
of the violin (which you detest) or hunger.
You were born and our house was a home conquered
      by war. And however
we spent a winter with pimentos and salted
      bacon. (And nights in silence).
You know nothing of the time when glory was a
      red rat—my poppy—roasted in the trenches.
Your labyrinth, Jutka, your labyrinth. Of madmen,
      not rebels.
The tall pasture grass grows in perfect silence. And
      you fear so much peace.
I love peace (not that of the sheep). I, the son
      of the plague, rebel.
Don't look like that. Here no one has sold his soul
      to the devil, nor am I a weed.
Memory shines over the fresh earth.
Kiss my hands, Jutka. Go to sleep."

III

Behind that door—for now—remain men
        and rats biting each other in the old memory
        of your father
awaiting the dream of laurel.
The young warriors have reached Fish Street. Uncle Miska—
        already dead during Lent—shouts in poor Russian:
        the devil take war, gentlemen, the war is ended.
And you dream also. But your dreams are not
        some soldiers on Fish Street.
(Silence of the howitzer and the rat—red like a poppy).

IV

You were born when the moss grew old between
        the new bridges over the river.
Order and construction of Socialism.
And the memory of war was but a little ash
        with the wind of winter.
Docile days on the green hills beneath the sun.
But order was also the moan or the dark
        cry under the lights
and the sheep's peace
—smile of he who seeks a little house on the green
        hills under the sun.
                                        (You kiss his hands).

V   [Jutka's dream]

The White Guard: Denikin
in the Ukranian fields.
The Red Guard rides on the frontier.
It does not accept the armistice or rest.
(Death to Denikin
and death to the bandits of Poland).
Ducks quack over a forest of silver firs.

VI

Ducks quack and youths make love under
        this sky as blue as their jeans.
They do not know the violin and operetta in the great
        labyrinth. They know nothing
of the time of the rats. And they fear the silence
        at midnight.

The big black cars crossing the (blue)
    Danube are witness
of some old men—rebels, neatly ordered
    like straight hair.

Café on Martirok Utja

There is a flowered lamp on the piano
and an iron stove.
You drink your wine beside the only window:
a silver and blue bus every five minutes.
You ask the girl for an ashtray
(tall flower of the fields, come to me).
The autumn light is a kingdom
of golden birds in your glass.

But soon night falls.
The buses are not blue and silver,
the ash tray is a dead rat,
the glass is empty.
The girl left when they turned on
the flowered lamp and you were looking at
the flowered lamp.

You can order another pitcher of wine,
but tonight
don't wait for the gods at your table.

Sunday in Saint Christina's in Budapest and Fruitstand Next Door

It is raining on the peaches and pears,
their skins shiny under the deluge
like Roman helmets in their baskets.
It is raining midst the snoring of the surf
and the iron derricks. The priest
is wearing Advent green and a microphone.
I know neither his language
nor the century when this church was founded.
But I know the Lord is in his mouth:
for me guitars, the fattest calf,
the richest tunic, sandals,
for I was lost
more than a grain of sand in Black Point,
more than rainwater midst the waters

of the turbid Danube.
For I was dead and I am resurrected.

It is raining on the peaches and pears,
seasonal fruit whose name I know not, but I know
of their taste and smell, their color
that changes with the times.
I do not know the customs or face of the fruitseller
—his name is a sign—
but I know that this holiday season and the fattened cow
await him at the end of the labyrinth
like all good birds
tired of rowing against the wind.
For I was dead and I am resurrected,
praised be the name of the Lord,
Whatever his name under this vivifying rain.

Translated by Wayne H. Finke

Juan Gustavo Cobo Borda (Colombia, 1948) has been the editor of the renowned magazine *Eco* since 1973. He has written books of poetry, entitled *Advice to Survive (Consejos para sobrevivir)* and *Tea Room (Salón de té)*. His latest publication is *All Poets Are Saints and Will Go to Heaven (Todos los poetas son santos e irán al cielo)*.

Errant Dwelling

In one-night cheap hotels
where a sleepwalking porter
inaugurates long corridors
filled with cages
I see always at my side
the woman of the night of foretellings,
with her feverish magic
and lips as sweet as sin.

It is there where a razing piety
breaks our hearts with its sweetness.

But the coming light of dawn
brings with it the blaring of the radio
or the noise of a neighboring workshop
where surely they alter stolen cars.
Upon leaving, the sky appears unreal.

In the Hotel of Your Soul

The farewells, at the airport,
are always a nuisance
and while going home on the freeway,
the foreseen litany:
you do not exist, torpid fable,
but a gust of sudden perfume
conjures unfamiliar surroundings
and the freshness of clean sheets.

Nevertheless, the bodies
lying on the hardness of the floor
seek a better form of union.

In the shower, desire is a tepid claw
except you no longer exist, worthless fiction,
you are no longer dampness and lust.

Sheer nonsense,
death stacks dirty dishes
while a woman remembers
her lover who has departed.

I Lost My Life

To Peter Shultze-Kraft

While my friends, honest to the utmost,
knocked down dictatorships,
organized revolutions
and with mangled bodies became
a part of banal Latin American history,
I read cheap books.

While my girl friends, the most beautiful,
evaporated in front of him who,
hesitant, no doubt was barely able
to tell them how much they were needed,
I continued reading cheap books.

Now I see it:
These cheap books
were about the wildest love affairs, the most just of wars,
all of which some day
will redeem so many empty causes.

Translated by Jennie Ibarra

HUMBERTO COSTANTINI (Buenos Aires, Argentina, 1924) during the military terror in Argentina was one of the important voices in exile to explore through fiction and poetry the effects of this terror on the common man. His widely reviewed novel, *Of Gods, Little Men and the Police (De dioses, hombrecitos y policías)*, winner of the Casa de las Américas Prize (1979), was published by Harper Row in 1984. His most recent novel, *The Long Night of Francisco Sanctis (La larga noche de Francisco Sanctis)*, appeared in 1985. He is the author of six collections of short stories, of which *Speak to Me of Funes (Háblenme de Funes)*, 1970, is the most well known. He returned from Mexico to Argentina in 1984.

Immortality

It simply happens I've turned immortal.
Taxis respect me,
they stop in front of me,
and lick my boots like lapdogs.

It simply happens I'm not dying anymore.
There's no angina to speak of
no typhus, falling rocks, war, barbed wire,
no cancer, knife, flood, Junin fever, no vigilantes.
I'm simply from the other side
of this side,
totally immortal.

I walk among gods, ambrosias, olympuses,
I laugh, or sneeze, I tell a joke
and the time grows, grows like a crazy weed.

How phenomenal the business
of being like this, immortal
celebrating birth each five minutes,
being a million birds,
an enormous yeast.
What a scandal, heavens
this swarm of life,
this plague called by my name
elephantine, growing,
totally immortal.

I had, of course,
the grip, dread, budgets,

idiot bosses,
stomach aches,
nostalgia, longings,
bad luck.

But that was a century ago,
twenty centuries,
when I was mortal.
When I was
so mortal,
so pig-headed and mortal,
that I didn't even love you.
You figure it out.

Gardel

The way I see it, we invented him.
Probably it was a Sunday afternoon
with mate
      old memories
           melancholy
soft dance music on the radio
after the football game.

Probably a photograph on the wall got to us,
a certain "I'm not in the mood"
a certain unreadable book.

I think that's the way we were,
stupid with boredom,
playing solitaire with old whys and wherefores
without a woman or without money,
vapid.

Probably we suddenly felt
terribly alone,
very much orphans, very much children.

Perhaps we touched bottom.
Perhaps someone thought of calling it quits.
Then, I don't know,
something strange happened.
He came to us like an angel from within,
we became prophetic,
we awoke biblical.
We gazed at the cobwebs on the ceiling,
we told ourselves:

"Let us make a God, then, in the likeness
of what we cannot, but wish we could be.
Let us give him the best,
the most magic and the most bird
of ourselves.
Let us invent him a name, a smile,
a voice that lasts for centuries,
a firm stand in the world, beautiful, easy,
like winking at Destiny with a poker hand of aces.

We longed for him and, of course,
he arrived.
He came out of us—Latin, glorious, pomaded,
eternal like a God or a record.

The heavens opened up a bit on the side
and his voice sang to us:
                    mi Buenos Aires querido . . .

It was about six
the hour when the dance music was beginning
and the football game was over.

Algebra

I shall try to prove
that the cars on the avenida Cabildo
Perform
the music of loneliness
precisely.

If we take an asceptic bar
with formica, windows,
jackets, atmospheric music,
tickets, et cetera.
Facing—a cinema or a garage
or a bright billboard
or simply a time T
(it is slow somber, tired,
viscuous and predictable).
Now then,
in the case of the bright billboard
hitting relentlessly ad nauseam,
and if we eliminate to simplify
(and for obvious reasons) the garage and the cinema,
we have left the following collected memories:
an unpaved street,

a magnolia tree,
a dog that one loved,
a little stream with weeds in the shade,
the bushes with raspberries,
and the siesta.
Factoring out then the siesta into its usual terms:
birds, dragonflies, indolence,
and a patio fresh with plants,
we could easily admit the existence
of another time T'
particularly blue
and identical to wonder.
But as by definition
there are cars on the avenida Cabildo,
adding to the smog,
to the nostalgia,
to the pitiless passing of the years,
and to what we can call provisionally X,
we multiply by neurosis,
we divide by the constant 1924,
and we have therefore, remaining:
X equal to fear, equal to the impenetrable shell,
equal to the poisonous and raving bitch, loneliness.

That is exactly
what we wanted to prove.

Translated by Janet Brof

PABLO ANTONIO CUADRA (Managua, Nicaragua, 1912) founded the renowned literary magazine *Vanguardia*. He has written *Song of the Bird and Wife (Canción del pájaro y señora), Nicaraguan Poems (Poemas nicaragüenses)* and *Book of Hours (Libro de horas)*. Since 1950 he has been the codirector of the Managua daily, *La Prensa*.

The Calabash tree

A hero rebelled against the powers of the Black House.
A hero fought against the gentlemen of the House of Bats.
Against the gentlemen of the Dark House
               —Queguma-ha—
in whose interior only sinister thoughts occur.
The Mayans called him "Ahpu," which means "chief" or "head"
for he led. And his foot was daring, he who opened the way
and many times cunningly fooled his oppressors
but finally he fell into their hands.

(Oh, shadows! I have lost a friend!
rivers of people weep beside his remains.
The old fortunetellers prophesized a time of desolation.
"It will be," they declared, "the painfully sad time
when butterflies will be collected,"
when words no longer transmit the golden pollen.
I imagined that time of treacherous light—a cold and
moribund sun and birds of long squawks
pecking at autumn—
but it was a morning, a false glitter
of heavenly joy, chirping
still fresh and then
               the trap!
That dry blow of the heavy tile trap which suddenly
     snares
the unprepared, smiling hero.)

"You will be destroyed, you will be torn to bits
and your memory will remain hidden,"
declared the gentlemen of the House of Obsidian
(the barracks—the Arsenal).
And they beheaded the liberator.
And they ordered his head placed on a stake
and immediately the stake became a tree

and was covered with leaves and fruit
and the fruit were like a man's head.
     I write on this tree:
"Crescentia cújete"
"Crescentia trifolia"
"Xicalli" in the Nahuatl tongue
calabash-tree of the savanna
with cross-like leaves:
fasciculate, beautiful
leaves of a sacrificial design,
memorial of martyrs

"tree of skulls."
This is the plant
which makes the tree of the plains worthy.
Its fruit is the Indian's glass
Its fruit is the vessel or cup
                  —the cup of his drinks—
which the peasant adorned with incised birds
                  —for we drink song—
Its fruit sounds in our fiestas in maracas and timbrels
                  —for we drink music—
And for ages in the Mayan dialect of the Chortis
the word "Ruch" signifies indistinctly
—as among us—cup or head
                  —for we drink thoughts—

But the gentlemen of the Shadows
                  (those who censure)
declared: "Let no one approach this tree."
"Let no one dare gather this fruit."

And a girl named Ixquic learned the story. A girl became brave and said:
"Why am I not to know the miracle of this tree?"
And she lept on the oppressors' prohibition
and approached the tree.
She approached so that the myth gathered us in her image:
for woman is liberty, which incites
and the hero, untrammeled will.

"Ah," she exclaimed. "Will I live or die if I cut one of these fruits?"
Then the fruit spoke, the head between the branches spoke:
"What is it that you want?
Do you not know these fruits are the heads of the sacrificed?
By chance do you want them?"
And the girl replied: "Yes, I do."
"Then extend your hand toward me," the head declared
And the girl extended her hand

And the skull spit on her palm
and the saliva disappeared instantly and the tree spoke:
"I have given you my descendency in my spittle.
For the word is blood
and blood is once more word."

And thus began our first civilization
—A tree is its testimony—
The dawn thus begins, germinates each time
like Ixquic, the girl
who from the breath of the hero engendered
Hunahpú and Ixbalanqué
the twins, inventors of Corn:
the bread of America, the grain
with which the communion of the oppressed is kneaded.

Managua, 1978

Translated by Wayne H. Finke

The Indian and the Violin

For Juana Rosa

When Mondoy plays the violin
December clouds crumble into feathers
and to the East celestial-beings cross in flocks of Calendar
larks, of Linnets, of Thrushes.
Mondoy closes his eyes and inclines his head like a blind man
because music is a sweet blindness
a lagoon of blue waters.
Along his scale
descend the seven maidens, the early risers
to gather in their net the morning star
—it flutters its tail amidst the rushes of marginal waters—
and Tonantzin takes it by the gills and dawn illumines it.

The breath of Tonantzin is the unlimited land
where Mondoy's violin flits and hurdles
fugitive with a plumage of secret words. I have heard
songs in the Chorotega potteries
—lunar ocarinas of slow winds that raise
waves in the lagoon like scales of fish—
but not this rain, not this tenderness when
Mondoy plays the violin and it rains
in Diriomo, in Diriá, in Dirita, in Nindirí.

(Have you not perhaps had on your breast, soaking you
in music, the face of a woman crying?)

     August, the oppressor, maybe will return
hallowing his dogs of fire in the dog-days.
They smell the roads of dream. They know
that freedom is a flight. Or a thought.
Or a song when Mondoy plays the violin.
But nothing dies. In the air
we have sown our stars and we can
raise thought and sustain it
over the pure blue. Mondoy
traces a cross of music in the constellation
of the South. Mondoy plays the violin
and our Indian people go on a pilgrimage
to the place of promise.
A white line marks the tender border of the horizon.
It is the hour in which the seven maidens descend
—the dreamers—with their white sheets
to gather the evening star
and Tonantzin takes it in her arms
           and we hear the crying of a child
when Mondoy plays the violin.

Translated by María Pita

Belkis Cuza Malé (Cuba, 1942) presently lives in the United States; she is the author of the well-known collections of verse *Time of Sun (Tiempo de sol)* and *Letters to Anne Frank (Cartas a Ana Frank).* She is the editor of the very prestigious *The Linden Lane Magazine.*

Pandora's Box

The danger is in the street, but you wander on aimlessly
and catch yourself near the bronze hand
on the doors. Just as you are about to make
                           some noise,
doing something stupid,
a gust of wind holds you for a moment,
makes you turn your head, and you notice the old woman
standing next to you
with her bulging straw bag and, shining inside,
                           hidden,
her Pandora's box.
You don't trust your imagination and don't give in.
You let the arguments of time
and the mere thought of love
pass by.
She walks on.
She was tempted to let you have it all.
Why weren't you stung by the wonder of curiosity?

Oh, My Rimbaud

See how Rimbaud and I head for the sea
on a great white elephant,
drown in the brooding mist in our eyes
and fall like school kids
in love again.
He takes my hand; I gasp and pull away.
Then
he rides out on the tide,
sails other seas, other eyes,
goes on without me,
leaves me the red hair of his dreams,
the pale rouge of his cheeks,
a mirror.

When the storm has passed and his horse
finds the way,
he'll come back lord of the Golden Fleece,
jovial, and he'll have had his fill of me.

Women Don't Die on the Front Lines

Women don't die on the front lines,
their heads don't roll like golf balls,
they don't sleep under a forest of gunpowder,
they don't leave the sky in ruins.
No snow freezes their hearts.
Women don't die on the front lines,
they don't drive the devil out of Jerusalem,
they don't blow up aqueducts or railroads,
they don't master the arts of war
or of peace, either.
They don't make generals
or unknown soldiers carved out of stone
in town squares.
Women don't die on the front lines.
They are statues of salt in the Louvre,
mothers like Phedra,
lovers of Henry the Eighth,
Mata Haris,
Eva Perons,
queens counselled by Prime Ministers,
nursemaids, cooks, washerwomen,
romantic poetics.
Women don't make history,
but at nine months they push it out of their bellies
then sleep for twenty-four hours
like a soldier on leave from the front.

The Nature of Life

There's always a man painting
the door of his house,
a woman cutting the grass,
an old man climbing on to the roof of his garage,
burly weeds growing all over the backyard,
a head decapitated by light
bursting into tears,
a car flattening human instincts,
a man machine-gunned in the night

and another thrown out, on all fours, in the street.
You are always in my dream,
I am there, and my children.
When I wake up,
light is coming from another world
filtered by a slight concern
as I catch a glimpse
of a real landscape.

Order of the Day

She needs a hat
elegant enough
to make her presentable
to the President
of who knows what charitable organization.
Truth is, it's more an order than invitation,
something she doesn't quite pick up on,
because they say it with a smile.
It happens like that to all of us.

Translated by Pamela Carmell

Roque Dalton (San Salvador, El Salvador, 1933) is one of the revolutionary poets of El Salvador. A staunch believer in guerilla warfare, he was sentenced to death but was able to escape. He sought refuge in Cuba, where he presently resides. His published works include *The Sea (El mar)*, 1962, *The Evidence (Los testimonios)*, 1964, and *The Tavern and Other Places (La taberna y otros lugares)*, 1969. This last work won for him the Cuban Casa de las Américas Prize for poetry.

Poet in Jail

I did not want to think about destiny. For some reason
I associate it with forgotten tapestries of shame and majesty
where an impassive face
(like that of Selassie)
struggled to impose upon itself an eternal mark. Only the air,
absurd from cold in this my frying-pan country, applauds
till it reaches the heart in this hour. Oh, assault!
Oh, words that I shall no longer pronounce the same!
site of commissions for returning grandfathers.

This morning the guard brought only scraps
for me—the poor man has not suffered—
scraps which, with the fog, have given meaning to the day.
They are dead pieces of salt of some dead shellfish,

corn tortillas attacked with that fury
without more warm places to annoy,
remains of wild rice like three haughty standard-bearers
occupied in sparing lives of lambs and crude logics.

The wall is full of dates that I bear sinking,
Pieces of the final fatigue, bare fatigue, that cry and are
the worst witnesses of something that not even my tears would erase.

Translated by Wayne H. Finke

The Art of Poetry

For Rafael Castellanos

Anguish exists.

Man uses his old disasters like a mirror.

112

Only an hour after dusk
the man pulls in the painful remnants of his day
worried sick he puts them down next to his heart
sweats like a TB victim fighting for his life
and sinks into his deep lonely rooms.
The man smokes in there thoughtfully
wants to invent ruinous cobwebs on the ceiling
hates the freshness of the flower
exiles himself in his own skin he can't breath in
stares at his grim-looking feet
believes his bed is his grave day after day
doesn't have a penny to his name
is hungry
and breaks into sobs.

But all other men
bare their chests to the sun without a care
or to the killing in the streets
they lift the faces of the loaves out of the ovens
like a generous banner against hunger
they laugh until the air aches with children
they cram tiny footsteps into the wombs of fortunate women
they split rocks open like fruit hanging on to their solemnity
they sing naked into the friendly glass of water
they joke with the sea taking it by the horns playfully
they build homes of light in the song-filled wilderness
they get drunk all the way like God
they hold up their fists against despair
their avenging fires against crime
their love with its interminable roots
against hate's vicious scythe.

Yes anguish exists.

Like despair
crime
or hate.

Who should the poet's voice be for?

From *The Sea*

III

A ship filled
with dead hours

a ship filled with quiet groups escaping
from the sargasso weed's jaws at a deadly crawl.

In the prow we cut through the great wall of air
thinking to ourselves about the country
where we have left love
trembling in its first loneliness.

The books are soggy with salt
and from here the water is a big deserted square.
there's so much hierarchy in its battered emptiness.
In its cold nakedness like a black stone
on the horizon limp in the wind's arms.

Translated by Hardie St. Martin

Matilde Daviú (Maracaibo, Venezuela) is a short story writer and novelist who won the Casa de la Cultura Prize for her story *Death Has No Master (La Muerte no tiene dueño)*. Her novella *Barbazúcar* was published in 1977. She now lives in New York and is completing a novel to be titled *Neerebusch*.

Ofelia's Transfiguration*

*Take what is best from me there are no fires,
just a smooth stream of waters . . .*

It was eleven in the morning and they were already out along the hillsides with the sun tied on the hood of the Volkswagen. Above on the mountains, the day seemed misty and cold. Three quarters of an hour later, they broke out into a valley embracing a little floating town. The road dropped down to the main street, ending in a deserted plaza. From one side to the other, old houses with large windows, shutters, and screens were stacked up in rows; and farther on, the rest of the town spread out among small streets of reddish sand and ravines bristling with groves of *cují* trees. The little car moved along slowly and the lawyer awakened Nueva, tapping her knee. She didn't trust this place at all; she was suspicious, guided by that instinctive doubt that penetrated her neck first like a sting and then like a tongue of rubies. The lawyer insisted they had arrived, but a shiver ran down her spine and she braced herself crossing her arms. They backed up on the road and stopped, getting out in front of an entrance with painted tiles and green walls: a town hotel with a small lobby, striped canvas chairs, a dark wood hatstand and to the right a small desk. The lawyer and Nueva: two people who seemed aggressive for the fat mulatto who was coming out from behind the plastic curtain. He didn't wait for a question, but hurried to say there were no rooms, though they hadn't come for that, but to find out if anyone had seen the professor. The mulatto shook his head no and advised them to go to the police station. Just as they were about to cross the entryway, a shrill scream forced them to stop. An almost nude woman was rushing down the spiral staircase that began on the left side of the lobby, asking for help: her half-moon mouth painted fire red, her dark hair wild, a *cayena* flower behind her ear, barefooted, with a little silver chain around her right ankle. An oily, smelly Ofelia, bitch-dog, seal, hyena, from other worlds, with her teeth darkened by tobacco and her alcoholic breath spilling over their surprise. She

---

*From *Maithuna* (Caracas: Monte Avila, 1978).

115

grabbed Nueva by her blouse and, shaking her desperately, screamed for
help against the man she had been with. And while she was screaming
hysterically, the necklace made of river stones and seashells danced around
her blushing neck.

The mulatto drowned out her screams with a burst of cold laughter. He
approached Ofelia, slapped her buttocks twice, and ordered her to go back
up to her room, explaining that she always did the same thing when she
smelled someone new in town, that it was part of her show. Ofelia calmed
down, made a blushing grimace, half-pouting, half-bored, grabbed her
necklace with both her hands and, her head bent with shame, went up the
way she had come down. Nueva was nervous; she wanted to swallow, but
couldn't because a slug of fear was stuck in her throat, a slug of fear like a
giant and rotten oyster. The lawyer led her by the arm to the exit. They got
into the car again and went back to the plaza,looking for the police station.
After crossing the bridge, they turned left onto a dirt road leading out to
the mountains. But a soldier, a teenager, hastily cut them off, stopping
them in the middle of the road. The lawyer stuck his head out of the
window and told him what they were looking for. The soldier said they had
to go back to the town plaza. The sun was slowly eating all the shadows,
bursting right on the plaza; scarcely a warm breeze moved the few crotons
and *olas-de-mar* which were drowning in the concrete. They didn't see any
police station, or anything that resembled it, neither a coat of arms nor a
sign, only the plaza and the deserted street. Nueva begged him to leave,
but the lawyer pointed at a window framing the torso and face of a man.
Decisively Nueva got out of the car and asked him if he had seen the
professor who was well known in Caracas and had been working around
the town for several months. The lawyer had already gotten out too and
trying to clarify the situation said that the professor was looking for enormous bones about a meter in length. The man in the window opened his
eyes wider, and without saying a word, staunchly shook his head no.
Frustrated, the lawyer and Nueva were circling the plaza for the last time,
when a man wearing an undershirt came out from a house surrounded by
an iron fence. He asked them what they were looking for and finding out,
said this was the police station and everything had to be reported there.
They got out of the car, following his advice to speak first with Sergeant
Chávez, a *coriano* with Indian features, who received them sitting in a chair
and asked what they wanted. The previous experience had shown that the
paleontologist's work was unknown and they avoided mentioning the kind
of discoveries the professor was making. They told him they were looking
for a man who opened big holes in the earth and took things out. "Treasures? Oh, yes. . . ." Of course they didn't know that man. "The one who
had lived for several years in a thatched hut, just at the corner?" The
sergeant pointed to an old woman who was coming out and emptying a
bucket of water into the street. Complaining, Nueva dragged the lawyer
towards the car. They had traveled more than one hundred and twenty-

four miles for nothing, to end up in this hellhole where the professor may never have come; and it would be better to go back immediately rather than risk going mad wasting so much time. The lawyer was thirsty and stopped for something to drink in a café at the entrance to the town, remembering having seen it when he arrived that morning. They were parking the *Fauvé* when Sergeant Chávez approached them waving, sweating from the speed of his bicycling, and asked them for identification. The lawyer showed his identification card, but Nueva only had a temporary one. The sergeant almost tore it out of her hands and after examining it thoroughly from top to bottom, he asked her with a trembling voice where the picture was, saying that this wasn't an identification card, that what she needed was a card with a picture, that little green piece of paper placed in a water-proof plastic casing where her face stuck out, gazing over a wall of numbers, that her name wasn't important, but her face with numbers, her tan, numbered face marked like a prisoner's, because that little yellow paper dancing happily between the fingers of the queer sergeant wasn't worth anything, that he was already suspicious about them, that this professor thing was an invention, and that they were going to jail just because and THAT'S IT; that suspects without documentation were locked up, not in the police station but in an antiguerrilla camp so that those guys could better take care of the matter: the bulldogs, the hunters, there, at the edge of the little bridge, would arrange it on that Carnival Monday, if it was Monday or Tuesday or whatever damned day it was, because anyone who comes into this town is up to something, yes man, something no good. . . . And Nueva saying that she wanted her identification back and the lawyer gritting his teeth with suppressed rage and the sergeant saying that the paper wasn't worth anything and Nueva that the picture wasn't important if she was there herself, that pictures were memories and that she was more important than a piece of paper, the damned picture, the numbers of shit, the town and the whole scare-story the sergeant had dreamed up; that her personal integrity, that justice, that he should take a good look at her, that she was who she was and the sergeant saying no, that they had to come with him, and THAT'S IT . . . ! From his holster, he took out his pistol, cold and shining like the light of day, and leaving the bicycle in the middle of the road, he got into the back of the car and sat down, grasping the damn thing as if it were a toy.

The lawyer, while they were on their way, yelling at him that he was crazy, a dolt dressed up like a sergeant with the law's permission and government orders to shoot arsonists, chicken thieves, and killers. . . . And Nueva, that she had just come from the beach, that he only had to look at her flowered bikinis and her peeling face, that he could search the car and if he found anything suspicious she would reward him with five bolívares as her forty-year-old mother used to offer to do when boasting that her daughters could not find even one gray hair. The sergeant pointed the way with the pistol and the lawyer swallowed with difficulty in his

Adamite pain, watching Nueva's deadly terror out of the corner of his eye in that neck-cutting solar hour. They reached their point of departure and the little soldier was nowhere to be found. The sergeant made the lawyer stop the car at the bridge, and sticking half his body out the window, he yelled into the air, "Come here . . . !" and waited. Almost immediately, they saw a group of soldiers coming from the bushes, some adjusting their cartridge belts, others slinging rifles over their shoulders.

Suddenly they were surrounded as if they were movie stars. There were shadows on the lawyer's chest and Nueva, dying of cold, sunk down in the seat when the eyes and teeth of the soldiers shined like knives under the sun, and the sergeant: "here are the ones who were circling the plaza and confusing people with that professor thing, but I found them out and she doesn't even have an identification card, don't let them go, this is the little couple we've been looking for." Nueva, with a sore throat, felt as if she had a ball of dry hay in her mouth and almost a total lack of saliva had stuck her lips together. The lawyer defended himself saying that he did have an indentification card and that everything else was totally absurd, that before putting them in jail they had to have proof, that they had made a mistake and that it wasn't Nueva's fault that the ministry had given her a temporary certificate while her face was still swimming around in the solution contained in the big developing tanks. The small group of soldiers, joking and laughing, elbowing each other and saying, "look how these cowards behave when they are trapped and don't know what trick to use to convince us that they are not who they are, and please get out of the car and this way," leading them into the woods, through bushes and *cují* trees to the bank of a deep dry stream bed. A little farther on, among shade trees and Josephine lillies with stems stripped by parasites clinging and ascending until they made the leaves look like flowers, appeared the triangle of a tent. One of the little soldiers whistled and another came out with a camera. "Take a picture of these two, but separately, you stay here, closer," and he raised the lawyer's face by violently hitting him on the chin. The photographer straightened up and looked for the right angle, the deadly angle, the whitest angle, where the pupil disappears and the cornea glints like an egg floating in a well of water. The damn *click*, and "now the other, it's her turn, I want her well placed," and again the arranging and her eyes more open than ever like a cow in labor on the plaza of a dead town. And again the *click* . . . and the scream; and "you are going to see, you bastards, how pictures are developed in less than half an hour." And Nueva saying, "This is crazy. My God, I want to leave, let me go, I didn't have anything to do with what you are looking for, you jerks. I'm thirsty, if you want we'll all go there and verify it! This Sergeant Chávez is a real man, yes, yes, they'll promote the damned guy. Oh! I want to leave, I want out . . . !" And the seconds burning her eyelids and she all clothed in fever in the hands of soldiers who are sheltered no matter what, diarrhea of a country without a cure, they know nothing about life or what it is worth, they know nothing but blindness and nights in their cots. Stinking flesh that endures the midnight sun and swollen sores. And there, in the green barracks, clouds pass in front of the sun while Nueva and the lawyer are judged, and the coldness of death painfully saws their ribs, and they want to run, and cannot, because there is always the belief that something might happen, something to break the dream . . . and all the names of the saints are called up, and even if one wanted to cry there are no tears and the saliva doesn't come while storm clouds pass smelling of light rain.

The photographer comes out of the tent handling a package of photos of the lawyer and Nueva, each one reprinted several times, and he places it down on the sand of the dry stream bed. The lawyer was dreaming of the high tide and the sun rising while they left the little house on the beach to travel to a small town lost in the mountains and return the same afternoon. He remembered the sandwiches Nueva had prepared for the road and put in the glove compartment while sliding lazily onto the car seat; he pictured himself taking the coast road, heading toward the coconut palms, small seaside hotels, wardrobes made of palms; Tucacas, a gray town stinking of muck. Then entering the hills and bordering the sea again till he reached the port with the sun still and soft, but longing to heat up towards noon. That Carnival Monday, with Nueva asleep while he was driving the *Fauvé* over the slavering asphalt and sliding on the curves. No radio, just the wind whistling through the car's half-opened little windows; and Nueva, with her hands crossed on her legs, was dying to be part of the new landscape of greens and scattered villages. Around eleven, they were already in the mountains with the sun packed on the car hood . . . and now, the soldiers were sharing their reprinted faces.

"Let's give them the usual walk. . . ." And they pushed them, forcing them to take the return route in the afternoon still opened by the gullies and ravines they had crossed over in the car hours before. When they dropped down into the plaza, about twenty men were waiting for them, some with questions and others upset without knowing why. And suddenly a shriek was heard . . . "Save them!" From the window of the hotel, the voice crossed the street, cutting it in half before bursting against the opposite houses. Ofelia transfigured, half-hoping, because she is the only one who dreams in this town of forgetfulness, and again the scream that bursts small bones, spine-chilling, from someone able to grasp the bright moment: scream of the witches' sabbath, escaping from the smelly mouth of a daughter of marshes. The shudders of the houses were half-open before kaleidoscopic eyes, accomplices in the fear. Nueva with her lips stuck to her teeth because of the fever and the lawyer, searching, in those who didn't exist there, for the look that leads to communication and love, heard the woman.

Ofelia, half-naked and shaking, goes out to the street and stops at the edge of the road with her crazed look, the *cayena* flower in her hair and her necklace made of river stones and seashells resting now on her quiet chest. In her right hand, the dead, fanlike dove opened while Ofelia's flat bare feet were buried in the earth like those of a clay idol. "Ofelia . . . !" Nueva screamed, "save us from this death; they want to kill us no matter what, piece by piece, skin by skin; conjure them, distract them, gather forces from other planets in your hands, burn this sun, this fake sun, come closer and touch me, you are the only real thing in this town of fear. . . ." "Shut up or they'll break *your* face . . . ! I am only queen in my temple, in my room. On the street I'm just a whore and one of the worst . . . not even the truck drivers want me and I tell them it's free and they come up, and the first word is what counts. . . . Can't you see? for free . . . !" Ofelia shrugs her shoulders and throws them a zigzagging, serpentine, pearl smile of flames. Stuck in place, she began to breath the air of dream again, the humid air of indifference.

They threw them into the middle of the plaza, facing the dogs, the crowd. They tore off Nueva's chain and the lawyer's watch and searched his pockets for his wallet. Nueva wanted to smell the ocean, the wharf, the port and to swim again on that warm and foaming sea-swell. She wanted to feel the burning salt on her recently shaved legs, her tan legs jumping like fish through the bursting whiteness on the shore. The memory of the voices of children playing in the distance drew the deepest moans from her. The lawyer tried to speak but his cavernous voice broke on his lips turning into a cry as if several pieces of glass had cut his vocal cords. He moaned like a blindman or a mute. "Save them!" Ofelia screamed again, waking from her trance; she threw the dead dove against the pavement, turned around, and disappeared in the darkness of the entryway. "It's time," the sergeant yelled. And bringing a rope, they tied them against the iron fence of the police station, next to each other, their backs to the executioners.

The lawyer and Nueva wanted to retrace their steps and make them fly like butterflies. The lawyer resisted before they tied him up, but several men subdued him. Even if he had never been a coward, this time he cried and screamed. Nueva felt that she no longer had any control over her muscles; something opened as when the waters of a woman in labor break. She pissed and that warm liquid running down her legs calmed her for a second. She relaxed all her muscles and waited. Ofelia's voice, with the help of a piece of cardboard as a megaphone, sounded at the same time as the shots. "Fall down! Pretend you're dead! Relax . . . ! Pretend you're dead . . . ! Damned fools . . . !" Nueva pressed her cheeks to the cold iron fence and stopped breathing.

Translated by Raimundo Mora and Eugene Richie

GERARDO DENIZ (Mexico, 1934) is the author of *Gatiperio,* a book of verse published by the Fondo de Cultura Económica that brings together most of his work.

Crisis

Preacher Cicindelli had no dark half. In vain
they spoke to him of Teilhard de Chardin, they spoke to him of the
     mysteries,
of the mysteries of the sea,
of life,
that positivism never explained. In vain
they tried to shake his enameled white footstool,
they spit on his histological preparations when he went out to eat.

On the rocky shore,
the unfinished, dilapidated mansion, lacking window panes,
to view the threatening sea in front
and receive the wind that carries saltpeter and saliva in the air,
     flays
the water's torso,
and receive midst the clamor of the wind your name,
     Preacher.

No one inhabited the house. But this afternoon cohorts of submarine
     beings,
green gelatins already rise from the waves,
they invade the great roofless salon, they corner you without fail.
Do you see, Preacher? How much missing link? What do you know? It is
     nothing to laugh at, no,
the look of so many fixed eyes, some on a stalk.
And you who declared that time:
"There are imbecilic gods and more
imbecilic gods; all have manias about food,
all explain too much;
             but the worst
are those who carry their zeal to an extreme even to poke where it does
     not concern them;
I call them urology gods."

Every fellow first tunes
strings and castanets, kettle drums, French horns;

three times they repeat the vulgar tune that pursued you in the summer
through the narrow streets of Naples
—and that big, impertinent one, who is raising the strident little trumpet.
Did you see him, Preacher? They are already returning to the sea.

On the character of the professor
                              Falls the Shadow
Between the professorship of malacology and the risotto
                              Falls the Shadow

He was fishing for specimens with two students and the net came back
          full.
The repulsive beast, almost vaporous, with pulsings and
          ostioles that go pffff
abandons furiously in Mercutio Tartaglia's hands a
          small trumpet that the master grabs from him smiling sinisterly.
Dissection.
The professor published a study in the Zeitschrift für die vergleichende
          Morphologie der wirbellosen
Tiere.
He took his many children and nephews to the merry-go-round.
Preacher Cicindelli had no dark half.

Tolerance

That you occupy a table before obese chairs, writing
          with ten fingers more slowly than I with five,
is nothing against you, to tell the truth; we are
          so depraved.
Simply, transubstantiation consumes in the   x
          elevator floors
so that upon reaching the street
you have wasted that penetrating vapor of emphyteusis,
          trusts, rights holders, surviving spouses
          and today's issue of the Federal Register
—well, then; it was not so bad. In the final analysis my
          poetry does not broach great topics.
All things considered, in an hour there is scarcely time
for six buttons, the zipper, a strap, while
          you meow (as if it were an order of the Procedural
          Code; vid., if by chance, Fargard 16 and 18
          in fine) for last night you moon-landed on the Mare Crisium
and you go around like a tigress, as you say.

Infancies, I

You will permit me to recall my birth
and thus prove that this was not written by Louise Michel.
It was a May night, that I indeed remember.
In the square turbans were spinning to the sound of the band, but many
     eyes flush with alcohol were turned toward the palace balconies.
Why can they be closing all the palace balconies?
Hundreds are wondering when the offspring of the *chakrávartin** will be
     born,
whether now, or later.
Yesterday the *majarrani*† was impossible.
A Sousa march sounds,
from the main entrance they throw handfuls of sucked candies to the
     masses.
I open my mouth and emit a howl traditional in the family.
Memorable: that is the word.
I was born.
Within, life went in shorts.

It was I

I was thinking once, again,
about that famous manner of so many little ladies,
alternately granting and denying;
above all about the goal,
it must be pure ego boosting so minimum
or of course something much more complicated
that novelists expound, but as I do not understand them
they bore me.
I heard something falling on the roof. I went
It was Uranus' balls.
I sent them away with a kick.
The following day I learned of the birth of Aphrodite and of all the rest,
     which is left unsaid for it is known.

Translated by Wayne H. Finke

---

*chakrávartin—Indian term for "emperor"; literally "wheel-turner"
†majarraní—Indian term for "emperor's wife"

RODRIGO DÍAZ-PÉREZ (Asunción, Paraguay, 1924) is a poet and writer who presently lives in the United States. His verse publications include *The Wind's Pores (Los poros del viento)*, 1970, and *Southern Beach (Playa del sur)*, 1974.

Edgar Allan Poe's Room

for Omar Domingo Sosa
University of Virginia, Charlottesville

Profound
remote
hallucinating traces
in the sand of memory.

I still touch the ashes
and the embers of your erased steps
burn me
on moonlit nights
and north wind.

Ghostly
long corridors
geometric piles of firewood
await December
as always and as before.

The same window
sometime
a thousand times perhaps
saw your absorbed eyes—
diabolical and genial student!—
and the same brick
–historically certain–
received the doubtful impact
of your bad nights . . .

I have seen it:
your books
your bed
the home
the age old elms are
as you left them.

And also the crow and Lenore
are
seeking you in the
sleepy echo of the seasons,
Edgar Allan Poe—
forever more!

Cycles

I am present
in the absence
of beings who deny me.
But fear not;
I breathe the same air
and am imbued with the same
identical disquietude
of those who remember me.
And days evaporate
and even years pass voracious,
vertiginous,
leaving traces of dark
outlines
on the calendar of my flesh.
How the mystery of music disappears,
how the angle of a smile escapes,
how the brimming warmth of a kiss
is lost,
or the crushing
kindled flame of an embrace!
It is a long journey
on the path to the return
of the new
ardent
multitudes
who await their turn
in the cellular allotment
of the cosmos. . . .

Fleeting Afternoon

The afternoon drawn between mists
outlines your evaporated silhouette
in the silent space of your absence
and in my hands filled with emptiness.

In your tranquil distant smile
I only find the gleam of some flowers
gathered from a tree rooted
in the melancholic fibers of my soul.

Tenacious persistence of a glance
shaped with the letters of memory.

That unfinished gesture of your face,
those eyes that penetrate my destiny,
burn me in the twilight of my life
and reach me, tranquil and calm.
How far are shared dreams!

Memories

I left Paraguay
one clear January day.
The sun bit the watersheds
of turbulent rivers.
The land of the dreams
of all the silences
so quietly
went on adding new dimensions
to the frame of my forge.

And today appear
solemn colors
disappeared,
vaguely touching some corner,
some burned corner
lost forever
on the long journey of no return.

My heart, my pulse,
my eternal ardor,
Oh chronological tortures
of blinding afternoons.
And when I arrived he said:
"Don't say, brother,
that you departed.
You will not depart, brother,
though you may leave."

Translated by Wayne H. Finke

JULIETA DOBLES (Costa Rica, 1943) is a poet and critic now living in New York. Her collection of verse, *Earthly Footsteps (Los pasos terrestres)* won the National Prize for Poetry in Costa Rica in 1976. She published *Faraway Time (Hora de lejanías)* in 1981.

Caged Laurel

The markets grow with the heat of day
and make a transparent tumult of the morning,
a broad balloon of color
and smells recently captured
on earth that rises, and infects
and drags along all who approach
its air of mint, voices,
caged laurel.

You and I, sister, sink
in its round warmth, as in proper work,
of survival we make peace:
there are no markets replete
with oranges and their incense of orangeblossom,
nor purplish song of the tomato,
nor rich green offering
of lettuce in the air
with their loosened drop of rain,
where the smell of mitraille
and dry blood
have emptied the sky.

Hence we raise this kingdom
of desires and aromas and apples,
this wave that shakes
the nutritive plains
of the avocado and cabbage,
and whitens beyond
the white rows
of eggs and cheeses
confronting hunger,
as if life were ordered on shelves
and the fields regaled us with rivers of milk,
in tribute to cities and their voracity.

Vital kingdom, loosened from dawn,
when woman's hands sealed
some small, initial barter,
perhaps dewberries
and their bittersweet ink,
of those that are snatched
thorn against thorn,
in exchange for some nuts
of winged, oily heart,
filched from the hiding squirrel,
wild defenselessness
of branches and heights in the wind.
They buy and sell polishes, carrots, cereals,
cloth, eggplants, shoes,
parsley, cherries,
with the urgent fire
of who has decided to live today,
survivor of dark hunger,
and to distribute—nutritive enthusiasm—
the amber honeys of the land.

Music in the Caress

The caress requires its musical womb,
its astonishing gestation under thirsty touch.
It is as though suddenly we discovered
the continent of its translucent veins
palpitating in the transparent gold of the muscle,
under the fragrant map of the skin
and its very fine hair
that lengthens furrows, tiny rivers
and forgotten mirrors in its recondite folds.

In love the body
is round midday,
without a single shadow,
perfect identity
of birth and transfiguration,
beach where eternity
for a second shines
in all its remote nudity.

The caress is a sea
that is extinguished stretching
over mortal waves,
the evocation and conclusion
on the fleeting frontier of ecstasy.

Without more shadow than the flesh we desire,
without more certainty
than the bone divined and gathered
that separates and maintains us,
each one in his flaming, silent sphere,
trying, forcing ecstasy
beyond its origin,
like a music that was
too sonorous
for the air it occupies,
like a music
that seeking emptiness
fell silent forever in the void.

Thanatos in Stone

In the light of the wind and its bonfires,
perfect continuity of summer
that returns blood to its destiny
constructing sensorial prodigies,
suddenly we come across
only death besieged,
with the stone and its shadow.

In Spain the stone,
song that was,
preserves murmuring
its pride of a prodigious beggar,
its beatitude and domain of ruins.
Anchored language and sun
in its presence,
terrible gift of air
that, overcome, confirms
the beginning of all silence.
The stone of Castile
falls inscriptionless.
Convulsed by secrets
it bespies the ash,
sheltered in its patina
of yellow mirrors,
repeating in itself,
hour by hour, its interminable twilight,
and the reflexion, sweat, clay or time,
that created it.

Lethal moss, surrounded
by grass and poppy where before

wars confronted desire and voices
in their obstinate wave of destruction.

Thus it stands erect, alone, snatching
space from oblivion,
a clinging witness
still crumbling
in the spun thread of the centuries
and their tenacious reason of dust.
Frightful is its solitary intent
defying height,
needle of ashes that treasures
—as a motionless prophecy—
the fatidic splendor of hate
in towers, battlements and ramparts.

II

How to drown the stone
under its anchorless solitude?
How to become immune to the beauty
the past grants it?
How to erase definitely
the dark rhizomes
from its echo that clings
to our mobile daily voice
and the hero's cruel fascination?

Death is intimate,
sealed in its bubble
of impure limestone,
like love.
Its abandon is intimate,
like the dream where returning matters not,
for the bare branches are also
total and beautiful
against the incessant sky.

But it remains there,
erect from within,
the stone and its high needle,
innumerable assault
around the heart
and its silent splendor of the world.

1980

Translated by Wayne H. Finke

Roberto Echavarren (Montevideo, Uruguay, 1944) is an important poet and critic now residing in the United States and teaching at New York University. His first book of verse, *The Sea Behind the Name (El mar detrás del nombre)* won the Editorial Alfa prize in 1967. His second book of poetry, *The Damp Plain (La planicie mojada)*, appeared in 1980.

For Tonight

Lovers do not speak to each other
when they listen to the radio.
They listen in silence.
They say what they do not say.
A gush of mercury
trembles on open lips. Smoke is forgotten.
Trills gather in corners of the piano bar
open to the phosphoric beach in stillness.
The music said what they had to hear
to let their abandon grow.
They are a single scene without a fixed limit.
Now a haunch curves
as much as the other wants but did not expect,
as much as the radio
prescribes.

Oyster Bar

The shoulder-blade a petroleum green flagstone;
painted flagstones on his back,
a greenish one in contrast to a grey-beige one,
which move when the body moves,
the cameraman—or the man-camera—
walks in front of me.
There is also an island of hair
by the Mar del Plata subway entrance further down.
At the waist—always on the back—
labels accumulate of lustrous grape green silk.
He is filming pink orchids and a magnolia tree
in the crescent of an Egyptian road.
I have never seen more beautiful ones.
We reach a darker zone
across the passage next to a lake.
In that idyllic spot he films me
with the woman I love, safe from danger.

Roberto Echavarren

The night darkens as the avenue enters the park.
Now it is necessary to pay for the hotel.
The cameraman, son of the owner, gets me a discount.
I reach my woman friend, who is leaving on a bus,
so she can give me some money.
Before this story, and after it, two others:
in the first a wild husband
wants to kill me and I leap behind a counter.
In the last a mediocre academician
requires my presence on a panel but I do not come
out of the Oyster Bar's underground hall.
When he comes down I avoid him
racing up the stairs to the women's restroom
from which there is no exit to the outside.
Next to the mirrored door
I bump into an undercover bodyguard.

Translated by John Neyenesch

DAVID ESCOBAR GALINDO (El Salvador, 1943) is one of the newer representatives of the literature of El Salvador. He is a member of the Salvadoran Academy of the Language and has collaborated in many European and American literary magazines. His published work includes *Book of Lillian (Libro de Lilián)*, 1967.

We

We,
mortals in passing assault against radiant
perpetual forces, carry
but a torch: our voice
hoarse from the silence that stones teach
from the dark springtime of cathedrals,
from the crypt of visceral daydream;
for we, mortals intoxicated
in a gust of pollen, burn
just like that torch, we are
integrally the resinous food of the flame,
and once more, after resting
for a second in the ash
—which is wingèd dust—we muster
the consoling strength
to continue at our work.

Myths and Flames

Myths and flames
challenge our fleetingness:
nothing fastens us to the earth but this unknown
thread of what now sleeps
—in marginal dream—
under the frightening holy waters.
Our life is an endless sea
if we sail on it
between forests of sea-lettuce where the intimate swaying
                           of the branches
is anticipation of nebulous spider,
suddenly breathing phosphorescent music
digging up light in the deep past.
                       And yet
there is a crack in our temples
the modesty of the eternal.

Dawn

Dawn arrives like a shadow:
—Let us invent the star,
let us remove it from the background of blood
                              And let it fly
celestial and explosive.

We Sprout Beneath the Soil

We sprout beneath the soil
beside the mushrooms whose fantasy
of splendor and poison
animates the blindest
darkness.
                    Our destiny lives
from that work: creating and destroying,
as if the fictions
that make us spirits or supermen
were simply
the irredeemable rapture of old clothes
sleeping in cellars.

Oblivion

Oblivion brushes against our brow,
but truth is a pellet
(a gust of eyes)
that rends the entrails.
                              And truth
is always time:
its ardent corrosive limpidity.

If I Walk

If I walk, I lose myself
within you,
like the bird grazing
against the dust.
And if I stop walking
I lose you in the peaks
of the loneliest dreams.
          (And moreover I carry
          a goshawk on my shoulder).

Suddenly Our Life

Suddenly our life seems to be
tinged sepia,
earth color that is rediscovered
in the whiteness of living anguish.

Maturation breaking the dike
with deep threat of impatience,
for a clock is no longer a sign,
but the very blood seized.

From there I emerge into the clearing
of this open winged morning;
and we breathe like children
on a holiday from schedule and alphabet
biting the pulse of a fruit
until the juice saturates us;
and in that juice our blood,
red of so much transparency.

But suddenly—in broad daylight—
our existence becomes earth,
earth bare as the gust
that illuminates and seals consciousness.

In the Light

In the light
our wounded hands
pick up the remains of the mirror
where the moon was seen
after the first day
of the flood.
                    We learn
                    —then—
                    to die in the light
like new born babes
seeking the nipples of darkness.

Translated by Wayne H. Finke

MAURICIO FERNÁNDEZ (Havana, Cuba, 1958) studied law at the University of Havana and is the author of *Region and Existence (Región y existencia)* and *On the Passing Days (En los días que suceden)*. He has served as the editor of the magazines *Punto Cardenal* and *Hombre de Mundo*.

Moon

There is a moon
on the archipelago of the West Indies,
on the largest island: musical lightning bugs.
A lit H. Upmann, layers of Vuelta Abajo
burning in the grace of the very tobacco.
Number one burns pleasurably and plays with the helices
becoming a perfect spiral, in harmony
with the illuminated letters of Fin de Siglo.
It is on Galiano and San Rafael*
towards Dragones or Zanja, salon of the Havana Sport Club
                  comay dancers
exchanging short steps: tangos, boleros, pasodobles
             how exquisite the mambo!
ten cents a dance, a hundred stampings one's anger.
Who will put a bell on the cat on a night of full moon
if we are wolves of the same litter?
There is a moon
on the meeting of the islands, on the cloistered patios,
on the backbone of the crocodile / deceiver
      there are watchmen who kill.
The sweat of the hold and the rhythmic tapping of the hides
arrive contaminated with the bitter heat of the bay,
negresses offering / enormous asses
second hand to Gringo sailors,
pesos and dollars count the same, the difference is in
             the taste:
"Cancha gives revenge and Piedra satisfaction."
There is a moon
on the plains, cane fields, valleys and pastures,
on the Mountain: a new song, an old promise . . .
There is a moon
on the lovers who seek each other like Tarzan and Jane
in the recesses of the Bosque Park of Havana,

---

*Streets in Havana

on the curious glances of the neighborhood
     (crickets of nocturnal tinplate)
ever ready for cheap gossip
at the most opportune revelation.
There is a moon
on the gulf current, on sharks and dolphins
on the islands that rise / remain . . .

Translated by Wayne H. Finke

PABLO ARMANDO FERNÁNDEZ (Oriente province, Cuba, 1930) lived in the United States for several years and returned to Cuba in 1959, where he codirected *Lunes de revolución*. A poet, essayist, translator and novelist, he has written *All Poetry (Toda la poesía), Hymns (Himnos)* and *The Permanent Site (El sitio permanente)*. In 1968 he received the Casa de las Américas Prize for his novel *The Children Bid Farewell (Los niños se despiden)*.

I Hope You Awaken . . .

I hope you awaken.
My hands have tried in vain
to tear from your eyelids
the wings of that dark bird,
to rip its claws from your neck
and its rapacious bill from your forehead.
Can it be that death is a bird of the night?
I see it grow on your body, its plumage
still; I am never going to reach its eyes,
although my hands squeeze its neck
and pull its enormous wings.
I am about to shout to frighten it
for it too sleeps.
I do not recall such a silence.
I am about to shout.
I am never going to reach your mouth, though my whole body
lose its blood, I know not how many times,
pulling on that nameless animal.
My hands are full of feathers and blood.
It seems you do not feel the weight covering you.
I do not recall such a blackness.

Steps and voices are heard, they open the door.
I am afraid. I am about to shout.
The doctor and a nurse enter, they consult each other
about something my ears do not catch.
They speak to you and you smile.
Zenaida gathers your wet hair, kisses you.
You seem like two young girls.
You float on a lake of snow
agilely undulating with your body.
The cowardly bird bespies me behind the window
pane, its eyes are faint,
but it does not take them off mine.

138

Zenaida adjusts you on the pillows.
This girl brings the summer sun;
(in Güira de Melena the thermometer went down to two degrees
centigrade, never did the wind tremble so much at
night, we have not seen the moon and it is January),
it is as if she were singing.
If some time I have heard the daily blessing
in the air, if some time I have felt
life burn, it is now.

But that odious bird is waiting for them to leave us alone.
I discover that it has laid its eggs
and soon they will fill the room with their wings, beaks
and claws; they will block the door, they will cover the window.
We will not be able to leave.

The doctor and Zenaida say good-bye.
The room shines white, it is snowing.
The snow accumulates, it will reach your bed.
I run trembling, my arms and my mouth
would like to be made of fire.
From the open sky fall frosted, silent birds
they become mixed, jumbled in a block of ice.
You seem asleep, white bird of the moon.

I want to open the window, I want to make two gigantic shovels
with my hands and tear out of the floors and walls
this enclosed, frightful whiteness.
Another hour and we will be two icebergs, or embraced beings,
an iceberg the size of the room.
It is useless to shout, we are frozen.
Though in some quiet part of us there rises
                    a flame.
Asleep as you are, you will not be able to share my vigil,
but in your sleep we will make a date with each other.
I will say that I love and that a snow woman awaits me,
who receives me with flowers and snow songs,
adorned with necklaces of pearls of snow
and between my arms she melts and becomes water
that tears from my eyes.

What time is it? At eleven the guard changes,
but in my frozen pulse the clock does not work.
Outside surely there is life with heat
and empassioned lovers seek the green shadow
of the trees.
But my belovèd is beautiful in her snowy season.
Love, do you dream perhaps of the birds flying
                    under the sun?

I hear voices and steps before the door.
The snow birds begin to hide.
When Milagros enters, my love sits up
on a white beach, and they speak of the coming morning
and of other mornings awaiting us,
sweaty, on a street full of activity.

I yet doubt that death is a bird,
but I know that life is always a girl.

National Hospital, 1970

My Wife

My wife,
what is missing in our life?
We have a little house
with beds, table and chairs;
four children
growing and enjoying
the sun and shower.
What do we recall that saddens us?
What bad dream,
                    what fatigue?
Like the sun the children
illuminate and warm
those noble objects, and towards them
they run
excited, when the skies
stampede in raindrops,
and slip on trees and walls.
What do we lack, my wife?
perhaps nothing, I do not know . . .
really very little.
Yet we sniff the storm,
the calm becomes suspicious for us,
nostalgia, fear.
                              1970

In a low voice

To say in a low voice, love, your name,
beside you, your ears, your mouth.
To be that happy animal that joins its halves,
and is only shoulders.

In a low voice, or silently, mute
the mouth returned to its unity:
inaugural silence that by word and flesh
grants new life.
Eyes, blind, returned to everything,
nothing, solitary light revealing worlds
as they are, as they were and shall be.
Again being the other's happiness,
one life another: yours, so belovèd!
To be once more origin without sadness,
pain, fear, nostalgia, or with them,
You and I, our memories and ashes.

May 1978

Translated by Wayne H. Finke

Rosario Ferré (Puerto Rico) is a young writer and poet whose works include *Pandora's Papers (Papeles de Pandora)* and *Half a Chicken (Medio pollito).*

Catalina

Catalina has decided to become penitent:
wrapped in her coiffure like a blanket of flames
she approaches the circle of guests
reclining on those sofas of purple velvet;
she bows before the nearest person
and brings her cheek near
the carved coldness of her hair;
she places her virility near the lip;
playfully she unwinds Fallopian tubes of lit seals;
she attempts to pray, curse, sing
but from her mouth there emerges only a fount of blasphemies
like moons of semen;
she takes the air standing beside a chair, a table, a tablecloth;
she smoothes over her thighs the crystal of her nylons
and strolls naked on the shore of the room
shaking her breasts, obscene little beasts,
in view of all.
She feels like urinating on the face of a second guest
gilding his hair with fine spurts of musk,
and giving him the saffroned liqueur of her desire to drink;
waving curls from one to another
Catalina unravels the wake of
her silver spittle on the floor;
she surrenders to her ten slaves
between sighs that crack like whips,
spawned from her mandarin bathrobe;
she sits on them
and gathers all the power of the world between her legs,
manipulating them with knees and loins;
she brings them on in Spanish style, English style,
Turk and Arab styles.
Nationality nor custom concerns her in the slightest;
irreverent and irredeemable
her heart's eye illuminated
by the dizzying sweat of death,
hearing the ax whistle bothers her not.

142

To the Cavalier of the Rose

In his embrace I embraced all roses:
the roses of stone and those of sleep,
the roses of the torrents and those of wine,
the raging roses chiseled
on the sun's skull, in continuous agitation,
those of pressed snow, roses with which I gird
my forehead in a circle of flames,
and the implacable ones that crown
the rose's thorn,
those that disperse ecstasy around
the banquets of love and those that rain
ashes and agony
on the face of the dying man,
the roses of the poem and those of smoke,
the roses of the rosary and those of the tiger,
the invisible roses of my blood and the blue ones
which my death will cause to sprout,
my swept terrace and the breeze of the roses
entering through the balusters of the afternoon,
the roses that climbed the stairs
and that which fastened itself to the keyhole
when he closed the door,
the roses of his sex and his foot
staunched and still warm on
the nurturing, nursing linen of the dawn,
the roses of he who arrived and has not yet gone,
in his arms I embraced them:
the rending rose still untrimmed
which rocks its oblivion on the stem
and the incomparable one which lasts
in all that it was, or could not have been,
the naked rose of the rose.

Epithalamium

Here, happy betrothed,
after being taught to darn, to gather
carefully, unhurriedly
the exact hem of her heart,
to stitch its measure in the safety of the lining
without even showing palpitations—the great grandchildren of her
desire—
she has decided to separate the frame from the cloth;
she then embroiders her smile on a corset cover;

it is the whitest organdy,
as she sings she unstitches the tablecloths soaked with resignation and
fasting,
she imbibes for the last time
the fragile flounces of love
around the imagined faces of her children;
she untacks—one stitch back,
one stitch in shadow,
one stitch on a cross—
the snowy collection of her trousseau
and the marriage sheets of the wait,
fragrant still of bitter milk; she unfastens
her bodice and removes
from her forehead her veil of tulle-illusion
in whose shadow she journeyed through life;
unstitched from her own flesh
she lets her feelings wither on her;
she presses them against her thighs, sweaty from activity,
balanced on the precarious breeze of her heels
she makes her feelings crackle like new silk around her waist
before pulling the thread and undoing the design.

Translated by Wayne H. Finke

HJALMAR FLAX (Bayamón, Puerto Rico, 1942) is a leading poet of Puerto Rico today. His recent publications in verse include *The Small Labyrinths (Los pequeños laberintos)*, 1978, and *Time of Adversity (Tiempo adverso)*, 1982. He is also interested in films and has published numerous movie reviews in *El Nuevo Día* of San Juan.

Our Father

Our Father who art in the office,
hallowed be thy name.
Thy will be done at home
as at thy desk.
Favor us in thy will.
Give us this day our steak, French fries,
and chocolate ice cream.
Force not upon us the Brussels sprouts
and we shall forgive the cook
if our steak is too well done
and our fries uncrisp.
Endow us with sports cars;
keep away the police.
Exempt us from serving in the army.
For thine is the country,
the power and the dollars,
for ever and ever,
amen.

In Tow

If I am to die, if each step
leads to nothing, what matter
Barcelona or Sarajevo, these immense
doses of solitude, always
the same drug,
be the wrapping Gothic or Turkish.

Advanced Course

Grammar lesson:
    You,

first person singular,
just as I.

Arithmetic lesson:
    One divided by one is one.
    One less one is zero.

History lesson:
    There is only one,
    but it will not be repeated
    for us.

Theology lesson:
    The infinite
    is a mirage
    that intensifies thirst.

Economics lesson:
    Offer more,
    ask for less.

Business lesson:
    Buy expensive.
    Sell very expensive.

Humanism lesson:
    Love today.
    Perhaps tomorrow you will love again.

Politics lesson:
    Who governs himself
    does not need borders.

Physics lesson:
    It is not just the impulse,
    also the moment counts.

Love Or Cult

Others
will find the answer.
In time of adversity we
will maintain
our faith.

Sic Transit

Where are you going?
Please, remain,
Today I am full of anguish
because of life that passes
like you
so near me without stopping.

Carpe

I am dying, you know?
You also.
One year courteously leaves way
and the new year,
with greater promptness and with the same
friendly politeness, gives way
to the following year.
                    Time
permits all, save
the lack of manners.
We die making bows.

The Departed of Spring

There are things that always remain.
Their presence does not change.
They have no size, or substance,
or any explanation whatsoever.
Time is one of those things,
space too.

Don't be deceived because love has no
explanation or limits,
or because its immense presence
seems unalterable to you.

We are love.

Translated by Wayne H. Finke

BLANCA GARNICA (Cochabamba, Bolivia, 1946) is a writer, critic and educator. She has written verse characterized by its candor, sentiment and lyricism.

The Letter

And you reached me
as the breeze comes
to unfold the arms
of the orange tree.

As the wind crouches
to the grass.

Like afternoon
to the tired land.

Thus.
Sweetly, and bitterly.

Thus you arrived, pilgrim,
on the forgotten wake
of the birds.

Sweetly, and bitterly.

I Do Not Know

I do not know
from whence
I came to stop
in this autumn train,
while sorrow rubs
the wing, tango
of the butterflies
and the path chews
the smile,
up the street,
from Monday to December.

How much this tour journey, unplanned,
weighs down!

But the complaint
withers
in the throat
and
ticket and stamp
go
from the arm already.

Ah, I do not know.
I do not know why
the soul
became a pupil
for the night
of tulips;
nor why I scratch
the ashy voice
of an absent
guitar.

And,   yet
I go on:
the ineffable face
of a cloud
keeps me company,
and at twelve noon
and twelve midnight
the rail
unfurls.

Translated by Wayne H. Finke

FREDDY GATÓN ARCE (San Pedro de Macorís, Dominican Republic, 1920) is the author of *Surprised Poetry (La poesía sorprendida)*, *Withdrawal Toward the Light (Retiro hacia la luz)* and *Common Songs (Cantos comunes)*. He is highly recognized as a poet in his homeland, where he was awarded the 1980 National Poetry Prize for his book *They Are Wars and Loves (Son guerras y amores)*.

Monday, October 10

I

Chaos or strife, the solitude of the falling trees
Rises towards the opposite side of their fall
And quickly substitutes them from trunk to top,
Their roots in the ground to continue supporting it.

The deserted shadows then rise musical
On hills and valleys, and sometimes lament,
Others—on nights of mist and full moon
But always windy—bewitch villagers and wanderers
who stray from their path and discover sorrows and illusions.

The girl with the abacus, solitude flattened on her belly,
Saw a tolling and a suggestion rising from herself
That opened up to her paths of life and death, her own and others',
Strife, everything struggles from the cry of new born babe to
                    the death rattle.

Monday, October 10

II

Woman is multiplied in the child, but also,
          possible loss, she becomes worn.
Man knows it and remains silent, or sings to that gain
          and to that loss.
It happens as with brushwood; what is lost on top
          is gained in music or silence.
This is the illusion, but equal certainty; they are the weapons
          of woman, man and their offspring
from the beginning to the end, from solitude to shadow, from number
          to number.

Ah: the foundations of the generations are there,
And on them cities are founded,
Fields are cultivated, hope grows lonely.
Strife or lineage, the girl with the abacus extended
      her calculation, legitimized history.
She was the mother.

Sunday, July 31

Muse or woman,
The seasons appear, changing, in the patio
Beside the flowers, as the year passes.

In summer or winter, in spring or autumn,
At dusk you water the plants
While here and there, nearer or farther,
Your presence informs that all flight over the world
Stops at your side, already perfume or skirt.
                        –You are, in the dance, the foot
                        on which the wind leans.

Translated by Wayne H. Finke

JUAN GELMAN (Buenos Aires, Argentina, 1930) is a poet of the vanguard, remarkable for his versatility. His work reflects not only the political climate in Hispanic America but also the mean hypocrisy of which some men are capable. Published collections include *The Game We're In (El juego en que andamos)*, 1962.

María the Servant Girl

She was called María all the days of her 17 years,
she was capable of having a soul and smiling with the birds,
but the important thing was they found in her suitcase
a dead child of three days wrapped in the newspapers of the house.

What a manner was that of sinning for sinning,
said women accustomed to discretion
and in sign of horror they raised their eyebrows
with a brief flight not devoid of enchantment.

Men reflected quickly on the dangers
of prostitution and the lack of prostitution,
they recalled their prowess with different little whores
and said gravely: ofcoursemydear.

In the police station they were decent with her,
only the sergeant and above fondled her,
but María was busy crying,
the birds lost their color under the rain of her tears.

There were many people displeased with María
for her way of wrapping up the results of love
and they felt jail would return decency to her
or at least, frankly, it would make her less brutish.

That night men and women perfumed themselves zealously
for the child who told the truth,
for the child who was pure,
for the child who was tender,
for the good soul,
finally,
for all the dead children they carried in the suitcases
of their souls
and they began suddenly to stink,
as the great city opened its windows.

Medals

They pinned a medal on the general,
they pinned a medal on the admiral,
on the brigadier, on my neighbor
the police sergeant,

and sometime they will pin a medal on the poet
for using words like fire,
sun, hope,
amidst so much human suffering,
so much sorrow,
without going any farther.

History

Studying history,
dates, battles, letters written on stone,
famous phrases, eminent men smelling of holiness,
I only perceive dark slave,
metallurgic, mining, weaving hands,
creating the luster, the adventure of the world,
they died and their nails still grew on them.

Poetic Art

Among so many vocations I exercise this one that is not my own,
like an implacable boss
it obliges me to work day and night,
with pain, with love,
under the rain, in the catastrophe,
when arms of tenderness or of the soul open,
when sickness plunges in its hands.

To this vocation I am obliged by others' sufferings,
tears, greeting handkerchiefs,
promises in mid autumn or fire,
the kisses of encounter, the kisses of farewell,
all oblige me to work with words, with blood.

Never was I the master of my ashes, my verses,
dark faces write them as though firing against death.

Juan Gelman

Nun on the Bus

Midst men and packages, out of date newspapers,
dry faces, sweat, cheeks reflecting rancor,
wrapped in the silence of her pale hood
the bride of God travels with Christ
on her breasts that never nurtured a soul.

Translated by Wayne H. Finke

Mempo Giardinelli (Resistencia, Argentina, 1949) is considered among the most important writers of the post-Boom era, even though his work has largely been suppressed in his homeland for political reasons. He presently lives in Mexico City, where he works as a journalist, professor and literary critic. He has published *Revolution on a Bicycle (La revolución en bicicleta)*, 1980, and *Heaven with One's Hands (El cielo con las manos)*, 1982.

Revolution on a Bicycle

Chapter 11

"You're like a child, Bar."

"Uh huh . . ."

"We'd be so happy if you weren't always so nervous."

"Don't start now."

"I'm not kidding. Honestly, you're very irritable."

"First, last night was horrible and secondly, I'm always waiting for something: aren't those reasons enough? And now there's news that Gelasio has come back to Resistencia after being away for nine years. What do you want from me?"

"Oh, dear Bartolo."

"What's wrong now?"

"I'm just surprised that you're not worried about being kicked out or not having enough to eat. You live in your own world."

"The thing is that certain of my worries have priority and what happened last night knocked me for a loop."

"Okay, but forget it now. It's over."

"That's right, I'll just forget it."

"And go to sleep."

"Good idea."

He turned his back towards her. Then he remembered the night before and thought that reviewing it would calm his nerves.

"This egg's also rotten," Elida had said. "That makes two."

He had been reading the morning paper under the kerosene lamp. Paulina and Margarita were quietly tracing over old magazines while Raulito tried shooing the mosquitos that landed on the ceiling by snapping at them with a dirty shirt.

"The poor own the worst hens in the world," he remarked.

"Don't make me laugh," Elida answered contemptuously. She glared at him, thumping her foot. "I have the best breed of chickens. The problem is that I have to trade my eggs for a spoonful of rice and sugar at the store. And then your three oldest sons steal my best eggs and sell them to get the money to support their vices. That's why we're stuck with only the shittiest eggs."

"I see . . . though we're poor, we have the best hens in the whole wide world."

"There aren't any clowns around here, so I don't know why you're laughing. I only see an idiot who slaves day in and day out while her husband and kids sit around doing nothing!"

He gently put the paper down on the table, stood up, and walked over to his wife in a threatening way. "First of all, I want you to stop talking in that shitty sergeant's tone of voice. Secondly, leave the boys alone; they're entitled to have some fun on their vacations. And third—"

"Vacations! For the little they've studied?"

Bartolo slammed his fist down on a pot. "And third, damn it, Elida, I want you to pipe down!"

As he returned to the table, he took up the paper, sat back down, and continued reading where he had left off. A few minutes later he realized that his concentration had been broken. He stood up again and walked out of the house.

It was already nighttime and the river reflected the moon like a mirror. He could see two moons from where he stood: the real one and the one reflected in the water. Across the river, he could see that another typically false summer storm was brewing above the orange trees and the fields beyond the corral. The silence was complete, and Bartolo listened to it till a barking sound interrupted him.

Approaching the small gate, he looked down the road. He saw shadows, heard laughter followed by another barking sound, and finally he recognized Bolito, Agenor, and Pablo. They were walking gayly, playing with a huge black-haired German shepherd with a big old hairy tail and raised ears. It was such a beautiful creature that Bartolo just stood there watching him for a few seconds until he realized how strange it was to see a dog with his sons.

"Hi, Pop," Pablo began. "Look at this great dog."

"I'm looking, but I want to ask a few questions."

The boys laughed as if their father had said something funny. Bolito cocked his head to one side and said: "It's a shepherd."

"And you're a human being . . . I know it's a shepherd, you idiot. Where did you get him?"

"We found him," Agenor said.

"What do you mean 'found him'? You just don't find an animal like that."

"Well, we were walking along and we found him about three hours ago on the bridge near the Boat Club. Bolito said it was a beautiful dog—we agreed—and then we went on walking. But a little while later we realized he was following us. Pablito threw a stick at him which he retrieved; then we threw him something else and that's how we began to play. We all became friends, and he came home with us."

"He's a terrifying dog," Bolito said. "He'll help to protect the house."

"And you won't have to worry about feeding him," Pablo added, "we'll take care of that."

Bartolo looked at each of his sons, squinting his eyes, and then at the dog for a few seconds more. It was truly an amazing creature. He had never seen anything like it before: it proclaimed its champion pedigree by its sparkling fur, noble expression, dignified walk, and by the way its chest swelled with pride. There wasn't a doubt in his mind that something was wrong. "You've thought it all through, eh? You have a good answer to whatever objection I might pose?"

"I guess so," Agenor smiled, scratching the dog's back.

"Let's go inside and eat," Bartolo said.

The dog followed them into the house. Elida watched the dog for a few seconds and began tapping her heel while everyone else looked at her. Suddenly she bit down on her lip, as if about to burst out in anger or begin screaming, and started to laugh hysterically, saying it was okay, this was proof enough that madness ruled their house. That dog, she went on, could eat more than a horse, would destroy the orchard, kill the hens, split the bricks, but maybe it was for the best that madness had decided to help hurry things along. Her laughter became more shrill and high-strung: she welcomed the big doggy, saying that his dinner was ready, he could sleep in the girls' bed, he could even piss on her face if she didn't take good care of him; how funny, ha ha ha, let the craziness begin, now that dinner was on the table.

And she went into the other room, still laughing but with tears in her eyes.

Everyone else ate quickly and quietly, glancing from time to time at the dog. When Bartolo finished, he said that it was probably around 9 P.M. and he wanted total quiet as he was going to bed. He asked the boys about their plans. Agenor answered that they would tie up the dog in the tool shed, lay down a few old blankets, a bowl of water, and some bones, making sure that the dog stayed far enough away from Pastor's expected squawks and shits. Bolito added that later they would go to the Friday night dance at the town bath house. Fine, Bartolo said.

Paulina and Margarita slept next to their parents in the bedroom while Raulito slept on a mattress thrown on the floor. The older kids slept in the dining room on thin, worn out straw mats that were piled in a corner during the day and simply tossed on the floor whenever they wanted to sleep.

Bartolo took off his clothes, lay down, and then blew out the candle. He stared into the darkness for a while wondering if it would be better to give Elida a kiss or to just try and sleep. Though he hadn't kissed her for days, now he could do it, say something like "night, honey," but he realized that for her everything was too difficult, too full of desires, sacrifices, and narrow escapes to find satisfaction in a kiss. He could do nothing but ask her forgiveness for the shitty life he had given her.

Half an hour later he turned over for the umpteenth time. "Damn it, I can't sleep," he said into the darkness. "It's the music from the dance hall," Elida calmed him. "They set up the speakers in such a way as to disturb people fifteen miles around."

"You're awake," Bartolo said/asked. "No, I'm talking in my sleep," she answered, stroking his hair.

They stayed like this for a while. Bartolo sighed a few times, Elida repeated "It's the music," and he replied: "It's going to be a shitty night." They ended up hugging each other, waiting, forcing themselves to try and fall asleep quickly.

They dozed until someone bumped into the kitchen table; a casserole fell, making a loud noise, and laughter and heavy breathing followed, a poor try to bring back the silence.

"You fucking pricks," Bartolo shouted.

He heard nothing till Pablo came to the bedroom on his tiptoes a few minutes later. From the doorway he whispered: "Pop . . ."

"What's up?"

"There's a car parked in front of the shed."

"What do I care? Two people screwing, that's all. Leave me alone."

"But it was a huge car, Pop, a blue Impala."

"It belongs to the state," replied Bartolo, feeling alarm. He lit a match, brought it towards the candle wick. He looked like a ghost, an absurd-looking spirit, with his hair completely mussed up. Suddenly his breathing had become heavier. Elida slept on, or so it seemed.

"Did you see anyone?"

"Bolito thought he saw someone hiding among the bricks."

"He thought! He thought! Either a man was hiding there or not, goddam-mit!"

"And . . ."

"Now what?"

"Nothing . . . just wanted to let you know."

"You've done that! Now get out of here!"

The boy closed the door. Bartolo blew out the candle in one puff and lay back down muttering curses, for he realized that he couldn't go back to sleep. He tried talking to Elida, but she told him she needed to sleep: if he wanted to make sure, he could go to the road and see if the car was there. As far as she was concerned, he could keep on going and not come back for a couple of days—that way they would both have a vacation. Then she prayed, insisted, that he let her sleep in peace, for the sake of the Virgin of Caá-Cupé.

He lay back down thinking about nothing for a time that later seemed endless to him. Then he heard the sound of two engines moving quickly and making a racket as they came closer.

He was immediately on his toes: a car in this neighborhood, especially late at night, is a bit strange, he told himself, but two cars is even stranger; and it's not a good sign that they're moving fast. He dressed quickly in the dark and went into the dining room; Elida, who had also woken up, followed him.

The boys were awake; they gazed out the window, protected by the darkness. Two cars rumbled closer with their headlights on.

"See the red light on the roof, Pop?" Bolito pointed out. "I think it's either an ambulance or a fire truck."

"No one's sick here and nothing's on fire, stupid. It's the police."

"Damn, Pop, they're going to pick you up again—" Agenor said.

"But why? You haven't done anything," Elida argued. "This time you're innocent. Maybe they have a judge's order to evict us."

"Don't be silly. They wouldn't come on a Saturday night."

"Sunday morning," Agenor corrected him. "It's 4:15 A.M."

"Whatever it is, Bar, get going. You can hide in the brush and then cross the river. I'll keep them busy."

"No, I won't leave. Maybe they're trying to snuff me out so they can just shoot me. Take it easy, I'll handle this."

He decided to go out just at the moment that a truck and a jeep stopped at the front gate. Bartolo opened the door and saw half a dozen cops with submachine guns spilling out of the two cars. They were being commanded by a huge, husky two-hundred-and-fifty-pound man whose shadow Bartolo immediately recognized: Lieutenant Colonel Pompeyo Estrada, head of Resistencia's Second Division.

"Gaite!" The man shouted. "Come out and give yourself up."

Bartolo calmly opened the door all the way; he raised his arms into the air, walking normally for a few feet as if he were beyond suspicion. When he stopped he asked: "What's up, Estrada? Why do I have to give myself up? I'm a peaceful citizen living quietly in this blessed country. I sleep at home with my family and you know that I don't have any weapons here because you've gone through my house at least a dozen times in the last twenty years. I have nothing to hide so you can search through it again if you want to. I'd only like to suggest that you not come in the middle of the night screaming and yelling, waking up all my kids, so if you don't—"

"Shut the hell up, you shitty good-for-nothing Paraguayan, and give me my dog before my men tear your house apart looking for him!"

"I asked you not to scream at me, and since you want me to . . . ah . . . return . . . " His voice rose in pitch as if about to go out. Suddenly he understood everything.

He swore that, no matter what, he would remain calm.

"I'm sorry, Lieutenant Colonel," he went on, his voice now gentle and soft and respectful, "there must be a misunderstanding. Are you perhaps referring to a beautiful black-haired German shepherd?"

"Exactly! What's more, his name is Sultán and he was trained in the Kennel Club of Buenos Aires and in the headquarters of the National Guard. Where is he? He's the thing I love most in this world!"

As if he had heard his master's voice—perhaps he had—Sultán began howling and yowling in the tool shed as if someone were about to slit his throat.

"Oh my god!" bellowed Estrada, "Sultán, Sultán!" He leaped over the little gate and ran towards the shed.

As the tear-wrenching reunion took place, Agenor came to the door and whispered so only Bartolo could hear him: "Pop, come here a second . . ."

"Sons of bitches," Bartolo mumbled, swallowing his own words. "You little sons of bitches, you'll pay for this."

"Listen, Pop, we only—"

"I don't want to hear one word from you bastards. Not a damn word, you hear? We're going to get to the bottom of this, believe me."

The lieutenant colonel returned with his dog. He told two of his men to inspect the animal, feed him, then put him in the truck.

"And now, Gaite, you better come up with a good explanation or you'll be listening to the Sunday Mass from a dungeon. I swear that you'll catch two hundred Masses before you get out."

"Calm down, Estrada," Bartolo replied gently. He turned towards the house and shouted: "Agenor, Bolito, Pablo, get your shit-fuck asses out here right now!"

The boys came out in a disorderly group, stopping a safe distance from their raging father.

"Well, it's like this," Bartolo began. "That beautiful canine you brought home this afternoon is the personal property of Lieutenant Colonel Estrada, head of the Second Division, this man here. It seems that this gentleman—I'm sure you know him well since this isn't his first visit here—rightly demands a good explanation of what happened or else he'll throw me in jail. That's why I'm asking you to tell him the truth. And it better be a pretty good explanation, the best you can come up with, because if he throws me in jail, I'll tan your hides. You understand?"

The boys eyed each other and Bolito decided to talk. But before he could, the shepherd—having escaped from the truck—ran over, jumped on Agenor, and began licking his face.

"Sultán!" commanded Estrada. "SIT!"

As if he hadn't heard his master, the dog kept on licking though Agenor tried to pull himself away tactfully so as not to hurt the dog's feelings.

"SIT! SIT! Damn it, you treacherous piece of shit!"

In one motion, Estrada yanked Sultán by the leash and pushed him down beside him.

"Go on," Bartolo said, "finish the story."

"Like we told you, Pop," Bolito explained, "the dog just followed us home. We didn't know that this man owned him."

"What?" Estrada asked, confused.

"Well, actually, I guess I knew because once I did see you two together, but I swear I didn't remember that this afternoon," said Agenor.

"You knew perfectly well that this was my dog! You come to watch him train every afternoon in the courtyard of the Commissary. Why, you were even there today! What I want to know is how you brought him here, how you got him to obey you!"

"But sir, he just followed us," Bolito calmly interrupted. "Sure, we stopped by the Commissary, but then we continued walking slowly. When we reached the corner, Pablo said look at that beautiful dog. We turned around and saw him. Then Agenor said that he looked a lot like the police chief's dog, but we just kept on walking. Agenor then said that if the dog was running loose, maybe he had no owner and if he belonged to no one, he could be ours. Pablo then called the dog, began petting him, and he followed us for a few blocks. That's when we decided to bring him home. We didn't steal him, no sir!"

Estrada covered his ears. "That can't be," he said bitterly, "it's not possible."

He looked at Sultán with unexpected resentment. "And you, you traitor, why did you leave me for these fat pieces of shit? What did you see in these long-haired peckers? Damn it, you betrayed me!"

He was so dejected that Bartolo, seeing a way out, came up to him with an idea to calm him down. "Listen, Estrada," he began, putting a hand on his shoulder, "what can you do? That's the way dogs are, it doesn't mean they aren't loyal. Sultán loves you; you can see it in his eyes. Yes, he really worships you."

Estrada eyed Bartolo scornfully. "What the hell do you know about dogs?" he said, flaking Bartolo's hand off. "I taught him to be mean and that's how I'm paid back. Can't you see that he betrayed me? If they didn't steal him, then he's a traitor."

And Bartolo couldn't say yes, maybe his sons had stolen the dog.

When the two cars pulled out, taking away the dog and his grieving master, Bartolo still didn't want to know the truth. He simply slapped his sons as hard as he could on the face and went back to bed, fed up.

Recalling that awful night, Bartolo felt he deserved to doze as his revenge, and he fell into a deep sleep.

Translated by David Unger

ALBERTO GIRRI (Buenos Aires, Argentina, 1919), while of the older generation, continues to write prolifically, and in his multi-faceted literary activities of writer, editor and translator is one of the vital forces in Latin
America today. Among his many volumes, significant recent works include *Selected Poems (Poemas seleccionados)*, 1965, and *Envoi (Envíos)*,
1966.

Lyric

The unforeseen,
        that which you drag along inside
with the name of sarcasm,
        brand-new honeymoon,
and outside, judged and isolated
by behavioral sciences
you will merit another title,
                brand-new
erotization of the link,
a clear case, ordinary,
in accordance with statistics,
personal reports,
        and which so surprisingly
as it was installed, it will revert back,
                late
exaltation when in the penumbra,
bridal bed, receptacle,
it is your turn to pay with the suspicion
that it only occurred in you,
                she intact,
the feminine, observing you, surpassing you
        by dint of not recognizing vicissitudes,
                feminine voluptuosity
of not yielding to transformations
of high tension and weak intensity
in low tension and great intensity!

Buenos Aires, 1978

Quartet in F Minor ("serioso")

Let your perception
go in an oblique sense,
never grazing,

162

do not be discouraged by
the relativity of his fidelity
to go on discriminating, if you prefer
that he move you to the beginning
of pleasure or brevity,
          if he commits
with what flows toward you
abusive interpretations,
mirages,

and being thus you acquire
confidence, the contact
not so much with sounds, pauses, codas,
as with a state
in which listening projects you
to transcending opposites, contraries,
a movement which has distance
for propinquity, immediacy for distance,
down for up, up for down,

and even recognize yourself
in what is most sought in transmitting:
          that which is autumn-like,
a certain opaqueness like a
censure that the very music
had inflicted on its own limits,
          its implicit
confession that there is itself no
music that does not reserve
its original secret,
                              none
dressed to project
the whole truth, plain and dry,
however much the will to insinuate it,
provoke it, propose to us several
slips between its canons.

Poem from Kierkegaard

We sink our finger—
does it plunge itself?—in the earth,
          and it is
to tranquilize ourselves, to ascertain
what we lean upon;
                    but tempted
from probable similarities, egged on
by just the pleasure of achieving it,
undertaking an identical operation

with existence attracts us,
and it is a failure:
          our finger plunging
into existence—digging in it?—
and without being impregnated by anything,
               not even
detecting to whom we are directing ourselves and inquiring
what brought us here and cast us off afterward,
how we take interest
in that enterprise called reality,
and if Anyone directs it.

               Nothing
of what can be done then
will intimidate,
                    it will be, manifestly,
another fall in the universe
of our long, constant
practices in the same proofs, decisions
where all is already ascertained,
               where at most
our babblings, groping do not demand
going beyond choosing between whether
a window has a curtain or not,
                    whether a closet
has a dark color or not, reflection
of bile, old angers,
or red vividness of impatience.

                    Translated by Wayne H. Finke

MARGOT GLANTZ (Mexico City, Mexico) is of Jewish parents, the daughter of the well-known Yiddish poet Jacobo Glantz. She is the author of *Genealogies (Genealogías), Two Hundred Blue Whales (Doscientas ballenas azules)* and *You Will Not Pronounce (No pronunciarás)*.

From Genealogies

Prologue

All of us, nobility or not, have our genealogies. I am a descendent of *Genesis*, not out of pride but of necessity. My parents were born in the Jewish Ukraine, very different from that of today, and very different still from Mexico where I was born—the Federal District where I was fortunate to discover life among the bellowing of the shopkeepers of La Merced. My mother, dressed completely in white, always stared at these merchants in astonishment.

No one can accuse me of preciosity or of Biblicism, as I studied neither Hebrew, nor the *Bible* nor the *Talmud* (because I was not born in Russia and because I am not a male). However, often I become bewildered, thinking like Jeremiah, or eluding the cries of the whale, like Jonah. . . .

Perhaps what most attracts me about my past and present Judaism is the awareness of bright colors, the variegated, the grotesque, this consciousness which makes Jews a minor people with a major sense of humor, with its simple cruelty, its unhappy tenderness, and even its occasional scoundrel. I am attracted to those old photographs—like the one of a Lithuanian money collector who, with his sharp-pointed beard, (poised for persecution) his ill-fitting coat, looks at the camera with a drunken and fat smile, offering trinkets. Appearing by his side, solemn but disheveled, is the salesman of the clothes of the dead, a jackal who knows how to sniff out the next death among the people to whom he sells clothes. What also attracts me is those children of the Jewish school (*jeider*) accompanied by their grandfather, the child without shoes and the grandfather with the wasted look and the white beard. But I feel I do not belong to them—only a half-awake part that touches me from my father's side feels a closeness. My own father was a little peasant boy, the Benjamin, or youngest of an immigrant family, whose older sister, Rojl, disappeared when she was small, perhaps to Besarabia, and whose brothers began to immigrate to the United States at the time of the programs of 1905.

If I see a shoemaker from Warsaw or a tailor from Wolonin, a watercarrier or a boatman from Dnieper, they seem like my father's brothers, even though his brothers became prosperous businessmen in Philadelphia and exchanged their caps and beards for the clothes of the big department stores, probably Macy's. If I see several children from Lublin who can scarcely reach the table and who sit uneasily, always with their skullcaps, in front of some ancient books, while the melamed (teacher) identifies the Hebrew characters with a pointer, it also seems to me that I am looking at my father. I see my father with his muddied shoes, finishing his labors of the field, not being able to play because he has to learn the Ten Commandments, Leviticus, the Talmud, and the laws of celebrations which often seem far away to me.

I did not have a religious childhood. My mother didn't separate the plates and the pots; there was no definite division between those vessels which kept meat and those filled with milk products. My mother never wore a wig as my aunt did, the kind which hid her hair because the husband is allowed to see the hair only of his legitimate wife, and my Aunt Sheine was his second wife. His daughter Rojl, the one who immigrated to the center of White Russia, was the daughter from his first marriage.

. . . I knew the fine, braided challahs which the bakery with the proud Hebrew letters offered. This was our trade because an uncle of mine introduced this bread to the city before his helper, Mr. Filler, marketed it in the stores. My mother came to the same bakery, carrying her pot of cholent, prepared with tripe, meat, potatoes and beans, and keeping it in the oven the Friday before nightfall in order to conserve the heat, so that we could eat the meal on Saturday noon without violating respect for the Sabbath. I remember my Uncle Mendel praying close to the window with his *talis* and his *yarmulke* moving to the sound of his chanting as if he were shaking with laughter; or more accurately, it was I who shook with laughter, just like today, when my daughters shake with laughter while some family member chants the prayers before Passover or the ones which sanctify Friday. . . .

I became involved with the bakeries. They were on Uruguay Street, and those other streets which bore the names of marshes and places reminiscent of the pampas and the River Plate, like a premonition, a nostalgia for the possibilities of immigrating to unknown lands. My uncle Guidale allowed us to enter the bakery on Saturday. Its oven produced delicate little quince cookies which I nibbled on endlessly. My aunt knew that my teeth were tender like those of the little mice that gave money in exchange for the teeth of good children. Those little cookies alternated with ring-shaped fritters laced with chocolate, whose firm texture contrasted with the soft consistency of the jelly topped by an unforgettable pastry. I always dreamed of owning a bakery and handing out breads, of filling up the pockets of clients with marvels, of displaying various goodies in the windows, carefully arranged to delight both the goyim and the Jews. . . .

LXIII

Jewish men are weepers and Jewish women even greater weepers. During the periods I wept a great deal, I was always perplexed because I was not able to figure out the source of so much humidity. One time, during a period of crisis, in Paris, more or less exiled from myself, I began to reread Dostoievsky. . . .I always identify with Raskolnikov, who was a plebian, a petty thief, and later a public orator, author of a very special rhetoric, rhetoric which is also mine.

Yes, just as that proverb and all its redundancies—the one about the onions buried in the earth—belongs to all of us Jews, because onions make us cry and not even the earth can obstruct the flood of tears from gushing forth . . .

And why this preamble? What is it about? It is simply a tearful reflection on the tears readily shed during my whole life (and that of my parents) (now I weep no more because I've used up all my tears; this was the fault of my contact lenses which blistered my cornea.)

But I continue because tears are good for eliciting other tears (or as the proverb says: "raining over wet ground"). A few days ago I attended a family gathering—at my young nephew David's house. My father was a witness before the reformed Rabbi who read in Sephardic Hebrew—as used in Israel. Afterwards he translated it into Spanish, explaining it all and taking away its mystery (as they do when they say the Mass today in Spanish).

My father was the only one who clung to the mystery: he returned to the table with tears in his eyes, soon becoming a deluge, in homage to the Great Flood, undoubtedly. Likewise, my mother's, my brothers', my brothers-in-law's, my cousins', and even my eyes which have no tears left, began to flood in homage again.

I ask why of each and they explain. My father remembers his sisters who died very young, and didn't have his good fortune to attend the wedding of their sons and grandsons. We cry as if contaminated because of our ancestral sadness, the memory of our ancient destiny of the onions.

But I will not persist or else even the paper I write on will get soaked. I continue with the old genealogies and I recall, without having known them, the tears of my maternal grandparents, who never saw my mother again after my father brought her to these lands of magic realism. . . .

Translated by Joan L. Smucker

Isaac Goldemberg (Peru, 1945) is a writer and critic, presently a member of the Spanish Department of New York University. His first novel, *The Fragmented Life of Don Jacobo Lerner (La vida a plazos de don Jacobo Lerner)*, 1977, received very favorable praise from *The New York Times* Literary Supplement, and his second, *Time to Time (Tiempo al tiempo)* appeared in 1985. Also a poet, his verse has appeared in bilingual form: *Hombres de paso/Just Passing Through*, 1982.

Body of Love

Two-headed love and face
of the other side of the coin.
Such is the woman, fair the man.
Such is the boy who embraces her foot
and says not even I in the mouth of the mother
not yet born.
Such is the girl who became a kneeling widow
in the hard fly of her father.
Love with two sexes, with two heads!
Counter and window
of the same feudal commerce,
unnecessary.
Love of idolatrous need.
Such is the female who didn't satiate
the thirst of woman.
Such is the male who didn't quench
the thirst of man.
Come back, man, to the woman's being;
and you, woman, to the man's being.
And both to their own beings
separately.

Origins

Bat with milk teeth
I enter your sex—! God, what an orphan
of flesh exposed to the sun!—
to gnaw in my cave
your heart so full of men
like me
But with a difference:
Bird of prey I recognize myself in your eyes

of sticky bee
Come, enter me if for you life is love
(Sorry: I meant to say death!)

The Beehive and Its Roots

My woman goes limping through the house
on one of her feet, doubt dances
with the other she drags a barefoot boy
They are finishing it, she says
That wall in the back, which crushes us,
is the last one
But who is sharpening knives
                           behind the door?
What ghosts rain on us from the ceiling?
The table is set, she says
Honey and vinegar
bread and stone
Time rests on us, she says
Yes, like the broom on the dust.

Translated by Raimundo Mora and Eugene Richie

Alexis Gómez Rosa(Santo Domingo, Dominican Republic, 1950) is a leading Dominican writer and critic. He has published in numerous literary journals of Mexico, Cuba, Venezuela and Spain. For two years he worked with the Chilean poets Nicanor Parra and Humberto Díaz Casanueva in the Writing Division of Columbia University. Besides his prose works, Gómez Rosa has published several essays on contemporary vanguard literature.

High Quality, Ltd.

Her eyes hear the sound . . .
—Sakutaro Hagiwara, 1886–1924

To Mayumi Hidaka,
in the distant nearness.

1

Two enchantments
drunkenly walk: the moon
and her serenader.

2

Yes, an icicle,
the one from the blind moon,
the one the dogs lick.

7

The bridal bed.
Opposite of joy:
Wood of the coffin.

8

The cup of tea,
(to surprise me) sprouts
a lemon root.

10

The ship sets sail,
drowned in an agony
of handkerchiefs.

14

Stillness of gold.
The barechested sun
claws the mountainside.

15

Little seahorse.
In which shipwreck
did you lose your whinny?

16

Drop of semen
without a name: I beg you,
don't repeat me.

24

The furious bees
buzz, the broken flower
of sex.

Translated by Kim Gerould

JORGE GUITART (Cuba, 1937) is on the faculty of SUNY at Buffalo. He writes both in Spanish and English, and his translations and poems have appeared in many literary magazines. He is the editor of the multilingual poetry magazine *Terra Poetica*.

Buffalo

I

"There's something here
that's definitely
innocent,"
said Mr. Hass to himself
as he strolled past
the dying elms.
"Yes, innocent and . . .
and reptilian!" he added.
His thoughts turned
to Millard Fillmore
lying in his heavy tomb.

II

The night of the mammal is on:
A Polish boy
is wooing an Italian girl
in a clump of surviving trees.

III

Millard Fillmore
is President of the dead.
Eddie and Donna
are jogging by the fine new snow.

IV

Buffalo levitates
and is the city in the sky.
The short skyscrapers

are upside down in a puddle.
The puddle freezes.
Buffalo lands upright.

The Book and the Child

The book is carrying
the child by the hand.
The book is the river of words
The book is the lake of sentences
and no one has drowned.
In the house at the shore
Grandmother dies
and the child leaves
and crosses the world.
The book is hard; the child eats of it
by a paper rock.

The Fire

A man opens his mouth.
Inside is a fire.
The firemen respond.
Someone pulled an alarm.

They prop up a ladder
against his lower lip.
They go up with axes
in the light of cheeks glowing.
Alas, it is too late:
the man starts singing
with his teeth in flames.

Something Neither Vivid Nor Concrete

I wish to speak to the real self
the one holding the pencil awkwardly.
But you write with a fountain pen
says the argumentative father in the brain.

Or is it the mind? Oh I prefer the heart.
The brain is the one with the wires.
The mind is an onion.
The heart looks like a Valentine.

How am I supposed to know, is the question
put to us by the son, who speaks for the father
who is asleep. Dummy, says the son, and the sawdust

shifts to the wrong side of the head
which awakens the father, who is rational
yet says in a pipe-in-the-mouth voice,
'One never knows,'

recalling as to how the search for the real onion
(peeling and peeling) made him cry.

Translated by the author

OSCAR HAHN (Chile, 1938) is a leading figure of Chilean poetry. He currently resides in the United States and teaches at the University of Iowa. His publications include *This Black Rose (Esta rosa negra)* and *Art of Dying (Arte de morir).*

Photograph

> *. . . someone developed*
> *the negative of his existence.*
> —Braulio Arenas

In the next room
someone developed the negative of your death.
The acid penetrates through the keyhole.
From the next room, someone enters your room.
You are no longer on the bed:
from the damp image you view your still body.
Someone closes the door.

Comet

The wound in my side
the wound in my side
Who has seen the wounds in my side?

It went skipping downhill
it crossed the city street
and passed before your door moaning

All the neighbors came out to see it
all the mutes wanted to speak to it
and children pursued it

The wound in my side
the wound in my side

It reached the boundaries of the city at night
and was lost silently on the horizon.

Top Sheet

Carefully folded I placed myself
between the white clothes in the closet

175

You took out your sheets
and placed me on top

You slipped under the covers
and I covered you inch by inch

Then we were swept away by the hurricane
and we fell out of breath into the eye of the storm

Now you lie bathed in sweat
with your gaze lost in the open sky
and the top sheet still tangled about your legs.

Doves of Peace

Suddenly the rose-colored mists, the dense
corpulent mists, let loose white doves from
their claws: winged teeth that formed in the air
the dentures of heaven. Then we saw nuclear
dentists blandish their uranium pliers and shoot,
and rain dental doves upon the luminous meadow
of lava and sapphires. The vibrating howl of heaven
made virgins give birth, and our faces met
the fall of celestial blood and the fruit of war.

The Last Supper

Corruption sits
on clean bodies
with napkin, knife and fork.

Ocular Landscape

If your looks
go out wandering at night
dark butterflies flee in fright:
such are the terrors
your beauty spreads on their wings.

Canis Familiaris

It will come. It always comes. The incessant bark
of the dog of death always arrives punctually.

It enters the window and fills your body
with prickly pointed sounds.

It is a long typewriter, with dog heads
for keys. The canine typing
of that scoundrel dog does not let you sleep.
The incessant bark of the dog of death
will come. It always comes. It always arrives punctually.

Translated by Wayne H. Finke

JAVIER HERAUD (Lima, Peru, 1942) was one of the poets of protest who perished during the liberation of his homeland. In his lamentably short career he wrote *The River (El río)* and *The Journey (El viaje)*. His *Complete Poetry,* along with a tribute, was published posthumously in 1966.

I Do Not Laugh at Death

You wanted to rest
on dead earth and oblivion.
You thought you could live alone
in the sea, or in the mountains.
Then you discovered that life
is solitude amongst men
and solitude among the valleys.
That the days circulating
in your breast were only signs
of sorrow between your weeping. Poor
friend. You knew nothing and cried for naught.

I never laugh at
death.
It simply
happens that
I am not
afraid
to
die
among
birds and trees.

I do not laugh at death.
But sometimes I am thirsty
and I ask for a little life,
at times I am thirsty and I ask
daily, and as always
it happens that I find not answers
but a profound black
guffaw. I already said so, I am
never wont to laugh at death,
but indeed I know her white
face, her somber garb.
I do not laugh at death,
However, I know her

white house, I know
her white garb, I know
her humidity and her silence.
Of course, death has not
visited me as yet,
and you will ask: What
do you know? I know nothing.
This is also true.
Yet, I know that when she arrives
I will be waiting,
I will be waiting standing up
or perhaps having breakfast.
I will look at her softly
(so that she will not become frightened)
and as I have never laughed
at her tunic, I will accompany her,
solitary and solitary.

the keys of death

Now and always I keep on
my face my unequaled voice,
the unique voice which will open the
untiring doors of life,
the inexhaustable doors
of death.
The only voice on my face
I preserve eternally, my
face which is immediate
at the noontime hour,
and is susceptible facing
the eternal sun, that is the score
of weeping before death.
The unique voice contains
my face
indefatigably. The unequaled voice
capable of opening the doors
of life, and opening
the doors of death.
My face and my voice
are confused in the dawn
of death,
both
face
and voice,
like
a
key,

like a
bunch
of keys,
like
eternal
keys
of death.

epilogue

I am only a sad man
who exhausts his words.

Translated by Wayne H. Finke

Francisco Hernández (San Andrés Tuxtla, Mexico, 1946) is a leading Mexican poet whose published work includes *Dispersed Body (Cuerpo disperso)*, *Criminal Texts (Textos criminales)* and *Background Sea (Mar de fondo)*, the last of which earned him the National Poetry Prize in 1982.

#8

The first woman who touched my body had
a magician's lips: green and blue lips, tasting of wild fruit,
with indescribable marks like honey or air.
Often she burned my hair with seven grains and seven
waters, with incantations that rang like clay bells,
with clouds of capal that mixed into an embryo which
crossed my forehead crowned with sprigs of basil.
All night the potion burned under my bed.
Next day, a child born after the birth of twins
threw her into the river on her back, so he wouldn't see
where she was falling, or the sudden flights of buzzards.
Meanwhile, my mother told me about what White Fang
didn't know about snow and the memory of sea was
a mirage under sheets.

#11

It's a waste of time to fill with words a woman going on a voyage.
The sea sucks her sinovia's drains, polishes
her breath, outlines her abdomen in the sand, or with
its rusty cutlasses cuts off her breath.
Don't talk of dry land or the wharfs of a state of grace
to a woman going on a voyage.
Don't play her fados or carve figureheads for her.
Because, whether her name is Paura or Escandra,*
dreams are drowned for a woman going on a voyage.

#17   Sea Bed

—You stop, facing the sea as if in front of a mirror.
Before the sea, your face was the shape of your hands,
the hollow you found in the pillow,
oval abandoned behind the moon.
You saw a woman with broken nose and unstroked belly
run through mosquito netting and curtains.
From then on sleep was the promised land,

---

*Paura means *fear*; escandra means *diving suit*.

181

the distant corner of enchantments,
the little forgotten metaphor.
Do you remember the matins of the church in flames?
And the voice that in the other house shook
at the name of Jack London?
To forget is to be born. And you went to the back of the house
with the same attitude as the floods.
The mud threatened to bury you. The mud, the stinking mud.
Perhaps that's why you hid in the twisting conchshell.
Maybe that's why you walked around the bed
until dawn's wind woke you.
From the stream rose unpronounceable gnomes
made like your masks.
The sea-swell covered you with eyelids of a hog.
Books drifted next to the furniture,
portraits and fear.

#18

Since September, the only thing the river's
done is grow.
It carries along what it finds in its path: houses, bridges,
cast off carriages
and walls of contention.
The hurricane's tail, wrapped in rain, fills my space
with nestless birds that invade like bad news.
My mother is serenely worried.
She says that if I weren't sick all the time,
she'd be able to go out and place the picture of Santo Domingo Sabio
on the armchair in the hallway. That way we'd be safe
from floods and the rest of water's evils.
Yesterday the river killed a girl. It sank its muddy fangs
into her neck, got in between her legs
until it came out her ears and made her float
on a stretcher of black snow.
The noise of the current gives off a strange stench
that sticks to things. A biting smell that overcomes
the doorframes is placed in odd-numbered pages, it sits opposite me
with crossed legs and looks at its heart in the mirror.
Under my pillow I keep a baseball and a hatpin.
When the tremors become stronger I rub the ball hard
so it will absorb this damned sweat that runs through my body
like a swollen river.
I stick the needle into my tongue until I faint.

Translated by Linda Scheer

FRANCISCO HINOJOSA (Mexico) is a young poet who presently serves as director of the Department of Publications of the Autonomous University of Mexico. His work has appeared in numerous literary magazines in his homeland.

The Green Lagoon

The Green Lagoon cast forth another cadaver,
and we, in the indestructible infancy
that feared the drowning victim every day,
the same color as the dead earth,
with the salt of one sunstruck stuck to the body
and the round worlds of dry branches
that the craziest wind of the month hurled at us,
we looked at the swollen body
(the sponge of water and steam that someone
would spill on our backs each night):
the nameless dead person, only dead
blindly cast to the useless sadness
of our nocturnal games in the water,
head on, without being able to close our eyes,
attentive to the wail of the broken-down ambulance,
to a soaked dead skin that too
dampened our frightened dreams.

The Dandy

There was an elegant fellow
dressed in a suit, cane and Derby.
The dandy was weeping at seeing himself alone:
"I'd better fall in love with some woman."

As a man of the world he left to conquer,
perhaps walking he would catch a prey.
With surprise girls saw him
and declared in a chorus: "What an ugly guy!"

But filled with pride he looked at a Chinese girl,
he told her: "Chickie, I'll be your master."
"That's a lot of ham for a pair of eggs,"
answered the feisty Chinese girl directly.

Very sad the dandy went to the cantina
to down some tequila and bemoan his defeat:
"Why should I look for arms in those vests
if I'll only find holes?"
He went mad and thought of suicide
with a strong blow to the heart.

He saw himself in the cemetery in a terrible tomb:
"Here lies a rifle that had no bullet."
Just then his cousin Chayito arrived,
and told him: "Cuquito, how really handsome you are.
I saw you as a seed, now you're a melon,
I saw you on all fours and now you dance up a storm."

Cuquito saw her and though she was very ugly
he thought: "I'll marry up with her."
He began to sing in a gallant voice,
"Let's see if we talk to the judge later."

They lived happily, with such joy
that they finally won the lottery:
for although the dandy dresses in silk
his little monkey awaits him with a percale shawl.

Translated by Wayne H. Finke

Davⁱᴅ Huᴇʀᴛᴀ **(Mexico, 1949) is a member of the young generation of Mexican poets. His works include** *The Garden of Light (El jardín de la luz),* **1972, and** *Version (Versión),* **1978.**

Nine Years Later*

I appeared in the blood of October, my hands were funereal
in silence and my eyes were tied to a thick darkness.

If I spoke, my voice sounded to me like something cast out,
my bones were soaked with the cold,
my legs flowed with time, moving out of the square,
in a strange, aimless direction: of rebirth,
calling me to the mirrors and disordered streets.

The city was leveled by the silence,
cut like a quartz stone, slashes of diagonal light cast tight beams
on street corners, bodies were stilled and crushed against their life,
but there were also other bodies, but there were also other bodies.

I speak with the whole of my blood and my personal memories.
I am alive.

I ask myself: How do we have eyes, hands, a brain and bones
since I left the square? All is dense, voluminous and flows,
after I left the square.

The air told me all was still, in waiting.

I moved out of the square, my mouth was burned by the memories,
and my blood was fresh and shining like a continuous ring
in the interior of my absolutely alive body. So I was moving
out from the square, whole and breathing.

I was breathing images, and since then all those images visit me in
        dreams,
breaking everything, like crazed horses.
The mirror of death was in the very daily bread.
And a word of my existence hung from an infinite ledge.

I would not like to speak of the enormity of that day,
nor write adverbs here, shout or even lament.

---

*Reference to the bloody student protests at the University of Mexico, in 1968.

But, indeed, I would like one to see a burning of anger
stain the mirror of death.
Where could I place my being, my words
but here, nine years after, in that cold wrath,
in that animal of ire that awakes sometimes to enamel my sleep
with its bloody breath?

All my blood circulates through my essence, whole, unquestionable.
But there I heard how it was stopping, anchored to my breathing, and beating, with the mute call of its immobility, beating
my interior voices, my gestures of a human being,
the love I have been able to give and the death that I
myself shall deliver
There came fear to my eyes to cover them with its cold fingers.

The immense silence of my body opened its honeycombs
before the demolished bodies, spit towards death by the heat of the
        machine guns:
those bodies shining, bloody and silhouetted against the shredded
        afternoon light,
their bodies different from mine and even more different,
for they had been rent from human life by an enormous slash,
by a dizzying ferocity, by hands of a painful force that
cast itself, howling,
against those bodies more feeble already than the afternoon
and more and more shining, in my dream of a human being yet alive.

It is true I heard the machine guns and now I write this,
and it is true my blood flows anew and I still dream
of a type of dead doubt, and I see at times my naked body
like a spacious meal for the devouring mouth of love.

Where were the ligatures of my life,
my mirrors and my days, when the afternoon in the square intervened?

If I take a piece, a sliver of my body to set it against
the recollection of that afternoon in that square,
I step back, frightened, from my life as though the feather-light fingers
of hundreds of phantoms had struck me on the mouth.

I speak of these immense memories because I had to do it sometime,
this way or in some other way.

I was leaving the square with a vivid stupor in my eyes and mouth
and I felt my saliva and my blood, still alive.
It was a cool night, given to the season.
But on streets, on corners, in rooms,

there were bodies crushed and sealed against their life by
a monstrous bitter fear.

A ring of fear was closing upon the city
like a strange dream that continued, and led
to no awakening.

It was the mirror of death that intervened.
But death had already, with its arms and its instruments passed
by all the corners and the abolished air of that square.
It was the mirror of death with its reflections of fear
that shaded us in a city that was this city.

And in the street it was possible to see how a hand closed,
how a winking intervened, how feet slipped with a
thick silence
seeking an exit,
but there were no exits: there was only
a vast open door in the kingdoms of fear.

October, 1977

Translated by Wayne H. Finke

JORGE IBARGÜENGOITIA (Guanajuato, Mexico, 1928) is a journalist, play-wright and novelist. He twice won the Casa de las Américas Prize for his novel *August Lightning (Los relámpagos de agosto)* and for his historical farce *Assassination Attempt (El atentado)*.

What Became of Pampa Hash?

How did she arrive? Where did she come from? No one knows. The first indication I had of her presence was the panties.

I had just entered the cabin (the only one) with the intention of opening and eating a can of sardines, when I noticed a clothesline strung lengthwise above the table, and on it, precisely at the height of the diners' eyes were hanging the panties. A short while later I heard someone flush the toilet and when I raised my eyes I saw an image which would later become more familiar: Pampa Hash coming out of the bathroom. She looked at me as only a doctor of philosophy could: ignoring everything, the table, the sardines, the panties, the ocean that makes us seasick, everything, except my powerful masculinity.

We did not get anywhere that day. Actually, nothing happened. We did not even say hello. She looked at me and I at her, she went out on deck and I remained inside eating sardines. One cannot say then, as some viperish tongues have insinuated, that we have been victims of love at first sight: rather it was the *ennui* that brought us together.

Not even our second meeting was definitive from an erotic viewpoint.

Three men and I were on the bank of the river trying to inflate a rubber raft when we saw her appear in her bathing suit. She was astounding. Possessed by that impulse that makes a man want to marry Mother Earth from time to time, I grabbed the pump and proceeded to pump away like a madman. After five minutes the raft was about to burst and my hands were covered with blisters that later developed into sores. She was looking at me.

"She thinks I'm terrific," I thought in English. We threw the raft into the water and navigated in it as Lord Baden-Powell once said, "on the river of life."

Oh, what a Homeric journey! I broke off pieces of enormous tree trunks with my bare and blistered hands in order to heat the meal and blew on the fire to the point of almost losing consciousness. Later I climbed onto a rock and dived from a height that normally would have given me a cold sweat; but the most spectacular feat occurred when I let myself be swept away through the rapids and she shouted in fear. They picked me up bleeding a hundred yards farther down. When the trip ended and the raft was packed on top of the jeep, I got dressed among some bushes. Seated on a rock, I was putting on my shoes when she appeared, still in her bathing suit, and told me while looking down: "Je me veux baigner." I corrected her: "Je veux me baigner." I got up and tried to rape her, but I couldn't.

I made love to her almost by accident. She and I were in a room, alone, speaking of unimportant things, when she asked me; "Such and such an address is in which postal zone?" I didn't know, but I told her to consult the telephone book. She came out of the room after a short time and I heard her calling me. I went to the spot where the telephone was and found her leaning on the book: "Where are the zones?" she asked me. I had forgotten our prior conversation and understood her to be talking about erogenous zones. I told her where they were located.

We had been born for one another, between the two of us we weighed three hundred fifty pounds. In the months that followed during our passionate and torrid love affair, she called me a buffalo, orangutan and rhinoceros . . .in essence everything you can call a man without offending him. I was in poverty and she seemed to suffer from constant attacks of diarrhea during her travels through those barbarous regions. At sea level, apart from her need for fourteen hours of sleep each day, she was an acceptable companion, but six thousand feet above sea level she used to breathe with difficulty and fainted easily. Living with her in Mexico City meant remaining in a constant state of alert in order to pick her up from the floor in the event of a fainting spell.

When I discovered her passion for pathology, I invented just to please her, a string of sicknesses in my family, which actually has always enjoyed the good health proper to privileged zoological species.

Another of her predilections was something she called "the intricacies of the Mexican mind."

"Do you like motors?" she once asked. "I'm warning you that your answer is going to reveal a national characteristic."

There were certain irregularities in our relationship. For example, she has been the only woman whom I never dared ask to pay for my dinner, in spite of knowing very well that she was swimming in money, which wasn't even hers but came from the Pumpernikel Foundation. With my face in my hands, and elbows on the table at both sides of my coffee cup, I contemplated her for several months as she consumed remarkable amounts of steak and potatoes.

The waiters used to look at me with a certain contempt, believing that I was paying for the steaks. She felt sorry for me at times and treated me to a piece of meat wrapped in a Mexican roll, that I naturally refused, claiming that I wasn't hungry. Furthermore, there was a problem with tips. She supported the theory that one percent was a sufficient amount; therefore, leaving forty centavos for a bill of twenty pesos was extravagant. I had never made so many enemies.

Once I had twenty pesos and I brought her to the Bamerette.* We ordered two tequilas.

"The last time I was here," she told me, "I had Scotch, played the guitar, and the waiters thought I was a movie actress."

I never forgave her for that remark.

Her size was another drawback. For example, if she left her arm under her body for two minutes, it would become numb.

The only historical figure that could illustrate our relationship was Siegfried, who crossed the seven circles of fire and reached Brunhilda. Unable to awaken her, he picked her up, found out that she was too heavy and was forced to drag her out like a rolled-up rug.

Oh, Pampa Hash! My adorable, sweet and ample Pampa!

Her curiosity was terribly scientific.

"Do you love me?"

"Yes."

"Why?"

"I don't know."

"Do you admire me?"

"Yes."

"Why?"

"You are professional, conscientious, and dedicated. I admire those qualities very much."

That last statement was an awful lie. Pampa Hash spent a year in the desert doing research which later resulted in a paper that I could have written in two weeks.

"And just why do you admire those qualities?"

"Let's not be too inquisitive. Let us be carried away by our passions."

"Do you desire me?"

It seemed like an interrogation at a police station.

We went shopping once. I have never seen a more difficult customer (than her). She considered everything either too expensive or not good enough, or else it wasn't exactly what she needed. Besides, some mysterious reasoning seemed to convince her that the salesgirls enjoyed ripping the store apart showing their merchandise and later putting it away without having made a single sale.

Panties were almost like the recurring theme of a symphony in our relationship. "I need panties," she told me. I told her how to say it in Spanish. We went to at least ten shops and in every one the same scene was repeated. We would be in front of the salesgirl and she would say, "necesito . . ." and turn toward me. "How do you say it?" "Pantaletas," I told her. The clerk looked at me for a split second and then went to get the panties. She wanted neither nylon nor silk ones, but rather something made from a

---
*The local cafe

material as rare as commercial spider web in Mexico. They were of such an enormous size that it was almost shameful. We never found them. Afterwards, we bought some mangos and ate them seated on park benches. I was fascinated by the way in which she tore off the skin from half the mango with her strong teeth and proceeded to devour the fruit and fibers until the pit resembled Father Hidalgo's head.* Later she would firmly pull the remaining half of the mango from the pit and eat it. Right then and there I realized that woman was not for me.

When she had finished her quota of three mangos, she carefully wiped her mouth and hands and lit a cigarette. She settled back in her chair and turning to me smiled and asked, "Do you love me?"

"No," I told her.

Of course she didn't believe me.

The day that rhythm possessed her was the Grand Finale.

We went to a party where there was a guy who danced so well that people referred to him as the Fred Astaire of the neighborhood. His specialty was dancing alone and contenting himself by watching his feet. After a short time a tropical beat began to play. I was speaking with someone when I got a feeling in the pit of my stomach that something terrible was about to happen. I turned my head and was paralyzed by the sight of Pampa, my Pampa, the woman whom I loved so much, dancing around Fred Astaire as Mata Hari around Shiva. I had never been so ashamed of her since the day she began to sing. "Ay, Cielitou Lindou . . ." in the middle of Juarez Avenue. What could I do? Nothing but lower my head and continue the conversation. The torture lasted for hours.

She later came, knelt down at my feet like a Mary Magdalen and asked me: "Forgive me. I became possessed by that rhythm." I forgave her right there.

We then went to her hotel (with the intention of mutually putting aside our differences) and were already inside the elevator when the manager approached us to find out the number of my room.

I told him I was accompanying the young lady.

"Visits are not permitted after ten," the manager told me.

Pampa Hash became angry.

"What are you insinuating? This man has to come to my room to pick up his suitcase."

"You bring down the suitcase and have him wait for it here."

"I'm not bringing down anything. I'm very tired.

"Then the bellboy will bring it down."

"I won't pay the bellboy anything."

"Young lady, the bellboy is paid by the hotel."

That was the end of the discussion.

---

*Priest and father of Mexican independence, almost completely bald.

The elevator began ascending with the bellboy and Pampa Hash. I was watching her. It was an old-fashioned one with iron grills; so when it reached a certain height I could see her panties. I realized then that was the signal. The moment for her to disappear had come.

I was already starting to leave when the manager told me to wait for the suitcase. I waited. Shortly afterwards the bellboy came down and handed me a suitcase that naturally was not mine. I left after having taken it and walked away more hurriedly with each step.

Poor Pampa Hash, she lost me and her suitcase on the same day!

Translated by John Chando

ROBERTO JUARROZ (Dorrego, Argentina, 1925) is a poet, essayist, professor and director of the School of Library Sciences in Buenos Aires. From 1958 to 1965 he edited the literary magazine *Poesía-Poesía*. All his verse, already translated into seven languages, is collected in one volume titled *Vertical Poetry (Poesía vertical)*.

I Do Not Hold God

I do not hold God between my hands.
Nor do I hold man.
But I hold an absence
that can become
either of the two.

And the problem is not
not knowing which to choose,
but simply not wanting
my absence to become either one.

Many are the presences
that must dissolve
in order to create an absence
to fit between one's hands.

Life

Life is a necessary precaution,
like shade for the tree.
But there is something else,
as if life should avoid its own leap
or the shadow be cast back, and not forward.

Nudity precedes the body.
And the body sometimes remembers this.

There Are Few Whole Deaths

There are few whole deaths.
The cemeteries are full of fakes.
The streets are replete with phantoms.

There are few whole deaths.
But the bird knows on which last branch it sits
and the tree knows where the bird ends.

There are few whole deaths.
Death is more and more uncertain.
Death is an experience of life.
And at times two lives are needed
to be able to complete a death.

There are few whole deaths.
The bells always toll the same.
But reality no longer offers guarantees
and it is not enough to live in order to die.

You Have No Name

You have no name.
Perhaps nothing has.
But there is so much smoke cast over the world,
so much motionless rain,
so much man unable to be born,
so much horizontal weeping,
so much neglected cemetery,
so much dead clothing
and solitude occupies so many people,
that the name you lack accompanies me
and the name that nothing has creates a place
where solitude is found in excess.

Vertical Poetry

I

Where is the shadow
of an object leaning against the wall?
Where is the image
of a mirror leaning against the night?
Where is the life
of a creature leaning against itself?
Where is the empire
of a man leaning against death?
Where is the light
of a god leaning against nothingness?

Perhaps in those spaceless spaces
is what we seek.

II

Words also fall to the ground,
like birds suddenly crazed
by their own movements,
like objects that suddenly lose their balance,
like men who trip without their existing obstacles,
like dolls alienated by their rigidity.

Then, from the ground,
the very words construct a ladder
to rise again to man's speech,
to his stammer
or his final sentence.

But there are some which remain fallen.
And at times one finds them
in an almost larvate mimetism,
as if they knew that someone will gather them
to construct a new language with them,
a language made only with fallen words.

XIII

The center of love
does not always coincide
with the center of life.

Both centers
seek each other then
like two troubled animals.
But they almost never meet,
for the key of coincidence is another:
to be born together.

To be born together,
as all lovers
ought to be born and die.

XVII

As you sleep
your hand unexpectedly transmits a caress to me.
What zone of yours has created it,
what autonomous region of love,
what reserved part of the encounter?

As you sleep
I know you again.
And I should like to accompany you
to the spot where that caress was born.

LXXII

Which to erase first:
the shadow or the body,
the word written yesterday
or the word written today,
the dark day
or the clear day.

One must find an order.
The apprenticeship of erasing the world
will aid us later to erase ourselves.

Translated by John Chando

José Kozer (Havana, Cuba, 1940) has lived in New York since 1960 and teaches at Queens College. His work has been widely anthologized and published in literary magazines throughout the world. He is the author of *This Jew of Numbers and Letters (Este judío de números y letras)*, which won the Julio Tovar poetry prize in 1974. Recently the prestigious Fondo de Cultura Económica published an anthology of his work in its "Tierra Firme" collection under the title *Under This One Hundred (Bajo este cien)*.

You Remember, Sylvia

You remember, Sylvia, how the women worked at home.
Papa didn't seem to do anything.
He held his hands behind him leaning like a rabbi smoking a
      stubby birchwood pipe, the curls of smoke
          giving him an air of mystery,
I'm beginning to suspect that Papa must have had a touch of
          Asian in him.
Maybe he'd been a nobleman from Besarabia who'd freed his serfs
          in the days of the Tsar,
or perhaps he'd been in the habit of taking his ease in fields
      of oats and dreamy at winnowing time had sat hunched
          over gently in a damp spot among the ferns
          in his ancient longcoat a bit threadbare.
It's likely that he became thoughtful when he came across an
          apple on the steppe.
He knew nothing of the sea.
Confidently eager for the image of the foam he confused anemone
          and sky.
I think the weepy crowd of eucalyptus leaves unnerved him.
Imagine what he felt when Rosa Luxemburg appeared with a tract
          in her hand before the Tsar's judges.
He would have to emigrate, poor Papa, from Odessa to Vienna,
          Rome, Istanbul, Quebec, Ottawa, New York.
He would reach Havana as a document and five passports, I can
          see him rather wearied by the trip.
You remember, Sylvia, when Papa would come home from the stores
          on the Calle Muralla and all you women in the house
          would start to bustle.
I swear he came through the parlor door, two-toned shoes,
          blue pinstripe suit, elegant oval-spotted tie
and Papa didn't ever seem to do anything.

This Is the Book of Psalms That Made My Mother Dance

This is the book of psalms that made my mother dance,
this is the book of hours that my mother gave to me,
this is the righteous book of precepts.
I appear wrathful and consuming before this angular book,
I appear as a rabbi to dance a mighty polka,
I appear at the height of glory to dance a courtly minuet,
arm in clandestine arm with death,
I appear goosestepping to dance while smoking,
I am a rabbi who lifted up his robe on Russian steppes,
I am a rabbi whom a great big Tsar makes dance before death's
       battlements,
I am grandfather Leizer who danced tied ceremoniously to grandmother
       Sara's waist,
I am a maiden who comes all lewd to open up the limits of the dance,
I am a maiden opened up by a sudden collapse of ankles,
but death mixes things up on me,
and there's a vase that falls over on the big bookshelves in my room,
and there's a glowing cabaret step that they've done wrong,
and my feet are like the great roar of four generations of dead.

Reminiscences of Grandmother at Home

Grandmother, her fermented mare's urine, the sprigs of juniper
                 to sweeten up the kitchen charcoal. You
have a strong smell of smoke of cockles of quiet little bits of
                 whitefish in their dish
and you knead
pastry dough, you get rid of your migraine smell, decomposing
             bridal veil if you lean your disordered shadow
             against a birch
and hug your rolling pin:
the two-toned apron with deep pockets and held up by a lily
      smell that you distill two-handed and gather in
             like a basket of puff pastry and unleavened bread
one Sunday
of soupspoons and tureens: the breeze came in and your throat
             opens to a still-life voice, you were
the blessed seed
that bloomed as David's line, you regaled us with the tasteless
      operetta of your dead, do you remember?, the
             flowery patina of the kerchief covering
             your shaven head

and furtively
at dusk on Pesach you handed us the herring in its cream, egg
                    whites in a spinach soup and your destiny
intoxicated us
with its raspberry smell and your pulpit for us was your oven
          with its fresh custard smelling of bowers and you
                    paid us homage, old figure of Israel on
                              your zither.

A Franz Kafka Triptych

For Jorge Rodríguez Padrón, with Pizca

Still Life of Franz Kafka

It fell to him to love sparrows.
As he was a broad and hateful man he tried to think himself obscure
      as if an inhabitant of the city of Vienna
                    condemned to view the world from the bay
                              windows Stalin thought of for the
          Kremlin.
But he dreamed of cane fields too.
One day he saw the image of Saint John of Patmos sculpted in his
                              eyes and torn by fire.
And he felt himself all surrounded by doves.
Vast to excess, he came to know momentarily the misfortunes of
          ambiguity.
He thought he saw himself in the bushes murdered by police.
By having no clairvoyance he came to know the future.
On the stone of holocausts he understood his meaning.
Nobody appeared! He summoned the prosecutors in piety.
He was leaving too many circumstances still unfinished.
They began to search for him in Prague or in Lima's incessant drizzle
but they only unearthed the verdict he had left in libraries.
No one in the midst of all those documents attempted to console him.

Franz Kafka's Wedding

To Miss Milena Jesenská, it is their pleasure to invite you and
                    your distinguished, etc.
Although the main thing is that Franz has said he wants no issue.
Understood, too, is his horror of flowers: they bring him such
          a bad memory of the future.
The ceremony is to take place on a streetcar.

Franz has understood what Milena is sacrificing; Milena understands
    what tranquility means to Franz.
Or wanting, for example, the following: detachment.
Since no friend can attend, the ceremony will have to take place,
    inevitably, in the Black Forest.
Please come.
In fact, a few celebrities have already accepted: Bertolt Brecht
      has approved and the poet Franz Werfel, of whom it
           is said he would be incapable of letting down
               a namesake.
Only, unfortunately, the poet Federico García Lorca will be
              unable to attend.
On receipt of the news and with the stupor of the gathering, one
          might have been inclined to call off the wedding.
Everything pointed to some disaster.
But Franz was most fearful of turning back: why deny it when that
         business was something pulmonary.
Or someone might have come to think Franz didn't know that in
         twenty years tuberculosis would be nothing but an
            illness of the past.
That in twenty years a sudden gust of wind against a flower
      would be unable to change the untenable quicksilver
          of repose.
Sincerely—and Milena knew it—Franz couldn't imagine any
          other heroism.
It cannot be denied that he showed courage along the hallways
         leading to the altar.
Or that the meeting was in the Black Forest: and Mrs. Milena
        wasn't to attend.

Franz Kafka's Sprout

It's a small two-story house not far from the river on a Prague
back street. In the early hours
between the eleventh and twelfth of November he had a start, he
      went down to the small kitchen with the round table
         and the basswood chair, the portable stove
            and the blue methylene flame. He lighted
the gas ring
and at the same time (three) the fire greenedflames on the three
         windowpanes: it smelled of brimstone. He wanted
to go
into the small dining room and drink some boldo-leaf and honey
      tea, he pulled out the chair and settled down in
         front of a sienna mug that he had placed who
         knows how long ago on the six-colored
           wicker glass rack a gift

from Felicia: and once more
Felicia appeared with a stripe in the middle, the two braids and
    a glow of candles in the white oval of that avid face
            of flour and consecrated bread, a face
three times
a flame on the windowpane: she appeared. And once more three
    times she was the little girl of her dead,
to the sound
of a triangle some chamber players came and to the sound of the
    bell (it's three) in the tall belfry not far from the
    river: they spread out, ten
cups, ten
chairs in the huge mansion with garrets, the house where the
    bay windows and the sideboards (stables and sheds)
            were open day and night, the water
and the sponges
gleamed. Well, yes: it was a different time and a chorus of girls
    watched over the tea kettles (bubbling) the
            eucalyptuses (bubbling) the marjoram and some
                digestive water (mint) waters
for breathing: everything
tranquil (finally) everything tranquil, he went up the steps and
    saw that he was leaning on the windowpane (at last)
            without a crowd of birds
at the window.

                      . . . because the harvest is come.
                      (Mark 4:29)

Saint Francis of Assisi

He stoops to feed all manner of cautious birds who had been
            terrified a while before.
He summons them: they flock.
He himself gets holy nourishment, excessively exemplary and
            unacceptable for centuries to come.
God denies him sight, bad for meditation.
Through his eyes he loves the things of the world: girls in
    the depths of pools, astonished fish on the surface
            of the sea, even the devotional scene of
                crucifixion.
And as he would a stream he loves the incorrupt concatenation
    of flowers on the fertile flat of blessedness.
Newts reflect the ass in a seeming divinity of face.
If not: how could a creature live through the anguish of its
            sleeping beast.
Within his own foundation Francis loves simple endless treadmill gears.

And even more—it's well known—than onager hide, than
                unpolluted tapestry of unicorns or the Gospel,
                                too obligatory.
Poor Francis: in sienna solitude he venerates the vermin above
                        the whiplash of a ladder.

Translated by Gregory Rabassa

PEDRO LASTRA (Chile, 1932) is a leading writer, poet and critic presently teaching in the Spanish Department of SUNY at Stony Brook. His collections include *And We Were Immortal (Y éramos inmortales)*, 1969, *News from Abroad (Noticias del extranjero)*, 1979 and 1982, and *Notebook of the Double Life (Cuaderno de la doble vida)*, 1984. As a critic he has published *Conversation with Enrique Lihn*, 1980, and *Julio Cortázar*, a critical anthology, 1981.

Later We Will Talk Of Our Youth

Later we will talk of our youth,
we will talk of our youth later on, whether dead or alive
with so much time on top of us,
with ghostly years that never belonged to us
and days that came from the sea and returned
to the depths of its continuity.

Later we will talk of our youth
almost forgetting it altogether,
confusing the nights with their names,
what was taken from us, the presence
of an obscure battle against dreams.

We will talk seated in parks
as we were twenty years ago, as we were thirty years ago,
indignant at the world
without remembering at all who we were,
or where love sprang up,
or in what vague cities we lived.

Drawbridges

Who is this monarch without scepter or crown
lost in the middle of his palace?
The innocent pages are no longer present
(now each one is fighting for a kingdom
and yet unowned). The ladies of the court
prepare for exile.
To whom then belongs this incompetent
hand, these eyes that see only vague
frontiers or the wind

203

that scatters the remains of the banquet?
I've come too late, I have
nothing to do here,
I didn't recognize the drawbridges
and that one in front of me
wasn't the one that I sought.
They will drive me out, those last sentinels
still awake on the turrets; and they too inquire
who I am and where is my kingdom.

Etude

For Juanita

Your hand is strange like that, raised in the air,
a hand and its fingers
that sometimes surround bread on the table
and lift up a glass, grasp and close
soundlessly upon the water,
soundlessly upon the bread, the glass, the water,
because a shadow is born from the air of your hand.

The Dissolving of Memory

I

The glint of a gaze
crosses the landscape
this gaze comes from afar

                                    oscillating

between your time and mine

II

Images   images
loaves   fishes
which your hand sketches and multiplies
I listened to other voices
my traveler
I was gazing at that which takes place between dream and sky
and hunger was unreal
and you were terrestrial

III

We saw the old flame burning
that which is renewed like a canticle
or a litany
that which is resolved in memory and silence
to become canticle again
and the unknown woman who came out of you
suddenly separated the earth from the waters
and she herself was the canticle
and ascended   vanishing

Translated by Elias L. Rivers

ENRIQUE LIHN (Santiago, Chile, 1929) is one of his country's most important writers and the recipient of the prestigious Casa de las Américas Prize in Poetry. Among his publications are *Force Majeure (Por fuerza mayor)*, 1974, *Beginning with Manhattan (A partir de Manhattan)*, 1979, and the novel *The Art of the Word (El arte de la palabra)*, 1979.

The Sewer

The personnel on this street are not renewed
the staff of prostitution spends its last cent on make-up
under a dusty light that sticks to one's face.
A double row of cavities, denture of crumbling houses,
is the scene of this Danse Macabre
trivial Saturday dance in the pustule of the city.

It is a known face filled with welts, with livid
        scars under a few cents worth of powder, and which emerges
from all the crevices
of the city, in this neighborhood older than that of
        the Alchemists
like the bodiless face of the snail offering itself in the two
        sexes of its androgynous neck
blandly phallic and oiled with vaginal spittle
the bust of a boxer showing his tits in the frame
        of a cave-in.

The river neither advances nor retreats in this white
        boiling space around the hatch
The mechanism of a broken clock hangs like the entrails
        of a fish
from the night table
between the curls of a pink wig
The fermentation of the waters of time which become entwined
        around the detritus like the snail in its shell
the ecstasy of what finally rots forever.

Isabel Rawsthorne

God spit and man was created
Man ejaculated and the gristly skeleton

of a woman named Isabel Rawsthorne appeared on a
    street of Soho
pools of membranous flesh showing through in clinical
    beds.

Isabel Rawsthorne, gristly skeleton of Soho streets
A face like vomit
like a soft mass that the bloody milker of reality
    tramples with his cow's feet.

In the meadow grass grows like hair in Isabel's pubis

The grass growing in the pubis of the meadow
blackened with semen
under those two figures
pools of membranous flesh showing through in clinical
    beds.

Old Woman in the Subway

Her skin is already a rag and packs the crumbled
flesh as though it were burlap or sawdust.
Her head has stopped rising above her rigid neck
bent like a handle; but she travels on the subway
at speeds incomprehensible for her
she lets herself be borne along by this need, half asleep
grasping her personal property
bundles of a weight that anchors her to herself,
half-empty, more filled with papers than things.
She has made herself up as everyday in order to arrive
at dawn at another station of the night
painted pink and white blended with a natural shade of
lilac, this flower of death
Destiny that is displaced
fulfilled but persistent
towards a street at the end of the world
Welfare Hotel on Broadway:
a bed like a grave
to die in life.

Edward Hopper

Stories alien to the Event
the place where events occurred and/or are going to occur

this Edward Hopper painted
a world of cold things
and rigid meetings between living mannikins
The extraterrestrial light with which an endless Sunday
begins or the glimmer of rails at twilight
this he painted: a path without beginning or end
a Manhattan street between this world and the other

Reality and Memory

The image of profundity that memory lends to everything
for it is by definition what is profound
that profundity consubstantial to things in memory, the reason
      why they are withdrawn from recognition
slipping in themselves constantly towards an apparent
      past.
In memory
we will never find ourselves before the things we saw
      sometime neither in reality before anything
But in reality—where exactly the opposite occurs—
things are pure surface
closing us to the knowledge of the same
things about which hence nothing can be said in reality.

Translated by Wayne H. Finke

Nineteenth Century Lions

The lion, a good family man
playful or cruel depending on how the wind blows
tameable, that's true, but never meek:
the ideal model for the nineteenth century.
Every sculptor made the circus into
his studio—beginning with the biggest frauds
(those kittens versed in the art of pleasing).
Millions of lions were transplanted
from the jungle to the world of metal casts
The marble roared, stone became lionlike
By the hundreds and thousands
artificial lions were scattered
about town, climbing up
all the palace stairs two by two

and there they kept guard in the name of the Law
But they weren't lions or even dogs
they were their own jailers, the guardians
of Power strutting about in the shape of lions.

Translated by David Unger

Roberto Lima (Cuba, 1935) has lived outside his homeland, mostly in Peru and Mexico. Widely known as a poet, critic and translator, he is a professor of Spanish and Comparative Literature at Penn State University. His verse has appeared in *Cielo Abierto,* a major literary journal in Peru. He has prepared a number of translations for this anthology.

Peripatetic

I walk
between the cobblestones
on bricks and paving blocks

Incessantly
the steps take on the tempo
of a funereal march
through grounds deserted, wet

until
beneath the feet
papered on the footpath
I come across
the Eye of God

The God Eye
looks up my sole
and through its darkness
sees it leathery

I salivate
to tread on Death
with expert feet
having overwalked
the Eye of God
without a consequence

Persona

You whiten mind
and leave it void,

210

blank as the space
outside these words

Lorca

Eyes breaking
against paving stones
of ashen streets

Roots of the cry
in the mocking of cacophony
and spit

Syntax of sound
without cursive sense
terrible in its length
and cavernous depth

Soul moan into night
of torn flesh
and severed heart

Head rolling to and fro
on impact of the hot lead's plunge,
the boot's emphatic thrust,
the coup de grâce

No longer a matter of
time or place

Earth's entrails in red damp
unmarked, apart from identity

The solitude of neverness

SILLUSTANI

I

The driving rain
tall upon the lake,
the red clay underfoot,
the often green or

sometime ochre mold
upon the moulded blocks
and on the boulders
strewn about the silence

II

Uneven stones
upright in patterns
of circular dimension
butting into hillsides
with their hard-cast edge

III

The chullpas rise suggestively
above the altiplano's height,
lithic tenements of death
stretched in rigor mortis to the sky

IV

The wasted lie against the stone
embraced by roundness
waiting for another birth,
perhaps the exit of some resurrection day
when stones that open out of earth
will service an eternal need

V

Monuments to death,
erect like phalli,
cathartic to the living

C I V I L   W A R :   S P A I N

L O N G   L I V E   D E A T H !

The charge
                    across the torn geography

The feet
                 once warm, now lying cold and still
The lives
                 prone each upon the side of strife
The sky
                 blood-red in the refracted light
LONG   LIVE   DEATH!

The cry
                 redundant on the crimson earth

CHILD ECOLOGY

When I grow up
litter will reach mountain tops

When I grow up
the ground won't grow food enough

When I grow up
rain will fall in dirty drops

When I grow up
snow won't be soft and white

When I grow up
water won't stop thirst or clean

When I grow up
rivers will run dry and die

When I grow up
oceans won't have fish alive

When I grow up
the sky won't be blue anymore

When I grow up
the air will be hard to breathe

When I grow up
the earth will be hard to save

Translated by the author

JUAN LISCANO (Caracas, Venezuela, 1915) is the director of the important publishing firm Monte Avila as well as *Zona Franca,* a leading Venezuelan literary magazine. He is the author of *From Dawn to Dawn (Del alba al alba), New Days (Los nuevos dís)*and *Foundations (Fundaciones).*

III

Buds of transparent capsules
thorny fruit flowers
sterile or inundating vegetation
metamorphosis of rock
populous kingdom of minerals
landscapes of subsoil
long tubular veins
             fisures
fields of metalliferous ore
             at rest
the wind pushing or obstructing
the shifts of ice
and between dusty clouds
ascending rivers.

IV

Variable and constant relations
limited in their direction by the atmosphere
effects of obedience to causes
cycles of resistence or surrender
of expansions or contractions
forces are interpenetrated
to raise and rejuvenate
to level and age
in an order bordering on eternity.

VIII

In the last days
everything for them was sepulchral
nostalgia of animal innocence
and for frightened beasts
nostalgia of being a plant once more.

XIII

Each element takes its part
in the cyclical work
of building and destroying

Water allied with the wind
erects monuments or plains
of erosion
                        —delicate arches
towers and excavated pinnacles
modeled unceasingly
hills of quicksand—
and patient boring
                              valleys and canyons

A persistent drop of water
is more powerful than lightning

Wind conquers all resistence
in its sowing of chance

XVII

A sweet water wave
                              brought a plant
to the shore
                  On the shore
the pregnant plant
                        cast an offspring
the offspring repeated the plant
on the shore
                  A plant brought
by the sweet water
                              dried up
without budding
The rain bore its remains
towards the sweet water
                                    which raised a wave
pregnant with a plant
                        pregnant with an offspring
on the shore. . . .

Translated by Wayne H. Finke

JOSÉ LÓPEZ HEREDIA (New York) grew up in Puerto Rico and studied at Columbia University and the Sorbonne. A professor of Spanish and French, he has devoted his energies to the narrative, and his short story *The Adventurer (El aventuerero)* won a prize from the Círculo de Escritores y Poetas Iberoamericanos in 1976. He published *Miracle in the Bronx and Other Narrations (Milagro en el Bronx y otros relatos)* in 1984 and is currently working on a second collection.

The Retiree

Seated before the partially open window which admitted a bitter cold draft, immersed in a world where apathy and sadness reigned like the wild Tradescantia vine, Primitivo contemplated the solitude outside in the street with indifference. For years the old man spent his melancholy in that position, before those fogged window panes. For a moment he harbored a fear of that immobility as though some unseen danger lurked beneath its cloak. He felt enveloped by a silence of that unfinished afternoon, a silence of the beyond that filled the room and gradually possessed his body to the point of placing his mind at rest.

In the window pane he thought he saw—for a fleeting moment—the anguished reflection of his own face, which heightened even more his sense of fear. Dozing, the old man appeared motionless before the afternoon silence, his head rocking in the air, in rhythm with the soft purring of a large, contented cat, tranquilly curled up in his lap.

"Cleo," he whispered into the animal's ear just as it shuddered, "now you're the only one I have left," and his gray eyes, of a metallic shade of gray, paled as he felt overcome by a wave of sadness, almost cold, of memories forgotten in a sterile past.

At nightfall, as the sun set, the trees transformed into phantoms by the reflection of the last rays of light, extended their branches towards infinity in an attempt to escape from this corrupt world of evil. They sought refuge in the heavens, in the crystaline pure air of far-distant atmospheric regions, far from this contaminating misery. In view of this picture, the old man stirred and in his subconscious, this gesture of supplication, repeated every afternoon like a penance imposed by destiny, seemed to him to sum up his whole life. Over the years he felt frustrated and abused by friends and relatives, constantly at the mercy of unscrupulous individuals who had exploited him for their own ends, and he thought of God like all those in dire need, wondering why He had abandoned him, surrendering him to that heartless pack.

He missed the gentle warmth of the hazy sun, and lamented deep within having to be cloistered up again in that dark room like a prisoner in a cell, closing the window and lowering the blinds only to find himself once again irrevocably and horribly alone. The sun when it was at its apogee would rejuvenate his arthritic bones, and angrily, with a despairing wrath, he would wish the sun to stop in its path, to burn for twenty-four hours a day, and he soundly cursed life's injustice.

He detested those sunless days. At night, the room grew cold and despite the heat that warmed the radiator, he felt frozen as his flaccid flesh trembled from the damp cold. During those nights he would spend hours twisting and turning in his bed, casting out disquieting memories.

From the night table he took out a bottle, opened it carefully and held it against the light, squinting to ascertain better how his reserves were faring: "Hardly anything left!" he complained in anger, and since he was retired, he was afraid of finding himself again without liquor before his pittance of a pension came in the mail.

He recalled unwillingly the words of his dead wife Jesusa, shortly before her death, when in one of those endless quarrels she labeled him a coward and a drunken sot and gave him a lecture on abstinence, insinuating that his was dubious, and chiding him for all his indiscretions.

"Someday they'll find you face down in some dark hallway, bloated with alcohol and your friends and cohorts won't even shed a tear, not even a single one; on the contrary . . ." and a dry, raspy cough interrupted her invective as she fell back, trembling from a slight fever that assailed her night and day. The only son she bore died at birth, and perhaps this caused her to dry up and become embittered prematurely, making her cross and cranky for the slightest motive.

When the sun was hotter, Primitivo exposed his hairy arm to its rays— "curative rays" as he called them—while he attempted to calculate how much longer the springtime sun would take to appear and prickle his shriveled skin. He missed those sunny days of old and experienced an infinite sorrow, a sudden despair that convulsed his meager body, as he recalled the tropical breezes of the longed-for land of his youth.

Oftentimes he lost his train of thought and remained in the shadows like a mummy, without perceiving the passage of the seconds, minutes and hours. And yet, in days passed, he was overwhelmed by a deluge of memories noisily overflowing in fierce cataracts which assumed the proportions of immense echoes and left him enervated. He managed to summon up all the strength he could to resist the recollections that assailed him, and involuntarily he uttered a deaf moan of acute shame in light of his dissipated life, a moan no one heard.

Some trees, dried and twisted by the wind, observed indifferently some pedestrian or another cross the little square. It was true that some shrubs were already showing their little green buds replete with springtime maternity, although the skeletal branches of the trees, undermined by the lack of rain, received the gusts of icy wind.

Discolored phantoms with flat faces like a wide open palm crossed his mind, treading strong and firm to be heard, resurrecting mouldy echoes, trying in vain to move his heart. In those moments Primitivo became nervous, almost aggressive, and in the darkness he glared as he received every recollection as though it were an intruder.

His inner being repeated daily that it was the most convenient attitude to assume, erasing every distant thought, and keeping it a prisoner, crushed in a strongbox in the back of his brain so that it would not emerge and perturb his accustomed tranquility.

That night, he let out a sigh, involuntarily. . . .

He recalled the little wooden house, down in his Antillean homeland—the house of his youth!—that creaked in the night breeze as the floors cracked and the tin roof trembled under the weight of the downpour. A sad echo soaked with tropical perfumes, for the coffee plants in flower on the slopes gave off a sweet aroma. Suddenly the atmosphere was filled with sorrow growing with the wind; only the uninterrupted percussion of the raindrops crashing furiously against the metal. In a dark corner of the house a small spider, surprised in its domestic chores, skittered away yielding to a shapeless form that entered the house, wrapped in cold air. A little old woman, hardened by the Caribbean sun, her swollen fingers strangely deformed, lay motionless, prostrate on a cot. Under a rag of a sheet there hid meager flesh, whipped with fever, stuck on bones.

As the man entered, the old woman felt pangs of pain and gave forth a sorrowful smile just as the wind's roaring exploded and drowned out her moan. In the penumbra, under the slight shadow of a smoked lamp, a mass was visible, head down and silent, propped against the wall with a lit cigarette between his lips. It was a man in the prime of his years, with a tight, agile body. The sick old woman caught in his intention a smile, a slight gesture of the lips and eyes.

"Primitivo," she gasped in a voice linked to life by a tenuous sigh, "don't leave! Wait a few days more before going, only a few more days . . ." and her voice was engulfed in the misty night. Despite the semidarkness, the man perceived the anguish portrayed in his old mother's countenance.

"I can't, mother, it's impossible, I have engagements, several of them, I gave my word; they're waiting for me in town."

The fatigue was so intense that instead of answering, she dropped her head deeper into the pillow. She had a premonition, however, a single fleeting flash of intuition, and envisioned some friends with worried faces gathered in a bend of Luna Street waiting for him with just-opened bottles of rum; and his telling yarns between sarcastic smiles, and in the back room shadows of streetwalkers from Sol Street, those with ardent eyes caked with make-up and mascara.

That night, dancing the latest tango by Carlos Gardel, he received the news of his mother's death to the strident sounds of a shrieking jukebox while customers struck their glasses against the bar in a constant repetition of slugs and curses. The next afternoon—since he overslept and missed his bus—he reached the town, only to find that they had already buried her, and friends recounted how up to the very last moment she had kept the sinister contortion of her death throes, and he recalled the previous night spent in the caresses of the lover whose passion now caused him to manifest a tired smile.

Sowing one's oats! for he lost reason when hot turbulent blood galloped through his body seeking thighs wherein to deposit his desires. In those moments of exaltation he savored his rum with a gastronomical look, without exhausting a mouthful, letting the liquid prickle his gums, and then descend soft and easy, tickling his throat, and he would smile, satisfied, with an approving air if it was a good brand of rum.

Suddenly, he was wounded by reproach in the glances of the old women of the town and assailed by the memory of his mother. He wanted to forget, he had always said so; evoking the past was like resurrecting the dead, who ought to rest in peace.

He had never known his father. He only knew he had worked in the merchant marine and that a few days after his birth his father sailed off never to return again. As a child, sometimes he would sit on the jetties watching boats dock and when he saw rowdy sailors disembark he would try to find out if his father was one of them. Once he thought he recognized one—tall, heavyset, good-looking—from an old photograph his mother kept in a drawer, and he raced home sweating and out of breath to find it in darkness as though isolated from the rest of the world.

Mama Tina had raised him up right and religious, working like a slave to educate him and dress him decently.

"With every ounce of my strength I raised him—and look how mischievous he was—," she used to declare, contemplating her hands, dry and caloused from so much washing and ironing for the rich folk of the town. She could not understand how the lad turned out so carefree, just like his father, when the latter saw him only once and apparently wasn't very impressed.

As a youth he was not afraid of ghosts or of the lights that lept around his room in the wee hours of the night, drawing diabolical shadows on the walls. On the contrary, when they appeared he would, fascinated, identify with those antediluvian forms dancing until dawn.

One afternoon as the rains fell in buckets, he sat against the window to read an amusing magazine with stories and pictures . . . His eyes sparkled with licentious visions and desire burned his face as he felt an exquisite dryness seize his throat. The seduction of forbidden pleasures enslaved his imagination. All of a sudden, Mama Tina appeared without explanation, in the most unexpected moment, and tore the magazine from his hands.

"You follow the devil's advice more than your own mother's," and with a look that crushed him she sent him scampering to his room to repent for his sins in silent prayer.

That night, with a burning confusion in his murmurings, he contemplated himself in the mirror and began to make faces, biting his fleshy lips and letting the edges of his mouth swell out like two enormous fangs. He wrinkled his forehead from the effort he made tightening up, and he turned as red as a beet. In the silence of the night, drenched in a satanic sweat, he perceived a spectre—red, cruel, with flat ears and two little horns appearing in the darkness—beckon to him invitingly. Reality and illusion became so tightly fused that he wavered between fear and desire, suddenly experiencing a profound fright. Dropping the mirror, which shattered in a thousand shards, he huddled in his bed and hid, afraid to confront that aspect of his personality. For a long time afterward he held a high regard for mirrors and avoided coming face to face with his double.

In that moment the lights of the city were coming on like stars appearing in the darkness of the night. Cleo stretched, lifted its ears on hearing the solitary wind and curled up in a ball for another sleep.

Primitivo did not understand why he had grown tired of Jesusa. In the beginning everything had been perfect, then, after two years he began to look at her with anger, feeling somehow cheated. She was neither beautiful nor graceful; on the contrary, she appeared timid and awkward in dress. She would always be a hindrance in life and now he realized it. True, her father had left her a small inheritance, but this was soon eaten up in a weak business venture that failed within two months. And she never helped him to prosper, leaving all the responsibilities on his shoulders. She was a vain woman, and did not encourage him to open new horizons as other wives did. After all, he too needed a well-meaning push from time to time. Rather, she rejected him and denied his rights as a husband, the obligation of all good wives. When he would come home after spending long hours with his friends in the bar and whisper little sweet nothings in her ear, romantically, with the smell of rum on his breath, she pretended to be asleep. He never wanted to have children. For him they were an obstacle in life and he knew that without offspring he would lead a carefree life, without hindrance or responsibilities. He observed his friends, surrounded by hungry mouths, always asking for food and eating like bottomless pits. They were slaves of these children, needy and with their hands extended, who when they grew up would abandon their parents without a word of thanks—a pack of thieves!—and he determined never to have any, never!

On her part Jesusa did not feel complete without children and she confessed it daily, averring that she only wanted one, for she was satisfied with little, when suddenly and unexpectedly she became pregnant after three long years of marriage. For several days she hid the truth from him, awaiting the opportune moment to give him the news, but the months passed without her speaking to him about it.

He had his suspicions seeing her so brimming and hearing her humming some nostalgic tropical melody in the kitchen, her maternity reflected in the bloom in her face. Jesusa kept the tidings to herself and did not look at him until she was sure it was too late to have an abortion, for she knew he would demand one. He divined it from her look and understood.

"You're sure," he was on the verge of uttering but he held himself back, conceding the point, for he felt in his bones that it was true.

As the months passed he watched the threatening belly grow and he felt handcuffed and chained as though he were a prisoner in the most fetid dungeon of Princesa jail, there in old San Juan, deprived of liberty and breath. Her belly grew evermore like a crescent moon, and her steps got slower and heavier as the date approached.

As the months elapsed his brain was drilled by a thought, like a drop of acid, an implacable desire that did not let him rest. He fell into a silence, pulling and tugging, showing his bad temper and free hand, smashing and breaking everything in sight.

A thousand times a day he would repeat that he wanted no children and offered pretexts: lack of money, the high cost of living, uncertainty at work . . . and many times he would repeat the words, almost biting them. Each day his expression became harder, like that of an individual who in secret, in silence is hatching a plan. He realized the date was drawing near and he had to make a decision.

One day when Jesusa was at the top of the stairs, he saw the dreamed-of moment. He stared at her like someone waiting to dominate merely with his eyes. She received his look and for the first time she endured that stare and looked defiantly right back at him. It provoked an argument and feeling shamefully insulted he gave her a slap that made her lose her balance. She fell tripping on the stone steps and lay there, stretched on the floor, her hair bathed in blood.

That night Primitivo heard the creature's crying and the mother's heart-felt prayers. Jesusa looked at the baby with maternal affection and saw a little male child, the only hope of her life. Primitivo saw only one more chain, a mouth like an abyss which would spend an eternity being nurtured by the sweat of his arm, and he made a silent invocation for his own liberation. . . .

The child had been born in winter and died a few hours later.

Jesusa swore she would never love the man who had killed the child of her womb and wept over that loss for many years, even after the tears had stopped watering her eyes. She bore a violent resentment against her husband until the day of her death, and he knew it.

One afternoon she arrived, sorrowful and fatigued, from the lawyer's office.

"How much did the old man leave you?" Primitivo asked her with great interest. He paid careful attention to what the lawyer had told Jesusa. She spoke in a monotone, still moved by the unexpected death of her father, so she did not note the gesture of disappointment in her husband's face when he learned the inheritance did not meet his high expectations. As he had dreamt of being a businessman since his youth, the boss of his own shop, he made plans, obtained a centrally-located spot on a well-traveled street and there opened a hardware shop, selling barbed wire, tin-plate, screws and bolts.

Jesusa was in a ruined state, fevers obliged her to remain in bed most of the time. As he had no one to help him in the shop, he was forced to bring his nephew Inocencio from the island. A young peasant, as good as the daily bread; he worked the poor lad day and night for a pittance; the youth slept in an old cot in the unhealthy back room. Inocencio worked seven days a week, receiving begrudgingly a couple of free hours off on Sundays, in order to stroll aimlessly through the city streets.

"Take the afternoon off," Primitivo would say to him, "but remember, I need you tomorrow, early, mind you, to look for a box of nails in the storeroom. And don't forget to count the boxes and weigh them to make sure everything is in order," and the young man wondered how he was going to lift them when they weighed more than 160 pounds each, yet he said nothing, for he respected his uncle. In view of the incredulous look on Inocencio's face, Primitivo replied, somewhat ruffled,

"Well, what? You think money is earned just like that. . . ."

The youth went off, not understanding how his uncle could be so unjust, making him work like a slave without rest, paying him a paltry sum, giving him only a couple of hours off per week.

Next to the hardware shop there was an elegant, fragrant-smelling establishment, La Boutique Gauloise, belonging to Mme. Grossein, a French couturière of high airs and even higher breasts, married to a blind farmer who spent his days buried in his farm labors.

Mme. Grossein paraded through the streets in an ultratight dress that attracted men's attention and Primitivo's covetousness. With satisfaction she perceived ardent glances following the lines of her calves and rising over her back to caress the skin on the nape of her neck. At times she felt trembling glances of passion electrifying the fibers of his being become entangled in her curly hair. In the morning as he watched her open the boutique, Primitivo felt a general well-being and spent long hours dreaming of her, as if they had poured hot coals into his veins, and at night, suddenly, he would get up sweaty and nervous, leaving Jesusa alone in their bed.

One day Mme. Grossein entered his shop, asking for a loan to pay an account (to some impertinent creditors demanding back payment) as he contemplated the smoothness of her breasts, and captivated he handed over much more money than she had requested. The French woman stuck the bills down her bosom, thanked him with a graceful movement of her head, and went out swaying to the rhythm of the latest guaracha dance playing on the jukebox of a neighboring bar. In ecstasy he spent the day in a state of exaltation and in the secret crannies of his imagination he sowed the seed of desire, nurtured it with hopeful appetite and waited for his little garden of whims to bear fruit.

Mme. Grossein was impressed by robust men, of staunch builds and flesh that gave off an odor of wild, fresh wind.

One night when Inocencio was working late in the storeroom, he entered the back of the shop—dead from fatigue—just before the storm broke. He entered through the side door, which he found ajar strangely. In the darkness he vaguely perceived two shadows separate brusquely, a movement so clumsy that he immediately intuited something wrong. He heard some sentences tinged with a foreign accent, and on closing the door, the hushed sound of the downpour.

Primitivo went to bed late that night, his thoughts unchained, twisting through the bends of his imagination. He recalled jubilantly that night when he placed his thirsty desire and beating heart in the hands of Mme. Grossein, who, naked and trembling, sunk into his arms as the rear of the shop vibrated with the storm's thundering. Again he felt how the couple's legs intertwined and how they slipped into that position of ecstasy and heard his name pronounced between ardent panting.

The whole night he spent wrapped in a euphoric state without falling asleep, just listening to the rain retreat, slowly and sadly.

The morning greeting Inocencio received the next day was a hostile glance and tightened lips. Wrathful looks quickly communicated to him that his indiscretion of the previous night would cost him dearly. At noon Primitivo announced he wouldn't be needing him any more and he offered him his return passage, taking out for a small advance; his uncle sent him packing without a single word of thanks.

A dévotée of popular music Mme. Grossein accompanied Primitivo to the cabaret where they spent evenings dancing cheek to cheek till the wee hours, surrounded by rough, aggressive types who between swigs and malicious stares desired the French woman and dreamt of the moment of carrying her off, but Primitivo held on to her tightly with his steel-like pincers.

Rough as a tree trunk, drunk and hair uncombed, he would spend the evenings demonstrating in spite of his years that he danced better than the young fellows. Reeking of liquor he dragged Mme. Grossein around the cabaret floor and then fell tripping over the edge of tables and chairs, causing a scandal and fueling the gossip of the other customers.

His shiny flesh covered with sweat, rivulets running down his back, bathed in burning desire, he would receive satisfaction afterward in the back of the shop. It was then during those moments that he truly distinguished himself as a lover. It was then that all those forbidden, sensual books (filled with perverse acts, crimes worthy of Satan, against God and humanity) he had read since his youth permitted him to enjoy all prohibited secrets and taboos.

Money flowed like water and business declined, his doors closed and his light out, as he silently rejected customers.

The whole street was up on his licentious behavior and all felt sorry for Jesusa, who lived forgotten, buried in her house, venerating the memory of her father and son.

One night of faceless shadows while Primitivo demonstrated his skill in a complicated pasodoble, Jesusa felt an unknown force sent from heaven, from the pure diaphanous horizon, and heard the voice from beyond pronounce her name in a soft, slight tone; like a morning bird she gave herself up to the Lord.

The neighbor women carefully wrapped her body in a shroud, placed flowers at her feet, a tall white candle at her side that in the darkness lent a supernatural aspect, and for the first time in many a year she seemed to smile as a beatific expression illuminated her countenance.

Primitivo squandered her money, mortgaged the hardware shop, till one fine day his best friend enticed Mme. Grossein away with murmured words in her ear and a little package of rolled-up bills. Without giving too much thought she abandoned him for another in order to enjoy the delights of new capitalism.

His life dissipated, his fortune spent and his body aged, bent and dry, without any pulse, everything embittered him. He never prepared himself to understand the mystery of life, and in the silence of the night, far far off, he heard the hushed, almost prophetic voice of his dead wife:

"He who plants love harvests love!"

In that instant a brusque wind woke him from his thoughts. He raised his tired eyes in order to see the city sunken in night like the mouth of a wolf. The lights almost out, his room reflected an infinite darkness. The very terror of old age, at such a late hour when the devil does his mischief, made him feel an infinite fear.

Before the sight of the mist that made everything immaterial, his members swelled and his heart clinched in agony. With the gesture of a sleepwalker, he manifested a fear of the immobility of the night, a fear that had grown in him since Jesusa's death.

The mist pressed against the panes, entered his room and little by little—with an arrogant lentitude—covered him with its cold mantle . . . of an inhuman cold.

Suddenly he felt light, almost young, on finding himself sunken into an uncertain cloud, a mystical, hallucinating atmosphere that left him bodiless. In the distance he saw in the darkness of the room the carcass of an old man with a withered face and weakened body that brought panic to his being.

Cleo, feeling wrapped in the old man's chill, lept from his lap and with cautious steps curled up peacefully at the foot of the radiator that still warmed the desolate room.

Translated by Wayne H. Finke

JAIME MANRIQUE (Barranquilla, Colombia, 1949) is a leading novelist and poet of Colombia. His collection of verse *The Worshippers of the Moon (Los adoradores de la luna)* won the Eduardo Cote Lamus National Poetry Award. He is the author of *Papa's Body (El cadáver de papá)* and *Confessions of an Amateur Critic (Confesiones de un crítico amateur)*. He is currently working on his new novel, *Rich Ladies of the Andes,* due out in 1987.

Ode to a Hummingbird

If you were one of those birds
who sing ancient songs,
I would bring you bread crumbs or even a snare.
But you cannot be caged
or deprived of your natural habitat.
On the steps that lead up to the park,
we fulfill the ritual of our daily visit.
No one announces my arrival or yours.
Today my monologue is about love.

I don't know if you make pledges to resist
unusual flutters in the chambers of the heart—
so you never get closer than the roses,
and when you stare at me,
your eyes are caverns brimming with dark beads.
On the park steps while I talk to you,
while you flirt and approach me,
I stand among the fuchsias to watch you;
and when your wings buffet the noon light,
you are a tiny whirlwind gleaming in the air.
Though I cannot follow the steps of your dance,
I can watch you pirouette from leaf to branch.
Like love, you are fleeting and resplendent.
So I come hoping you'll learn to trust me
and that one day, without having to ask,
you will come to me and surrender.
Others think I'm looking into infinite green;
a hummingbird is only visible to the eyes of love.
But you are not just another hummingbird.
You are a beauty
and your loveliness stops me from knowing you.
Yet you have always been with me.
In my childhood, I wanted to climb the highest trees
and take your nestlings in my hands.

Even when the sea floated in my bones
you were a promise of the unreachable.
In my dreams, you continued growing.
Over the years I've learned that we leave each other
for other climates with other roses,
looking for the promise of voluptuousness
in the gardens of flesh.
But I'm sure today, if we weren't afraid of each other,
we could meet among the flowers
and astonish the passers-by with our daring.
Only I have not been able to conjure up love
with the proper offerings.
If I were truly courageous enough,
if I could still believe it was enough to climb a tree,
the tallest one, to reach what has a name,
but which is beyond words,
if I believed that a daring gesture
could bring us together and carry us beyond darkness,
thinking neither of death, nor of happiness,
if after so much thrashing among others
I had learned to make only the proper offerings,
my temples wreathed with orquids,
I could come to you—
my ration of light, my green helicopter of the soul,
to offer the rarest flower, the most treasured nectar.

In Amherst, your visits to someone
who had chosen silence for entertainment
suggested Brazil's exotic blooms of purple and cochineal.
Now I know that the body I love
is a Brazilian orchid;
it is your mouth seeking mine without fear.
But today I cannot offer you an orchid.
You have chosen to look for other climates,
to freeze yourself on the outer boundaries.
Some day you will come close enough again.
I'll look into your nocturnal eyes,
I'll marvel at your rainbow plumage,
I'll recall childhood memories,
though I know now that to reach you
it is not enough to believe in miracles,
or climb to the crown
of the tallest tree that life has to offer us.

Translated by Eugene Richie

JUAN CARLOS MARTÍNEZ (Valparaíso, Chile, 1959) is a young poet of Chile who during the recent political unrest suffered internal exile in Selva Oscura in the south of the country. His plight was dramatically highlighted in a feature article in *The New York Times* in December, 1982. His poems appear for the first time in this anthology.

Luis and Clara

Luis and Clara love each other,
they said so,
        till death do them part.
He
is a gentleman
who arrives with flowers and candy,
he is attentive to anniversaries,
he has a checking account in the Bank of Chile,
he bought a new car with his earnings,
        now they go out on weekends,
he amuses himself doing crossword puzzles
appearing in the daily papers,
he is informed about his country and abroad,
he is a good catch, as they say.
She,
a dedicated and self-denying housewife,
worries about all the little details,
a woman who dreams of hordes of children
        if the budget permits;
from time to time she buys clothes in the boutique
and goes to the hairdresser;
in confidence
she is called princess.
They live in a residential neighborhood,
their house is called the house of good fortune,
it is adorned with violets.
One has tea at five o'clock sharp,
        a family tradition,
the house is full of appliances,
with a maid and everything.
All goes as one wishes:
love sprouts from the radios
in the mouth of Julio Iglesias.
At night they make love
and fall asleep with a kiss

and may you dream of the angels.
One day. . . . one fine day
as he kissed her good night
the princess
turned into a toad,
tears flowed
and soaked the pillow,
what a shame!
Today
they no longer write tales like before.

I am by nature

I am by nature
a city dweller
for I remain at home
stuck to the wall
with a nail in my breast
so that I do not slip.

My Country

My country
is something like a migrain,
like one of those big ones
that appears in the ear,
almost feigning,
and after
gaining one's confidence
one gives it the eye
and the forehead is taken;
and the more pills
one takes for it
the more it hurts,
the more it says "here."
I make an effort with it,
with repose, away from all noise,
but there is no relief;
I relax and there is no relief.
It goes away a little,
it passes half slowly
almost so that I get its taste
for a day or hours.
I rest
but again it seizes me

suddenly,
for occurring so much it seems not to exist,
and it enters more forcefully
like a people united,
so strong.
This is my country,
it enters with such pain
and keeps me
waiting constantly.

The Plastic Flower

The plastic flower
lost its leaves with so much procedure,
its petals withered by taxes
beside the famous "Made in . . . ."
It is displayed in the business of
direct imports to the public.
Next to it
                    lies its metallic bee,
                      dead.

Translated by Wayne H. Finke

ARISTIDES MARTÍNEZ ORTEGA (Panama City, Panama, 1936), though from Panama, has strong ties with Chile, where he studied and worked. A keynote of his poetry is a strong anti-Yankee sentiment. *In the Manner of Protest (A manera de protesta)* is representative of his work.

Words Before the End

Before you destroy the earth
seeking peace
with your atomic bombs,
seeking peace
with your hydrogen bombs,
seeking peace
with your rockets
launched like fireworks in honor of your gods,
listen to me, Uncle Sam!
harken, old man of the Rio Grande, giant
in a clownish jacket.

We are content with the unrivaled robust Army boys
sweeping over us in jeeps to the rhythm of chewing gum;
have no doubt, these unrivaled robust Army boys:
attentive, groomed, polished, combed,
and comical. They have their picture taken
with their behind on our monuments,
their cap on one side, their Kentucky whisky in hand
and the SOB whore daughter and granddaughter of a whore.
Oh, the incomparable Army boys!
attentive, groomed, polished, combed.
And comical. They reach us by air or by sea
without a passport but with their M1.
I don't dispute it: they are your pride
and that of the world so much aided by you.
To Caesar what is Caesar's!
The world so aided by you cannot forget
that you help us to maintain your might.
The world so aided by you cannot forget
that you have us allied for your progress.
The world so aided by you cannot forget
that with facilities of payment you sell us our riches.
The world so aided by you cannot forget
that you bring relief to our catastrophes with your surplus.
The world so aided by you cannot forget

your mines in our land.
The world so aided by you cannot forget
that you do your best for our forces of order.
The world so aided by you cannot forget
that you finance witch hunts.
The world so aided by you cannot forget
that you reward with dollars rubbery weak backbones.
The world so aided by you cannot forget
that you let the Canal owned by you to be known as
          Panamanian on post cards for tourists.
The world so aided by you cannot forget
that combatting savagery—as your westerns depict—
you exterminated the wild red-skins.
The world so aided by you cannot forget
that to appease divine furies you offer Blacks to your gods.
The world so aided by you cannot forget
that you point out our path as the good cowboy does with his cattle,
To Caesar what is Caesar's!

Then, like devils they cry out in the streets
Go home, Yanqui! Get out! Son of a bitch!
I had forgotten; they're the damned Communists!
Uncle Sam, aren't you the one who appears
                    in a novel of Faulkner with the name Benjy?
May hell swallow me whole if I'm Benjy!
You are Benjy!

That was all I had to tell you
before you destroy the earth
seeking peace
with your atom bombs,
seeking peace
with your hydrogen bombs,
seeking peace
with your rockets
launched like fireworks in honor of your gods.

Translated by Wayne H. Finke

Pedro Mir (San Pedro de Macorís, Dominican Republic, 1913) is considered the country's national poet. He is the author of *There Is a Country in the World (Hay un país en el mundo)* and *Countersong to Walt Whitman (Contracanto a Walt Whitman)*.

The Hurricane Neruda*

The hours have passed over the volcano neruda
and delirium and fever over the quake neruda
and the dormant lava of the eruption neruda
over the din of the imposing situation neruda.

All is at rest, Father. The velvet sleeps
on the ivory keys of the oldest pianos.

There is a woman named Luisa from her brown
eyes to the sound of her hair, from her needlelike
voice to the end of a threat at whose bare end
a small child slumbers. The delicate dawn
gently rocks in her glance and slips in her hand,
rolls bleeding, falls to the ground and suddenly
we are confronted with the rising hurricane neruda
the gust neruda and the vortex neruda and
                              neruda
the storm,
                    reconstructed by the grave
explosion of infernal horror neruda.

2

What has happened, Father? Suddenly everything harms us.
Everything, even the water itself has become unbearable.
The floaters in the city aqueduct, who
not long ago, carried clouds to their temples and
thought calmly about tuberculosis and sponges
have suddenly become thoughtless.
                    One knows now
of many torrents that have slept in the forests.

---

*Fragment of an extensive poem dedicated to the memory of the Chilean poet Pablo Neruda.

Of youthful waters that have spent the night naked
in the streets.
               And of steam turbines that have returned
and sent the water back to its former clouds.
               And the same
with recently washed sheets that have dried, sooner
than expected.
               And decidedly the same fate
is known for sweat, oranges and mirrors . . .

What has happened, Father? Everything has died. Everything
has been displaced. Everything has sunk. The snail
neruda in the vast depths of the seas neruda.
The captain neruda in the breakers of the archipelago
neruda.
        And everything neruda burning in the essential wood
of that night illuminated in emotion neruda:

"I wish to write the saddest verses tonight . . ."
And suddenly the celestial thunder in the vaulting of
                       heaven neruda.
Neruda midst the stars of the infernal displacement neruda.

3

What has happened, true Father of the hurricane
volcano and new lava? What has happened
on the ivory keys and the velvet of the old pianos
and on the breakers of the archipelagos?

4

The story is very simple.
                   The discovery
neruda on the sides of the mountains
and at times on the sand of the rivers.
The vestiges neruda in the highest layers
of the atmosphere and in the backbones
of some insatiable individuals,
has revealed the decisive link
of the people with the reins of the dawn.

Felicitous discovery capable
of emancipating infinite regions
of the oceans and the desert

and above all eliminating the night
and the poppies' eclipses.

And that is all. And it has been enough
for everything. After, everything has sunk.
Everything concealed, and inundated.

For it has been dawn and not metal
that mangles the people in its mills.
Rather the people itself in place
neruda. Or if one wants the very people
in place of dawn.

                And thus it is told
in numerous ballads of the people
and it appears in children's tales:. . . .

                        Translated by Wayne H. Finke

EDUARDO MITRE (Oruro, Bolivia, 1943) is a poet and essayist who has written on the poet Vicente Huidobro and has authored *Good Lieutenant (Teniente bueno)* and *Residence (Morada)*.

You tread . . .

You tread
          on the grass
                   unhurriedly
Musician of green sounds
The wind retreats
              It messes long hair
            Birds arise:
Stationary   A
      Stone   peach
         Behive of   falls
            dizziness
             The city
        Casts smoked cries
The sun absorbs your footsteps
I hear how they do not resound
My thoughts are weightless
Clarity murmurs:
Dig
  Below
      Beatle:
There is only ascension towards earth.

From Dark to Light

From dark to light
Tense dawn
You
  L
     e
     a
   p
Its
  a
    r
  c
From whiteness.

For it is law . . .

For it is law
May your
Flesh grow old
But not
    Your nudity.

Twins

Twins
    Like your breasts
Innocent
        Like the hills
That childhood traces
Oval
    Like temples
White
    Your buttocks.

It was . . .

It was
    Only
        A hummingbird
And laughter does not succeed in making it unattainable

In   mit
    ter   tenT
      suicide
          your
voice
    fr-
      om
        thE
Mul
    ti
      ple
        B
alconies   of
  L a u g h t e r.

Translated by Wayne H. Finke

Alvaro Mutis (Colombia, 1922) is a short story writer who presently lives in Mexico. His collection *Lecumberri Diary* was written during his imprisonment. He is the author of the collections of verse *The Elements of Disaster (Los elementos del desastre)* and *The Lost Works (Los trabajos perdidos)*.

CARAVANSARY

1.

They are chewing betel and they spit on the ground with the monotonous regularity of an organic function. Ochre stains spread about the gnarled feet planted like tough roots that have withstood monsoon rains. Above, all the stars track their unwavering course in the clear Bengali night. Time is as if softly stopped, tangled in the interstices of dialogue. Talk is of voyages, of clandestine harbors, of precious cargoes, of vile deaths, of famine. All is as always. The modest matters of men are spoken in the dialect of the Birbhum district, in Western Bengal, stringing a sordid rosary of cunning, of miserly ambitions, of tired lusts, of ancient fears. All is as always, facing the sea, tame as nut-milk under the countless stars. On the earthen ground shiny from the rubbing of immemorial soles, the betel stains disappear in the anonymous tracks of men. Sailors. Businessmen in their time. Blood-stained. Dreamy. At ease.

2.

If you persist in believing the lies of camel drivers, the truculent stories bruited about in every courtyard of every inn, the foul promises of veiled women offering themselves; if you persist in ignoring unwritten laws on the watchful behavior that must be followed when crossing the land of the infidel; if you persist in your foolishness, then, you will never go through the gates of the city of Tashkent, the city where plenty reigns and where diligent and wise men rule. If you persist in your foolishness . . .

3.

Stop! Stop you feverish madmen who with screechy voices demand what is not owed you! Stop you fools! The hour of disputes among voluptuaries, strangers to the protocol of these rooms, is over. It is the turn of the women, of the Egyptian Queens from Bohemia and from Hungary, of the treaders of all roads. From their beckoning eyes, from their high haunches, forgetfulness will distill its best liquor, its most efficacious domains. Let us settle in our laws, let us sing our song, and for a last time, let us deceive the specious call of the old weaver of battles, the mistress sister already standing in front of our tombs. Silence then. Let them come the females with the pox, the ladies from Moravia, the Egyptians for hire to the condemned.

4.

I am a Captain in the 3rd Lancers of the Imperial Guard, commanded by Colonel Tadeuz Lonczynski. I am going to die in consequence of the wounds I received in an ambush by the deserters of the Hessian. Each time that I try to turn, looking to ease the pain of my bones shattered by shrapnel, I slide on my own blood. Before the blue glass of agony invades my arteries and confuses my words I want to confess my love, my disordered, secret, immense, delicious, drunken love for Countess Krystina Krasinska, my sister. May God forgive the arduous sleepless nights of fever and desire that I went through for her on our parents' country house in Katowicz. I have always known how to keep silent. I hope that this will be taken into account when I appear in front of the Ineluctable Presence. And to think that she will pray for my soul kneeling next to her husband and children!

5.

My work consists in carefully cleaning the tin lamps with which the gentlemen go fox hunting among the coffee bushes at night. With these complex artifacts, stinking of lamp oil and soot, they dazzle the animal. So bright is the flame that it blinds the yellow eyes of the beast. I have never heard one emit a sound. They always die from the shocked panic caused by that unexpected and unexplainable light. Their last glance at their executioners is that of someone who meets his gods on turning a corner. My task, my destiny, is to maintain always polished these grotesque devices of tin for their brief nightly use in hunting. And I who once dreamed of being a laborious traveler through lands of fever and adventure!

6.

Every time the King of Cups turns up we must return to the ovens, to feed them with the strained sugar cane that keeps even the heat under the vats. Every time the Ace of Gold turns up the syrup begins a bubbling dance and to emit the unmistakable smell that gathers in its sweetest matter the most secret essence of the hills and the fresh gentle vapor of the ditches. The syrup is ready! The miracle of its happy presence is announced by the Ace of Swords. But if the Ace of Clubs turns up, then one of the workers must die, covered by the syrup that consumes him like voracious bronze poured on the soft wax of fear. In the dawn of the cane fields they deal the cards to the high song of the crickets and the splashing of water falling on the wheel that moves the mill.

7.

He went across the chasms of the mountain thanks to an ingenious device of pulleys and ropes that he himself managed, working himself slowly above the abyss. One day, the birds devoured most of him and turned him into a bloody puppet that danced to the frozen winds of the wilderness. He had stolen one of the women of the men who were building the railroad. With her he enjoyed a brief night of endless desire and he fled when the offended males had almost caught up with him. It is said that the woman had impregnated him with a substance born of her most secret entrails, and whose smell drove wild the large birds of the highlands. His remains ended by drying up in the sun, and they waved like a mocking flag above the precipice.

8.

In Akaba he left the print of his hand on the wall above the fountain.

In Gdynia he complained of having lost his papers in a tavern brawl, but he did not want to give his true name.

In Recife he offered his services to the bishop and ended by stealing a tin reliquary.

In Abidjan he cured leprosy touching the sick with a scepter and reciting in Tagalog a page from the book of the Custom House.

In Valparaiso he disappeared forever, but the women of the High Quarter still keep a picture of him in which he is dressed as a traveling salesman. They insist that the image is good for menstrual cramps and that it protects the newborn against the evil eye.

9.

None of our dreams, not even the darkest of our nightmares is larger than the sum total of failures that make up our destiny. We will always go farther than our most secret hope, but in the opposite way, following the path of those who sing on waterfalls, those who measure their self-deceit with the wise standard of usage and forgetfulness.

10.

There is a trade that should prepare us for the most silent of battles and the most subtle disappointments. But it is a trade for women and it will be forever banned to men. It consists of washing the statues of those who loved with neither measure nor forgetfulness, and to leave at their feet an offering that with time will make marble crumble and corrode the strongest metals. But it happens that this trade disappeared so long ago that no one knows with any certainty the order that must be followed in the ceremony.

Invocation

Who convoked these characters here?
With what words were they called?
Why have they been allowed to use the time
and substance of my life?
Where are they from and where does the anonymous
destiny that made them parade before us
take them?

Lord, let forgetfulness gather them.
quiet their impertinent pain,
give rest to their impure souls.
Let them find peace within it.

I don't know, in truth, who they are,
nor why they came to me
to share the brief instant of the white page.
They are vain people,
and liars besides.
Lucky that their memory begins to vanish
in the merciful nothing
that will house us all.
So let it be.

Translated by Roberto-Selim Picciotto

Luis Rogelio Nogueras (Havana, Cuba, 1945) has been a journalist, film maker and editor-in-chief of *El caimán barbudo*. He has written two novels, *The Fourth Circle (El cuarto círculo)* and *If I Die Tomorrow (Y si muero mañana)*. His collection of poems *Imitation of Life (Imitación de la vida)* received the Casa de las Américas Poetry Prize in 1981.

Poetic Material

What do the verses I shall write afterwards matter
now
close your eyes and kiss me
madrigal flesh
let me touch the lightning of your legs
when I have to evoke them on paper
cross my throat, whole,
deliver your voracious cries to me
your fleshy dreams

What do the verses where you will float intact matter
            when you depart
now give me the moist certainty that we are alive
now
pose intensely naked
for the madrigal where without fail
you will flower tomorrow.

Non Omnia Morior

Oh, bard of the XIXth century
who in a honey-like dirge
affirmed that the skin
of your beloved was of snow.
In the ever so brief space
of a hundred years, your poetry
lost freshness
till it "changed color."
What remains of that love
but dust and distance?

There Is a Poem

There is a poem that has been seeking me for some time.
I suspect we have been in the same places, without
           seeing each other,
and it is not improbable that we have loved the same woman
           some time,
that together we have laughed heartily over little
           jokes,
and that we have grown gray from the same suffering.
There is a poem that has been seeking me for some time,
and it does not tire,
and it has already lasted 34 years.

Time Maude

Time Maude,
time is not like the sled dogs
that stop at their master's voice.
Time is not like the white she-bear
that turns her head to see if the whelps
      are pursuing her,
not like the hunter
who returns to his igloo following his own footprints
      on the snow,
tracks that the wind already begins to erase.
Time does not stop,
it does not look back,
it does not return.

I was old when your parents had not been born;
I shall have died
when your breasts still remain firm
under the sealskin coat I gave you yesterday.

I love in you
the infinite universe, not your fleeting beauty;
I love in you the endless human race,
not the mortal clay of which you are made.
I love in you the way you will remember me
when you too approach the winter of your life
           with hesitating step,
not the springtime of your laugh.
But above all, Maude,
I love in you the one I was,
I love in you all the girls who burned their wings
there in the distance,

in the fire of my youth
and who were unable to survive me.

Love the Wild Swan

Do not attempt to place your hands on its innocent
neck (even the softest caress would seem to it
the brutal touch of the hangman).
Do not try to whisper your love or sorrow to it
(your voice would frighten it like a thunderbolt in the middle
of the night).
Do not stir the water in the lagoon, do not breathe.
To be yours it would have to die.

Accept its wild distance
and its alien beauty
(if it turns its head hide yourself in the grass).
Do not break the spell of this summer afternoon.
Swallow your impossible love.
Love it free.
Love so that it knows not that you exist.
Love the wild swan.

Translated by Wayne H. Finke

Julio Ortega (Lima, Peru, 1942) is a poet, critic, essayist and novelist. He currently teaches at the University of Texas at Austin and is the author of *Rituals (Rituales)*.

Syllables and Lines

*

Phosphorous and doors
that breathe

    furiously

against the night my body
burns solitude

    furiously

these footsteps
and one street are enough
place of the sea

    a crowd awaits

and I descend to drink
after the anger
beside the river
which blazes

    burning the city

debris of the sun

    lament of the wind

the names of this solar matter
are enough for me

    beloved field of voices

we belong there

*

Another day is lost
and I write the name of water
time enters
the palaces of water

*

like incomplete time
this street coincides
with me and with hunger

Someone stands up
in my nameless body

*

My eyes bring news
of this street without memory
in its abyss

things light up
at doors,
their names were burning
without doubting me,
I bring
that longing

because the day finds me
in an interrupted dream, time
judges my body

discovering all the reality
I possess, I bring
that brief joy

in the errors of memory
this sudden street
returning to oblivion

*

This world tells lies
living in its wounded
law.

The water that recovers
its own ardour
is more real.

Greater passion in the thirsty
struggle.

Of a river without measure—

a syllable

*

Other men already established
the name of the night
pleasure in disaster

My naked hand repeats
the occupied misfortune

A word that at the end
adds its own scream
which another man obeys.

A hand in the night
names the tempest.

A brief line explains
the brilliance of another day
the form that gains
a sure light—
        and kindles
the joy of memory
and oblivion.
        The diaphanous
evening and your hard light
return to time—
in its life
you are another of its names.
        Time itself
nameless.

Translated by Amelia Simpson

JOSÉ EMILIO PACHECO (Mexico, 1939) is a well-known poet, novelist and short story writer. He published the novels *The Elements of the Night (Los elementos de la noche)* and *You Will Die Far Away (Morirás lejos)*.

First Degree Equation with One Variable

In the city's last river, by mistake
or phantasmagoric incongruence, I suddenly
saw a fish that was almost dead. It gasped
poisoned by the dirty water, lethal
as our air. What a furor
    its round lips
    its mouth's zero in motion.
    Perhaps nothingness
    or the unspeakable word,
    the last voice
    of nature in the valley.
The only salvation for him
was to choose between two forms of asphixiation.
The double death throes haunt me.
The torture of the water and its inhabitant.
    His pained glance at me,
    his wish to be heard,
    his irrevocable sentence.
I will never know what he tried to tell me,
this voiceless fish that only spoke
the omnipotent language of our mother,
death.

The "&"

In the chapel's ruined walls
moss thrives, but not as much
as inscriptions: jungle
of razor-carved initials in the stone
that devours and confuses them
as time goes by.

Blurred letters, sloppy, crooked.
Sometimes confessions and insults.
But invariably
mysterious initials

joined by ampersand:
hands that approach,
legs that entwine, the copulative
conjunction, perhaps a vestige
of couplings that happned, or didn't.

Because the "&" of the meeting also symbolizes
roads that split: E. G.
met F. D. And they loved each other.
Did they live "happily ever after"?
Of course not. That's not very important.

I repeat: they loved each other
for a week, a year, or half a century,
and finally
life or death separated them
(one or the other; no choice).
Whether it lasts one night or seven lustrums, we know
no love ends happily.
But even separation will not prevail
compared to what they shared:

Although M. A.'s lost T. H.
and P.'s no longer with N.,
love existed and burned for an instant and left
its humble mark here on the moss
in this book of stone.

In Defense of Anonymity

(a refusal to grant George B. Moore an interview)

I don't know why we're writing, dear George.
And at times I wonder why we later publish
    what we've written.
I mean, we throw
    a bottle into the sea filled
with garbage and bottles with messages.
    We'll never know
to whom the seas will deliver it, nor where.
    What's most likely
is that it will succumb in the storm and abyss,
    in the sand below that is death.
    and yet
this grimace of a man adrift isn't so useless.
    Because one Sunday

you phone me from Estes Park, Colorado.
      You say you've read everything in the bottle
(across the seas: our two languages)
      and want to interview me.
How can I explain that I've never given
      an interview,
that my wish is to be read and not "famous,"
      that what's important is the text and not its author,
that I don't believe in the literary circus?

      Then I receive a long telegram
(how much must have been spent to send it).
      I can't answer and can't not answer.
And these lines come to me. It's not a poem.
      It doesn't aspire to the privilege of poetry
(it's involuntary).
      And I'm going to use the verse, as the ancients did,
as an instrument for all that
      (anecdote, letter, drama, story, agricultural manual)
we say in prose today.

      To begin *not* to answer you I will say:
I have nothing to add to what is in my
      poems,
      I'm not interested in discussing them, my
"place in history" (if I have one) doesn't concern me
      (sooner or later disaster awaits us all).
I write and that's it. I write. I give half of the
      poem.
      Poetry isn't black signs on a white page.
I call poetry that piece of the meeting
      with another's experience. the reader
will or will not make the poem I've only sketched.

      We don't read others: *we read ourselves* in them.
It seems a miracle to me
      that someone I don't know can see himself in my
      mirror.
"If there is merit in this," Pessoa* said,
      "it corresponds to the lines and not to their author."
If by chance he's a great poet
      he will leave four or five worthwhile poems
surrounded by failures and drafts.
      His personal opinions
are really of very little interest.

---

*Fernando Pessoa (1888–1935) was one of the most important poets of Portugal in the first half
of this century.

Strange, this world of ours: each day
it's interested more in poets
        and less in poetry.
The poet has ceased to be the voice of his tribe,
        he who speaks for the speechless.
He's become one more entertainer.
        His drunken bouts, fornications, his medical history,
his alliances or fights with the other clowns in the circus,
        or with the trapeze artist or elephant tamer,
have guaranteed him numerous fans
        who no longer need to read poems.

I keep thinking
that poetry is something else:
        a form of love that only exists in silence,
in a secret pact between two people,
        almost always between two strangers.
Perhaps you've read that Juan Ramón Jiménez*
        planned to put out a magazine fifty years ago.
It was going to be called *Anonimato.*
        He would publish texts, not *signatures,*
and it would be made with poems, not *poets.*
        Like the Spanish master, I want
poetry to be anonymous since it's collective
        (that's how my verses and versions are).
Possibly you'll say I'm right.
        You who've read me and don't know me.
We'll never see each other but we're friends.
        If you liked my poems
        what's the difference if they're mine/another's/no one's.
        In reality the poems you've read are yours:
You, their author, who invent them as you read them.

Translated by Linda Scheer

---

*Juan Ramón Jiménez (1881–1958), Nobel Prize winner, was one of Spain's leading poets of the
first half of the twentieth century.

JUANA ROSA PITA (Havana, Cuba, 1939) is the author of *Sun Bread (Pan de sol)* and *Sea Between the Bars (Mar entre rejas)*. Her poetry has been translated into English and German, and she is the editor of *Solar*, published in Miami.

Stroke the Back

Stroke the back of the least
beloved moment

sing each drizzle of your blood
toward the sea

let the sun shoot
all your anguish

and in round numbers
you'll find out what life is all about.

The Height Of Letters

Poetry is written by hope
and desire subscribes it between the lines:
the letter that results
              from the irrational rite
of filling inkwells with blood
and opening experience by its whitest face
setting it on the table
under the moistened fire

Poetry is the unreasonable letter
openly registered and addressed to everybody
with nobody's address:
              intended for tomorrow
the only letter that we consider lost
if it just reaches somebody

Poetry is the height of letter:
              inside are the powers
destined by love
for endless communion.

Walls Like Tears

I've tumbled down the walls of my house
and now it has transparent curtains,
accomplices of the night
and the winds.

You came to visit me
(everyone must know it by now),
exchanging your imprisonment for transparencies.

For I know you only through your writings,
of all my friends you are
the least unknown:
I beg you to stay forever
kindling dream.

Translated by Donald Walsh

ALBERTO LUIS PONZO (Buenos Aires, Argentina, 1916) belongs to the 1960 generation of Argentine writers. He is the author of *Occupations and Limits (Ocupaciones y límites),* as well as two collections of chapbooks titled *Encounter (Encuentro)* and *Labor (Mano de obra).*

History

In what place of one's face are memories lost?
In what parcel of centuries is birth forgotten?
The fantasy of the world burns beneath a secret wood.

Powers

Splendor of metals and kindled stones
face of spoons lights of wood
remains of blossomed tongues
moist tools of paradise
world borne on shoulders through eternity
filling each mouth with customs and
                              different loves.

Languages

Wings speak and the rings of the snake
speak and landscape moves without wasting a leaf

The world spells death after giving life
in its quick beating under the firm skies of blood.

Inscriptions

Cities fell under stains of earth
traces of absence on forgotten walls and ceilings
when night hangs from its infinite wire

Stories of wizards
dross that in shadow is transformed into dream.

Tutmosis

In the Cairo Museum
he was waiting to die
fooling eternity.
And he dreamt his mouth
was the delight of the centuries.

According to a Native American

I don't know what to do or to live
The human race has forgotten me
and I am under the heavens
naked to thunder
                    to blind dawn

I don't know what to do or to live
My head deserted
my weeping fallen in the light
a dead smell in the kitchen

I don't know what to do or to live

With the door torn
from my gums
pains and arranged pertinencies
in my eyes of fire
I don't know what to do or to live

And I forget nothing.

Eleven O'Clock

What is born as the clock strikes eleven
under the eleventh hour on this date?

I, in the shadow of the room made of myself,
grown from my dream of the void
of thinking and desiring,
only from the offspring of the dead,
one part of being and another not being
alive.

What is born as it strikes eleven in memory
to follow second by second

through my childhood in silent circle?

What is born:
                    the seed, impatience,
terror, sweetness, ignorance,
misfortune, the end
of eleven o'clock in another hour
that remains encased below
naturally certain?

Translated by Wayne H. Finke

Ulises Prieto (Havana, Cuba) is a short story writer and poet who has lived in exile since 1960. His verse has appeared in the *Diario Las Américas,* and a collection of his poetry, *The Olive Masks (Los mascarones de oliva),* was published in 1978.

I Come Painting Dreams

I come painting dreams
along the paths of the dawn,
and the wind practices leaps
over the sugar cane fields.

The green palms stand high
kissing the white clouds.
A peasant walks along singing
a joyful, sweet air.

The far-off countryside
is a watercolor of a thousand lights.
The sun gilds the green valleys
and the blue hue of the mountains.

II

I come painting dreams
between paths and ditches
and hazy lines arise
that turn into phantoms.

The stars are on vacation.
It is a very sad, bitter night,
and from the arm of a cloud
the moon silences its complaints.

From afar the echo of cheerful
bells reaches us.
As the masks descend from the sky
the bells sound in alarm.

With its red and black rags
this sad party begins.
Their hoarse olive-colored cries
are the trumpets of the farce.

257

Gusts and whirlwinds
shook the morning,
and a crazed, damned fire
punished us with its flames.

The olive masks
that pinned on medals,
and were painted green
to sell out our Homeland on us.

Red and Black

Somber winged birds
with rosaries and medals
and sad olive plumage
came down from the mountains.

Peace on the wide roads,
freedom with white crumbs,
naive faith of a noble people
who did not dream of the farce.

And the daydream broke
very early in the morning.
Farewell to peace, crumbs and roads:
long night overtook us!

The jails became filled,
and voracious animals
wrapped in fire and smoke
shot the dawn.

A flag foreign to my land
with your colors of a muddy pool.
In carnivals of mourning
you were the mask's clothing.

Flag of dark insignia,
you paid in bad money,
red, the people's blood,
black, the Homeland clothed in sorrow.

I'm on the Road to Varadero*

I left heat, fatigue behind,
I'm on the road to Varadero.
The afternoon is fused in gold
in the azure jewel of the sky.

My heart is filled,
I carry illusion in my breast,
I already feel the white foam
caressing my body.
I swim on beaches of my Homeland
and the sun burning me is our own!
But the blue afternoons
turned to gray,
and shadows of long night
painted them black on me.

I departed from your shore,
you will continue in time.
A shadow travels with me,
I want to dispatch it, but I am unable.

Miami

Walking sadly
under an endless sorrow,
we roll along, land-less
on the paths of the world.

With our bile as baggage,
our heart turned to ashes,
thousands of pilgrims
have reached many ports.

And Miami was the lighthouse,
bay and refuge of white sails.

A piece of Florida
with its channels and sands,
and a bitter dream of Ponce
that buried his reveries here.

And thinking of Ponce—at times—
I implore God to provide

---

*Varadero: the renowned beach of Havana

a sip for my dry mouth
from his miraculous fount.

Under your bewitched sky,
your palms also sing.
I don't know what daydream lulling
our palm trees have.

You were like a godmother
when the good mother was lacking.
With the magic of your spell
you changed salt to cinnamon.

With your blue sea and sky
your image is already ours,
and we have buried loved ones
left on your sands.

We will return without barriers
to the land of our birth,
and your beautiful image
will travel fastened on our breasts.

Your beaches were whiter
and your sun was a watercolor,
where your warm mouth
planted a kiss on our sorrow.

Before the Coastline

The waves form foam
on the Florida coast,
and its sea, covered in mists,
bathes my distant homeland.

From my watchtower corner
my tired eyes, gazing,
contemplate the beach
but remain glued to the South.

I should like to see it calmly,
sorrow breaking my tears,
and to the lee of the breeze
a song of my homeland arrives.

My mother, good mother,
never will I be able to kiss you;

I will return plunged in sorrow
to cover you with flowers.

The horizon becomes lost
between the pearly clouds,
and remembering naught
my stare has clouded over.

A cross, like a sign,
do I pursue in vague chimera;
Ay! From the South a breeze arrives
blowing cruelly upon my wound.

Translated by Wayne H. Finke and Bary J. Luby

LILLIANA RAMOS (Puerto Rico, 1954) is a young poet and translator whose verse has been published in *Avance, Sin Nombre* and *El Mundo*. She has prepared a Spanish translation of Charles Baudelaire's *Fleurs du mal*.

The Island's Economy

We flee from things
here is when artifacts arise
taking on macabre forms
this is the infinite market where we sell
the bones and warmth we had left
and everything departs

a people with cards on their sleeves
here time has been hanged forever
and we stand before
its blue tongue
haggling over its revolving shoes
here we are once more
and its budded eyes scratch
the walls

This is the place of the sale
the slight cut and the auction
of man and his back that bends
gathering the world
in tatters
the handled world
licking its coins

this is how you contend with anger in Río Piedras:
you look at it
you dance in rhythm with it
perplexed everyone takes its measurements
counting its hair
you cut it short
men gather its features
and from its lips the terror
of seeing it alive hangs them
en masse
they wander
they place it in bottles
shouting

changing its name
hammering it

for this is the island
where one comes to die
mouth agape
swept up by the broom
one comes to die
seated in La Torre*
pushed and shoved
with one's tongue riddled by coffee
one's head striking against evil
touching it repeatedly

here is how men fall like flies
deceived
their wrath plucked bare
their warmth lost
corpses lining up
the government asks the bigwig not to leave the Island:

who doesn't enjoy the leisurely grace of the stars here?
we legalize a parcel of heaven
license to
kill

we turn the crank of the Island
by its head
and we know
full well
where to carry out
the act of justice
yes
by obligation
when friends are alone and dream crouched
we stab them with justice in silence
ah
in the back
in cold blood we carve up truth
with a clean blow
we bear truth to the most hidden places
and everyone walks
erect
who says that
there's hunger here?
ah

---

*La Torre: the belltower of the University of Puerto Rico, in Río Piedras

they lie
and all liars will spread out
to go unheard

we set our rumps on death
are we not perhaps
extraordinary?

The Golden Age

Here
the golden age is awaited
like a memory
one waits and assembles it
piece by piece
but no one knows the master plan
morning and night is it sought
in trunks
in the cavitied soul of the corpse
in the cold dawn
in newspapers
but no one locates its form
no one perceives its smell
no one has seen it

different epochs are probed
yet there is no one who hits on the golden nail of its name
they raffle it in tickets
they think of it effortlessly
they prick up their ears make calculations and cry
because another has it had it or will have it
and it is
the repeated plaint
of all the Island's men

what map of the planet contains its route
which its countersign
people whisper and wonder
on the way to the post office
on buses
of the provisioned city

what world was that which was not
world
what place was that where there were men
at what time did death never occur there

children in school
learn to lose
patiently to remain defeated
they learn to live with their eyes blank
like us
more wise than statues
less nervous than sleep
we remain watching the tiny heads
fall hard against the wall
each day
meticulously attentive
and the boat slips away from the Island
leaving behind those late comers
and the passengers in port do not view the path
that brought them
and the path in its lassitude will never again touch
the house where they were born

how far

there is the flag of that phantom ship that
dies at full sail
how remote too are house plates and daily bread

there
quiet on a dock covered with sea waste
the planks and the thoughts of a thousand men
betrayed
there
stands waiting like
one singing
like one not wanting the object
the initial lapsus
the
sentence of clinking
gold

Translated by Wayne H. Finke

Julio Ramón Ribeyro (Lima, Peru, 1929) is a distinguished author who emigrated to France, where he first worked for the France Presse news agency and then for UNESCO. He has published *Chronicle of Saint Gabriel (Crónica de San Gabriel)* and *Change of Guard (Cambio de guardia)*.

The Double

At that time I lived in a small hotel near Charing Cross, and I spent the days painting and reading books about the occult. As a matter of fact, I have always been a devotee of the science of the occult, perhaps because my father lived many years in India, and in addition to a terrible malaria, he brought from the shores of the Ganges a complete collection of tracts on the esoteric. Once I read a sentence in one of these books that awoke my curiosity. I don't know if it was a proverb or an aphorism, but in any case it was a secret revelation that I have not been able to forget: "Each of us has a double who lives at the Antipodes. But finding him is difficult because doubles always tend to move in completely opposite directions."

If the sentence interested me it was because I had always been tormented by the idea of a double. On that matter I had had only one experience, and that was when getting onto a bus one day, I had the misfortune of sitting across from a person extremely similar to myself. After a short time, we became hypnotized, looking at each other with curiosity, until, finally, I felt uncomfortable and had to get off several stops before my destination. Although this kind of encounter did not repeat itself, it struck a mysterious chord within my spirit, and the subject of a double became one of my favorite speculations.

I thought, in fact, that in view of the millions of human beings who populate the globe, it would not be rare that by a simple calculation of probabilities several features would have to repeat themselves. After all, with a nose, a mouth, a pair of eyes and a few other complementary details, it is not possible to make an infinite number of combinations. The business of look-alikes existed as a particular example to corroborate my theory. It was the fashion at that time for state officials or film artists to hire persons similar to themselves in appearance, to have them run the risks of celebrity. This, however, didn't leave me entirely satisfied. The idea that I had of a double was more ambitious; I thought that the identity of features should correspond with the identity of temperament and—why not?—identity of destiny. The few look-alikes that I had the opportunity to see were related by a vague physical similarity—made complete with the help of make-up—with an absolute absence of spiritual congruence. It appeared to be a general rule, for example, that the look-alikes of the celebrated financiers were humble men who had always failed mathematics. But a double constituted a phenomenon decidedly more complete and more exciting for me. The reading of the text I have been referring to contributed not only to confirming my idea but also to enriching my conjectures. At times I thought that in another country, on another continent, at the Antipodes in short, there was another human being exactly like me, who acted as I did, who had my defects, my passions, my dreams, my manias, and this idea entertained me as well as annoyed me.

In time, the idea of a double came to obsess me. For many weeks I was not able to work and I did nothing other than repeat this secret revelation, hoping perhaps, that by some magical charm, my double would emerge from the earth's bosom. Soon I realized that I was tormenting myself unnecessarily, that although those lines from the arcane text posed an enigma, they also proposed the solution: to travel to the Antipodes.

At first I rejected the idea of a journey. At that time I had much work pending. I had just begun painting a madonna, and moreover, had received a commission to decorate a theater. However, passing by a shop in Soho one day, I saw a handsome globe exhibited in the window. I bought it on the spot, and that same night I studied it meticulously. To my great surprise, I discovered that at the Antipodes of London was the Australian city of Sidney. The fact that the city was a part of the Commonwealth seemed a marvelous omen to me. I remembered, likewise, that I had a distant aunt in Melbourne whom I would take the opportunity of visiting. Many other equally preposterous reasons were emerging—a crazy passion for Australian goats—but the outcome was that in three days, without saying anything to my hotel manager in order to avoid indiscreet questions, I took a plane with the destination of Sidney.

We had barely landed when I realized the absurdity of my decision. Reality had returned to me en route; I felt the embarrassment of my fantasies and was tempted to take the same plane back. To make matters worse, I found out that my aunt in Melbourne had died years before. After a long inner debate I decided that after such a tiring journey it was worth my while to stay a few days and rest up. In fact, I remained for seven weeks.

To begin with, I will say that the city was very big, much bigger than I had envisioned, so much so that I immediately gave up the idea of pursuing my supposed double. How would I find him? It was patently ridiculous to stop every passer-by on the street and ask if he knew a person like me. People would think I was crazy. In spite of this, I confess that each time I confronted a huge crowd, at the exit of a theater or a public park, I couldn't help feeling a certain anxiety, and against my own will I carefully examined the faces. On one occasion, seized with an intense anguish, I followed for a whole hour a person of my stature who walked like me. What drove me to distraction was his obstinate refusal to turn his face. Finally I couldn't stand it any longer and I spoke up. Turning around, he showed me a pale face, inoffensive and sprinkled with freckles, which—why not say it?—restored me to a tranquil state of mind. If I remained in Sidney the extravagant time of seven weeks, it was certainly not to carry on my search, but for reasons of another kind: it was because I fell in love. This was a strange thing for a man who was more than thirty, above all for an Englishman who dedicates himself to the occult.

My infatuation was tremendous. The girl was named Winnie and she worked in a restaurant. Without a doubt, it was my most interesting experience in Sidney. She also seemed to feel an almost instantaneous attraction for me, a fact which I found strange, since I had always had little luck with women. From the beginning she accepted my attentions, and for a few days we strolled through the city together. It is of no purpose to describe Winnie; I will only say that her personality was a bit eccentric. Sometimes she treated me with great intimacy; at others she became disconcerted with my words or gestures, a reaction which, far from making me angry, charmed me. Deciding to cultivate the relationship to the best of my ability, I resolved to leave the hotel, and telephone an agency. I obtained a little furnished house outside the city. I cannot help but feel the powerful surge of romanticism which this little villa evokes in my memory. The tranquility, the taste with which it was decorated, captivated me from the first moment. I felt as if it were my own home. The walls were decorated with yellow butterflies, figures to which I took an instant liking. I spent the days thinking about Winnie and chasing the most beautiful butterflies through the garden. The moment came when I decided to settle more permanently, and was thinking about obtaining painting materials, when there occurred a singular incident, perhaps explicable, but to which I insisted upon giving exaggerated significance.

It was a Saturday in which Winnie, after tenacious resistance first, finally agreed to spend the weekend in my house. The afternoon passed in a lively manner, with her customary spells of tenderness. Towards nightfall, something in Winnie's behavior began to disquiet me. At first, I didn't know what it was and I studied her features, trying to detect some change that would explain my ill feeling. Soon, however, I realized that what made me uncomfortable was the familiarity with which Winnie moved around the house. Several times without wavering she had gone straight to the light switch. Could it be jealousy? At first it was a kind of gloomy anger. I felt a true affection for Winnie, and if I had never asked her about her past it was because I had formulated certain plans for her future. The possibility that she had been with another man did not distress me so much as that it had happened in my own house. Seized with anxiety, I decided to test out this suspicion. I remembered that snooping around the attic one day, I had discovered an old kerosene lamp. I promptly suggested a walk around the garden.

—But we don't have anything to light our way—I mumbled.

Winnie got up and hesitated a moment in the middle of the room. Then I saw her go towards the stairway and resolutely climb the stairs. Five minutes later she appeared with the lighted lamp.

The scene which followed was so violent, so painful, that I find it difficult to recall. One thing certain is that when my anger arose within me, I lost my composure and behaved in a brutal manner. With one blow I knocked the lamp from Winnie's hands, taking the risk of starting a fire, and seizing her roughly, I tried by sheer strength to extract an imaginary confession. Twisting her wrists, I asked her with whom and when she had been there before in that house. I can only remember her face, incredibly pale, her eyes popping out, looking at me as if I were crazy. Her confusion and agitation kept her from uttering a word, a silence which did nothing but double my fury. I finished by insulting her and ordering her to leave the place. Winnie grabbed her coat and ran out through the doorway.

During the entire night I did nothing else but reproach myself for my conduct. I had never believed that I could be so easily agitated, and I attributed my distress in part to my limited experience with women. In the light of reason, Winnie's behavior seemed completely normal to me. All those country houses resemble each other greatly, and it was most natural that in one of them there would be a lamp and that this lamp would be found in the attic. My explosion had been unfounded; worse than that, it had been in bad taste. To look for Winnie and to present my excuses to her seemed the only decent solution. It was useless; I was never able to meet with her again. She had left the restaurant, and when I went to look for her at her house, she refused to see me. One day, at my strong insistence, her mother came out and told me in no uncertain terms that Winnie wanted to have absolutely nothing to do with lunatics.

With lunatics? There is nothing that frightens an Englishman more than the label of "lunatic." I stayed for three days in the country house trying to get my feelings in order. After calmer reflection, I began to realize that all that happened was trivial, ridiculous, worthless. The original idea of my trip to Sidney was insane. A double? What folly? What was I doing there, lost, anguished, obsessed by an eccentric woman whom I perhaps didn't love, squandering my time away, collecting yellow butterflies? How could I have abandoned my paintbrushes, my tea, my pipe, my walks through Hyde Park, my beloved morning mist over the Thames? Sanity had returned to me; in the twinkling of an eye I packed my things, and on the following day I was flying back to London.

I arrived in the wee hours and from the airfield I went straight to my hotel. I was completely exhausted, and had a great urge to sleep and recover my energy for my unfinished work. What happiness I felt to be again in my own room! For a few minutes it seemed to me as if I had never left. For a long time I remained lolling in my armchair, savoring the pleasure of finding myself again among my things. My gaze fell upon each of my familiar objects and caressed them with gratitude. Leaving is a wondrous thing, I told myself, but most marvelous is returning.

What was it that suddenly attracted my attention? All was in order, everything was as I had left it. However, I began to feel great discomfort. In vain I tried to ascertain the cause. Getting up, I inspected the four corners of my room. There was nothing strange, but I felt, I sensed acutely a presence, a trace on the point of vanishing. . . .

A few knocks sounded on the door. Half opening it, the bellhop stuck his head inside.

—They called you from the Mandrake Club; yesterday you left your umbrella at the bar. Do you want them to send it or will you go by to pick it up?

—Have them send it—I answered mechanically.

Immediately I realized the absurdity of my response. The day before I was probably flying over Singapore. Glancing at my paintbrushes I felt a shiver go through me: they were damp with fresh paint. Rushing to the easel, I tore off the cover: the madonna which I had left as a mere sketch was completed with the dexterity of a master, and strange as it seemed— her face was Winnie's.

Overwhelmed, I fell into my armchair. Circling around the lamp was a yellow butterfly.

Vultures Without Feathers

At six in the morning the city rises on tiptoes and begins to take its first steps. A fine mist diffuses the profile of the city's objects and creates an atmosphere of enchantment. People who frequent the city at this hour seem to be made of another substance, as if they belonged to a realm of the spirits. Pious women crawl laboriously until they disappear into the porticos of the churches. Nightwalkers, wasted by the night, return to their houses, wrapped in their scarves and their melancholy. Garbagemen, armed with brooms and carts, begin their sinister passage on Pardo Avenue. At this hour one can see laborers walking toward the street car, policemen leaning against trees yawning, paperboys turning purple from the cold, and servants taking out containers of trash. Finally, at this hour, as if beckoned by a mysterious watchword, the vultures without feathers appear.

At this hour, the old man, don Santos, puts on his wooden leg, and sitting himself up on the mattress, begins to bellow:

—Time to get up! Efraín, Enrique! Get going!

The two boys run to the water ditch in the vacant lot, rubbing their gummy eyes. Undisturbed in the stillness of the night, the water has become stagnant, and in its transparent bottom, weeds can be seen growing while quick-moving water insects slither around.

After rinsing his face, each boy takes his own can, and together they shoot out into the street. Meanwhile, don Santos approaches the pigsty, and with his long stick, strikes his pig which is wallowing in the waste.

—You still need fattening up, swine! But just wait; soon it'll be your turn.

Efraín and Enrique delay along their route, scaling trees in order to snatch blackberries, or picking up stones, the sharp ones that whiz through the air and hurt you in the back. Even though it is still dawn, they arrive at their post, a long street adorned with elegant houses which look out onto the sea road.

They are not the only ones. In other vacant lots, in other slums, someone has sounded the alarm and many have arisen. Some carry cans, others cardboard boxes, some only an old newspaper. Without knowing one another, they form a kind of clandestine organization which spreads out all over the city. There are those who prowl about the public buildings; others have chosen the parks or the garbage dumps. Even the dogs, expertly taught by poverty, have acquired their habits and their routes.

After a brief rest, Efraín and Enrique begin their work. Each one chooses a sidewalk. The garbage cans are lined up in front of the doors. They have to dump the garbage out and then begin picking through it. A garbage can is always a treasure chest of surprises: sardine cans, old shoes, pieces of bread, dead mice, filthy cotton balls. The only thing which interests the boys is leftover food. At the back of the pigpen, Pascual eats anything, but he prefers slightly decomposed vegetables. Each little can filled up with rotten tomatoes, pieces of fat, and strange sauces that do not appear in any cookbook. It is not unusual, however, to make a valuable find. One day Efraín found some suspenders with which he made a slingshot. Another time he found an almost perfectly good pear that he devoured in a second. Enrique, on the other hand, has luck in finding boxes of medicines, shiny bottles, used toothbrushes and similar things that he collects greedily.

After a rigorous selection, they dump the trash back into the can, and dash on to the next one. It isn't good to delay too much because the enemy is always on the watch. Sometimes they are surprised by servants and have to flee, leaving their booty scattered. But more often, it is the municipal garbage truck which appears, and then the work day is lost.

When the sun begins to show over the hills, dawn comes to its close. The mist has burned off, the pious women are submerged in their ecstasies, the nightwalkers sleep, the paperboys have delivered the newspapers, the laborers climb the scaffolding. The light banishes the magic world of dawn. The vultures without feathers have returned to their nest.

Don Santos would await them with the coffee ready.

—Let's see; what've you brought me?

He would sniff around inside the cans, and if the find was good, he would always make the same comment:

—Pascual will have a banquet today.

But most of the time he exploded:

—Idiots! What have you been doing today? I'll bet you've been playing! Pascual will die of hunger.

They would flee towards the tangle of vines with their ears burning from the blows, while the old man would hobble towards the pigpen. From the back of his hideaway the pig would begin to grunt. Don Santos would hurl food at him.

—My poor Pascual. Today you'll stay hungry because of these dumbbells. They don't spoil you like I do. They'll learn after I beat them hard enough!

When winter began, the pig changed into a kind of insatiable monster. Nothing seemed to please him, and don Santos avenged the hunger of the animal on his grandsons. He would make them wake up earlier in order to invade the nearby territory to scavenge for more garbage. At last he forced them to go as far as the garbage dump which was by the seashore.

—There you'll find more things. And since everything's together, it'll be easier.

One Sunday, Efraín and Enrique arrived at Barranco, an area where the cliffs overlook the ocean. The municipal garbage trucks, following the makeshift dirt road, dumped the garbage onto a hill of stones. Visible from the sea road, the garbage dump formed a kind of dark and smouldering cliff, where the vultures and dogs scurried around like ants. At a distance the boys hurled stones in order to frighten their enemies. One dog retreated howling. When they came close, they smelled a nauseating odor which penetrated the lungs. Their feet sank down into a heap of feathers, excrement, decomposed or burnt matter. Burying their hands, they began the exploration. Sometimes, beneath a yellowed newspaper, they discovered a half-devoured carrion bird. On the nearby cliffs the vultures spied, impatient, and some came closer, hopping from stone to stone, as if to corner them. Efraín screamed to intimidate them, and his screams resounded in the gorge, causing the surrounding pebbles to fly loose and tumble down into the sea. After an hour they returned to the vacant lot with their bucket full.

—Great!—exclaimed don Santos—you'll have to go there two or three times a week.

After that, on Wednesdays and Sundays, Efraín and Enrique made the trek to the garbage dump. They soon became a familiar part of the strange fauna of that place; the vultures, now used to their presence, worked at their side, squawking, fluttering, scratching with their yellow beaks, as if they were helping them discover the clue to the precious filth.

It was on the return from one of these excursions that Efraín felt a pain in the sole of his foot. He had cut his foot on a piece of glass. The following day his foot became infected; nevertheless, he carried on with his work. When he returned, he was hardly able to walk, but don Santos did not notice because he had a visitor. Accompanied by a fat man whose hands were stained with blood, he looked in the pigpen.

—I'll come back here in a few weeks—said the man.—I think he should be ready then.

When he left, don Santos' eyes flashed with fire.—To work! Get to work! From now on we'll have to increase Pascual's rations! Now this business is on the right track.

When don Santos woke his grandsons on the following morning, however, Efraín was not able to get up.

—He has a cut on his foot—explained Enrique.—Yesterday he stepped on some broken glass.

Don Santos examined his grandson's foot. The infection had set in.

—This is nothing! Go wash his foot in the ditch and wrap it up in a rag.

—But it hurts him!—intervened Enrique—he's not able to walk very well.

Don Santos thought for a moment. Pascual's grunts could be heard from the pigpen.

—And me?—he asked, whacking his wooden leg—don't you think my leg hurts me? I'm seventy years old and I work . . .! No more excuses!

Efraín went out into the street with his can, leaning on his brother's shoulder. A half hour later they returned empty-handed.

—He couldn't go on!—said Efraín to his grandfather.—Efraín is half-lame.

Don Santos looked at his grandsons as if he were contemplating a sentence.

—All right, all right—he said, scratching his straggly beard. And grabbing Efraín by the scruff of the neck, he shoved him into his room.—Off to bed! Go rot on the mattress! And you'll do your brother's work too. Get to the the garbage dump—now!

About noon, Enrique returned with the containers full. A strange visitor, an emaciated and mangy dog, had followed him home.

—I found him at the garbage dump—explained Enrique—and he followed me.

Don Santos grabbed his stick.

—One more mouth to feed!

Enrique clutched the dog to his chest and fled towards the door.

—Don't hurt him, Granddaddy! I'll give him part of my food.

Don Santos approached, his wooden leg sinking in the mud.

—No dogs here! I've got enough with you boys!

Enrique opened the door.

—If he goes, I go too.

His grandfather paused. Enrique insisted:

—He eats hardly anything . . . look how skinny he is. What's more, since Efraín is sick, he'll help me. He knows the garbage dump well and has a keen nose for trash.

Don Santos reflected, looking up at the sky where the mist condensed into a light drizzle. Without saying anything, he let go of the stick, picked up the containers, and went hobbling towards the pigpen.

Enrique smiled with gladness, and hugging his friend to his heart, ran to his brother.

—Pascual, Pascual . . . Pascualito!—sang the grandfather.

—I'm going to call you Pedro—said Enrique; he petted the dog's head, and then entered the room where Efraín was.

His happiness vanished: Efraín, bathed in sweat, twisted and turned with pain on the mattress. His swollen foot looked like rubber, bloated full of air. His toes had almost lost their shape.

—I've brought you a present, look—he said, showing him the dog.—His name is Pedro; it's for you, to keep you company . . . When I have to go to the garbage dump, I'll leave him with you and you can play together all day long. You can teach him to bring you stones in his mouth.

—And what about Grandfather?—sighed Efraín, reaching out to the animal.

—He doesn't say anything—sighed Enrique.

Both of them looked toward the door: the mistlike drizzle had begun to fall. Their grandfather's voice reached them:

—Pascual, Pascual . . . Pascualito!

That night a full moon appeared. Both children were nervous, for during this period, their grandfather had become impossible. In the late afternoon they saw him pacing around the vacant lot, talking to himself, waving his stick against the vine. At times he would advance towards the room, throw a glance inside, and seeing his grandsons silent, would spit at them bitterly. Pedro was afraid, and each time he saw the old man, he crouched down and remained as immobile as a stone.

—Filth, nothing but filth!—the grandfather repeated all night, looking at the moon.

On the following morning Enrique woke up with a cold. The old man, who heard him sneezing at dawn, didn't say anything. Deep inside, however, he sensed a catastrophe. If Enrique became ill, who would provide for Pascual? The voraciousness of the pig grew with his girth. He began to grunt in the afternoons with his snout buried in the mud. The people who lived near the vacant lot a block away began to complain.

On the second day, the inevitable occurred: Enrique was not able to get up. He had coughed all night, and morning found him trembling and burning with fever.

—You too?—asked grandfather.

Enrique pointed to his chest, which rattled. Grandfather left the room furiously. Five minutes later he returned.

—It's very bad of you to trick me like this!—he grieved.—You both take advantage of me because I can't walk. You know that I'm old and lame. Otherwise I would send you both to the Devil and would take care of Pascual myself.

Efraín woke up in pain and Enrique began to cough.

—But it doesn't matter! I'll take charge of him. You're both trash, nothing more than trash. You're just poor vultures without feathers! You'll see how I'll come out ahead. Your grandfather is still strong. But I'll tell you, one thing is sure: there won't be any food for either of you today. No food until you can do your work.

From the doorway they saw him pick up the cans and stumble out into the street. A half hour later he returned, crushed. As he lacked the agility of his grandsons, the municipal garbage truck had won over him. The dogs, moreover, had tried to bite him.

—Worthless scum! Mark my words; you'll go without food as long as you don't work!

On the following day he tried to repeat the operation, but had to give up. His wooden leg had lost the ability to walk on the asphalt roads, on the hard pavements, and each step that he took was like a shot in the groin. On the dawn of the third day he remained collapsed on his mattress, without any spirit other than to insult.

—If he dies of hunger—he screamed—it will be your fault!

From then on, the days became agonizing and interminable. The three spent the day buried in the room, without talking, suffering a kind of inescapable seclusion. Efraín twisted and turned without respite, Enrique continued to cough, Pedro got up, and after taking a turn around the lot, returned with a stone in his mouth which he deposited in the hands of his masters. Don Santos, sitting up halfway on his mattress, played with his wooden leg and threw them ferocious glances. At noon he hobbled toward the garden patch in the corner of the lot and prepared a lunch which he devoured in secret. Sometimes he would throw a piece of lettuce or raw carrot to his grandsons with the idea of exciting their appetites, believing that this would make the punishment more devilish.

Efraín now had no strength even to complain. Only Enrique felt a strange fear growing in his heart, and looking into his grandfather's eyes, believed that he no longer knew them; it was as if they had lost their human expression. At night, when the moon was rising, he would take Pedro in his arms and hug him tenderly until the dog groaned. At that hour the pig would begin to grunt and the grandfather complained as if he were being hanged. Sometimes he put on his wooden leg and would go out to the vacant lot. By the light of the moon Enrique could see him go ten times from the pigsty to the vegetable garden, raising his fists, trampling whatever happened to be in his path. At last, he would return to the room and remain staring at them fixedly, as if he wanted to make them responsible for Pascual's hunger.

On the last night of the full moon no one could sleep. Pascual cried out with roars and bellows. Enrique had heard that when pigs were very hungry, they went crazy like men. The grandfather remained on watch, without once extinguishing the lantern. This time he did not leave the lot or curse between his teeth. Sunk down into his mattress, he stared fixedly at the door. He seemed to stir up an old anger inside of himself, to toy with it, and to make ready to let it fly forth. When daylight broke over the hills, he opened his mouth, and displaying its dark cavity, turned towards his grandsons and uttered a roar.

—Up, up up!—the blows began to rain—Get up you lazy good-for-nothings. How long are we going to stay here? It's all over! This is it! On your feet . . .!

Efraín began to cry. Enrique got up and flattened himself against the wall. His grandfather's eyes seemed to mesmerize him to the point that he became senseless from the blows. He could see the stick, as if it were made of cardboard, rise up and then fall on his head. Finally, he was able to react.

—Don't hit Efraín. It's not his fault! Let me go alone; I'll leave, I'll go to the garbage dump!

Gasping, grandfather controlled himself. He slowly recovered his breath.

—Right now . . . to the dump . . . take two cans, no four. . . .

Enrique moved aside, grabbed the cans and set off at a run. He was shaky from the fatigue of hunger and from sickness. When he started to leave the lot, Pedro tried to follow him.

—No. You can't come. Stay here and take care of Efraín. And he dashed out into the street, sucking the morning air fully into his lungs. On the road he ate herbs, and he was on the verge of eating the ground. He saw everything through a magic mist. His weaknesses had made him light, ethereal: he flew almost like a bird. In the garbage dump, he considered himself one more vulture among the others. When the buckets were overflowing, he began his return homeward. The pious women, the night-walkers, the barefooted paperboys, all the lowlife of dawn began to disperse itself throughout the city. Enrique, having returned to his world, walked happily among them in this world of dogs and spirits, touched by the dawning hour.

Upon entering the vacant lot, he felt an oppressive, resistent air which made him hold back. It was as if there, on the threshold, one world ended and another began, made of mud, of howling, of absurd penitence. Surprisingly, however, a calm reigned in the vacant lot this time, a calm charged with evil portents, as if all the violence remained in equilibrium, on the point of crashing down. Grandfather, standing on the edge of the pigsty, was looking towards the back. He looked like a tree growing out of his wooden leg. Enrique made a noise, but his grandfather did not move.

—Here are the cans!

Don Santos turned his back on him and remained motionless. Enrique let go of the cans and ran puzzled towards the room. Efraín scarcely saw him and began to groan:

—Pedro . . .Pedro . . .

—What's wrong?

—Pedro bit Grandfather . . .Grandfather took the stick . . .then I heard him howling.

Enrique left the room.

—Pedro, come here! Where are you, Pedro?

No one answered. With his eyes fixed on the wall, the grandfather continued immobile. Enrique had a bad premonition. In one leap he came close to the old man.

—Where is Pedro?

His gaze fell upon the pigpen; Pascual was devouring something in the middle of the mud. Only the legs and the tail of the dog remained.

—No!—screamed Enrique, covering up his eyes.—No! No!—and through the tears he searched his grandfather's eyes. His grandfather shrank from his questioning glance, swinging awkwardly around on his wooden leg. Enrique began to dance around, tugging at his grandfather's shirt, stamping his feet, trying to look into his eyes to find an answer.

—Why did you do this? Why?

The grandfather didn't answer. Finally, impatient, he slapped his grandson so hard that Enrique went tumbling to the ground. From there, Enrique looked up at the old man, who tall as a giant, stubbornly watched Pascual feast himself. Reaching out, Enrique took the bloodstained stick into his hand. With it he raised himself on tiptoes and moved close to the old man.

—Turn around—he screamed.—Turn around!

As Don Santos was turning around, he caught a glimpse of the stick swirling around just as it banged against his cheek.

—Here!—shrieked Enrique, and he raised his hand again. But suddenly he stopped, frightened by what he was doing; throwing the stick to the ground, he looked at the grandfather, almost repentent. The old man, holding his face, stepped backwards, his wooden leg touching the soggy ground. He slipped, gave a yell and fell into the pigpen on his back.

Enrique retreated a few steps. At first, he pricked up his ears but he didn't hear a sound. Little by little he crept closer. The grandfather, whose wooden leg was broken, lay flat on his back in the mud. His mouth was hanging open and his eyes were searching for Pascual; the pig, who having taken refuge in a corner, was sniffing suspiciously in the mud.

Enrique drew back, as stealthily as he had approached. Probably the grandfather had time to catch sight of him, because as he was running towards the room, it seemed to Enrique that the old man called him by name, with a tone of tenderness he had never heard.—Come here, Enrique, come to me! . . .

—Right away!—exclaimed Enrique, hurrying towards his brother.

—Hurry, Efraín! The old man has fallen in the pigsty! We have to get out of here!

—Where are we going?—asked Efraín.

—Anywhere, to the garbage dump, where we can eat something, where the vultures are!

—I can't stand up!

Enrique took his brother with both hands and clasped him to his chest. Embracing so tightly that they seemed to form one person, they crossed the vacant lot slowly. When they entered the street, they realized that dawn was over, and that the city, awake and alive, opened its giant jaw before them.

From the pigpen came the murmur of a battle.

Translated by Joan L. Smucker

GONZALO ROJAS (Chile, 1917) is a leading writer and diplomat who has traveled extensively and lived in Cuba and China. He is the author of *Against Death (Contra la muerte)* and *From the Lightning Bolt (Del relámpago)*.

Love Letter

I venerate you by typewriter without praise
beyond this shoddy
keyboard with its A to Z, I tell you how
I love you from heel
to hair, be that hair
where it may, at your zenith or
in the secret recess of your fragrance, I await you
waiting for you, standing here at
7 beneath the smoke
of the clock. And

something else: take note of the clouds
but without crying whereon is written
almost everything
the white and fleeting nature of this
page in verse, call me
on the telephone at
000–0000

Translated by Robert Lima

Lost Port

All is narrow and deep
in this weightless earth, flowers
grow on knives, face down on the sand
one can hear a volcano; when the rain
moistens it, the mystery
clears up, a fantastic
chair appears in the heavens,
and seated there the God of lightning
like an aged mount of snow.

All is narrow and deep, persons
leave no trace, for the wind
casts them to their north and nothingness,
so that
suddenly
I go out on my balcony and no longer see anyone,
I see neither house nor blond women,
the parks have disappeared,
everything is invulnerable sand, all
was illusion, there was
no one on this bank of the planet
before the wind.

Then I run towards the sea, I sink
in its kiss, birds
form a sun on my forehead,
then I take possession of the air and the momentary rocks
in name of the wind, the blue stars,
Valparaíso, the wind.

The Farce

Death amuses me when it passes
in its splendid carriage, followed
by sadness in luxury cars:
one speaks about the weather, the deceased
                    is dispatched with roses.
                              Each bereaved relative
finds his wine better during lunch.

Sunday Daimon

Between the Jerusalem Bible and these flies flying around there, I prefer
    these flies. I prefer them for three reasons:
1) because they are putrid and white with blue eyes and they procreate
    everything in the air as though laughing,
2) therefore extremely rapid from their circumstance which already
    knows everything since long before Genesis,
3) for reading (besides) the World as one must read it: from putrefaction
    to illusion.

Visiting Professor

Doves vs. decrepitude, bloody
artifice, old semestral

artifice in which he who loses
blood is one and not
these airy six foot female beauties
of white hide whom I teach here in
the Angloworld for good pay with the pardon
of Socrates, who not for a moment
looked askance at these hips: tobacco
and armpit, sparks
of hemlock and whisky:
                                        the party
begins when you arrive businessman
of being all Apollonian frenzy
to the aeronautical Areopagus
but, by Jupiter, listen carefully, the
forger is not this movie mask of
Rome of
questionable light but yourself: the Phoenician
who for three drachmas
signed such a hasty contract.
                        Golden damsels,
barefoot.

October 2, 1983

Translated by Wayne H. Finke

Juan Sánchez Peláez (Caracas, Venezuela, 1922) is a distinguished poet who has spent the past decade living in Paris and Madrid. His collections of verse include *Common Traits (Rasgos comunes)*, 1975, and *For What Cause or Nostalgia (Por cuál causa o nostalgia)* 1981.

To Humberto Díaz Casanueva

The Circle Opens

The circle opens, you see? Don't you hear as if a great gust in the trees, don't you listen to the senseless words of a mandolin? That our good fortune and the wide barren plain should return to us. At bottom, my memory, in order that you not lose in the final season even an atom in the count of the anguished crop. Don't go sniffing memories, the singing garden proceeded; do not abandon us, queen mother, our family of orphans murmured; give me a point of support or a precise arrow, continued the childhood while it ate some strawberries. Don't go away, arduous autumn, I now exclaim, leave me to seize you and dance upstairs, puppet of my heart who knows so well to waste the catmilk and pitcher of seeds, and who with the help of time rectifies me and rises with the sound of a ball in the rain.

Today

I'm going to arrange in single file a thousand spears against the asphalt of the sky. I'm coming to seal up engraved jugs; to stop myself in the marrow, in the skin, in the flower. At the depth of an underwater cave, I'll yank out a fish, every bit of it, with a shaft of stars. Today, the world finds itself within reach of my tranquil eyes, and I live in the reflection, in the straight line, its concentric clarity.

VI.

From my
house

to
a street of rails

from a street
of rails
to my old suburb

incandescent
I'm going to reveal myself
with magnificent gestures
before my elders

there's always
also some other
ritual buzzing in memory:

          I'm going to scorch myself in you, deep
                            fragrance.

VIII.

With
     painted flowers
on   our
     body

and
     the candle
in   each
     hand

all
     that passes
is silence

but
     memories
     are faithful
     and

next
     to
        us
        they murmur
on
     the mask
the skin

or the word enormous:
"Hear my love to you"
"Hear my scream
for you"

XIII.

Which brilliance or foliage
and on the fountain of the rumbling garden

I have died   and I live
at once alive and dead

With an almost absurd patience
I live

walled-in or hidden

free

dead.

Translated by Marc Nasdor

SEVERO SARDUY (Camagüey, Cuba, 1937) participated in the literary movement known as Ciclón in collaboration with José Lezama Lima. He has resided in Paris since the 1960s and is the author of a book of verse,*Daiquiri*, and the novels *Gestures (Gestos)* and *Where Are the Singers From? (De dónde son los cantantes)*.

[untitled]

Entering you, head with head,
hair against hair, mouth against mouth;
I breathe the air you breathe—firmness
of memory—and in the feeble

afternoon light—unceasing beam
between seared bones—it touches
the contours of your body: light grasping
form. Already its climax calls it to

another aperture where its whiteness
erases your figure, marks it with sand.
The day devoured by sounds

burns its thickness from time to time
and overturns its texture with ashes
in the voracious night of the senses.

[untitled]

The shiny greased piston
jubilantly assails the fissure
and spills its white brand
more searing the slower it is.

A fleeting disguised witness
salivates and scrutinizes the opening
that its volume dilates and its own lava
sutures. And in the ovaloid

tangential quicksilver on the carpet
(the tower, penetrating besmeared,
pouring forth its honey, exciting, entering)

deciphers the ideogram of shadow:
thought is illusion: that which is unnamed
comes slowly softening.

[untitled]

Neither voice preceded by echo,
nor the voracious reflection of naked
bodies in the quicksilver of the mute
windowpanes, only the disengaged, dry trace:

fruit on the table and the colonial
landscape. When the siesta hour
enveloped us in the density of its waves
or in the murmur of its hushed festivity,

when one's thirst was quenched
in the other, when the light reddened by the flamboyan
advanced over the orchard

We would then open the great door
to the island's noonday sounds
and ever punctual still life.

[untitled]

Though you oiled the threshold and put saliva,
it could not penetrate, licked yet soft,
or even plumb so vast a vessel
because of its volume or weight.

My caution deceived and in contrast
—linaments, modesty or care—
with small forgotten anals
you entered suddenly, without warning.

Never more tolerance or welcome
will find in my disguised inertness
that invites to antipodal pleasures

and is inverted in symmetrical rigors:
death forming part of life.
(Life forming part of death).

Translated by Wayne H. Finke

Javier Sologuren (Lima, Peru, 1922) is a foremost poet, translator and editor of *Cielo Abierto,* one of the leading literary magazines in Latin America. He has published numerous collections of verse, including *Determinants (Determinantes), Sojourns (Estancias)* and *Seeking the Dark Air (Buscando el aire oscuro).*

love and bodies

i approach
              the dark
abundance of the roses
              i feel
the slow space of your breast
caressed
by something which is not
only my hands
nor looking at you
neither enough

in the center
             of my body
                     the secret
of your reply
             stirs
transferring
             its breath to me
its young years
its unruly ripeness

then
     then
i stammer
saliva and tears
spill over me
silent shift

instant in which
i am
totally myself

in which
i am not
myself

but
the wrench and pulse
and you
the sweet
        accomplice

beaten
infinitely
beaten.

in you

the grass gave way softly
the sand molded to you

pure blind syllables
the canticle of the water

the water   irridescent mirror
a red
wine like love
transcended the morning

your soft belly was
a nest
a chrysanthemum
golden feathers

one thigh separated from
the other thigh
for me to sing
deeply

for me to enter
with the fire
of blood

more scorching
than the sun.

celebration

for Ilia

i ride in the far reaches
of the night   perhaps
to see you better

perhaps not to see you
my joy takes in
the frontiers
of your mind
like
the warm catch
between the teeth
or the first
blood
in the kingdom
of the birds

stones of black light
your eyes   your hair
and a secret fire
which
is not alien to me

over us
the fox tail
motionless
in the sand
and the dark sea
wafting
its fecund nausea.

better yet, dreamed

day nests among the dark green spears of foliage

i spy

the raging apparition
of the wayward beast's
silhouette
   the insect's violet rays
the honeycombs of time
the rough hooves in the dust

the old   the gray   the cunning
spider
sets the table
for
its imminent repast

drinks belch
in the wineskins
tribal voices interweave

memory takes on an amber color
the webs are singed imperceptibly

everything rots away to the beginning
the law emits an acrid nocturnal dew

the earth drinks in everything
like a newborn
it sanctions everything
like the old matriarch
shrouding
with her lean and withered buttocks

the endless cycles.

Translated by Diane J. Forbes

GUILLERMO SUCRE (Venezuela, 1933) is an eminent South American poet and critic; his publications of verse include *As Days Pass (Mientras suceden los días)* and *The Dwelling (La morada)*.

Whitebodied Lady

Whitebodied lady
                       when you emerge from the cascade of the
shower
naked (oh slim) I see you distilling
transparency
                       the halflight rises and blossoms in the freshness
of your legs
                     you dry them   you flex them
you hold them out
                     smooth stones in the stream of the Manacal
there I slide happiness washing over me
I do not want you to cover yourself
                       you laugh
with a sad glow in your eyes
                       you shake your hair
long and still soaking
                 midday ferns
drowsiness weighing
you kiss me   you know (you say)
                     that I am a beauty ("my beauty")
you embrace me (as your freshness brazes me) "you
a beauty"
     you take me in your arms
                     you dress me and we go
into the yard (once again) under the trellised vine
surrounded by the passion
of the heat.

Not Keeping Silent

Not keeping silent but making silence flow
is what makes us younger

neatness is not concentrated: it is cast

closer and closer, farther and farther, each time
more   each time less

in the snow-covered meadow, only a green circle under
the maple of tan, wrinkled leaves

birds of Morris Graves: resistance to inclemency:
zen birds

praise of life: reconciliation with death

Is it not shameful already to speak so much of life and death?
speak of something else: for example: of not having anything else

to speak about except life and death.

Atlantic April

this tacit body still without sound
dark
this inheritance of the salt now awakening
is the sea
                    preparing its claws   its new
war
its fight or reconciliation with the
                    elements.

Translated by Wayne H. Finke

DAVID UNGER (Guatemala) is a poet and translator whose works have appeared in the *Paris Review, Persea* and *Street Magazine.* He cotranslated the poems of Enrique Lihn for New Directions Press in 1978, and has supplied translations for this anthology.

The Limbo Bar

In the doorway, a skinny cat
swishes her tail
like a cow swatting imaginary flies.
A rooster cheeps, she flexes her limbs,
the baby that has kept the night up
sleeps again, it's morning, in a back room.

The whore on the balcony,
after so many washings of her crotch,
wipes it once more
and squeezes the cloth dry over the railing—
the cat below jolts, takes the drippings
for the first drops of rain
and scoots back inside.
And the whore draws the shutters.

How the morning hums.
Nothing, but nothing moves
till a grizzly old man in suspenders
sails out of the bar:
on his hands and knees, he sweeps
bottles and shucked rinds to the street.

At sundown, the scratchy music repeats.

Insomnia

Yes, I finally understand why
Mayan priests plucked out
still blossoming hearts:
"Now that I've known you
I can never live alone again."
A threat? Perhaps,
but more likely a confession
with thousands of aftershocks

that leave me jumpy,
a cut so deep
mere sleep becomes a chore.

I've given up
on permanence, rather believe
we'll pass the passing years
with slight betrayals
that, complemented by inflation,
leave holes in our pockets,
a residue of Kleenex and lint.
But we're past the penny-ante stage
and, despite doubts,
we've staked our hearts,
this spare change.

Hotel Canada

A stretched out night in the Hotel Canada,
bloated dreams of Indians and slings
discolored by walls
that seemed to emit tiny bedbugs.
Several times shuffling feet
came to the door, hesitated,
wouldn't knock and didn't move on.
Heavy breathing wet my face,
the alarm clock ticked 3:45 A.M.
as if it had no time to lose,
and the night oozed on
turning my bed into a cocoon:
I dropped into sleep.

Hotel Canada. Loose bricks in the shower,
blades rusting everywhere, trash
building an altarpiece around
a brick fireplace,
floors spotted with footsteps,
the memory—hidden in a lightbulb—
of being here years ago
inside the perfume of a lover
I wanted to meet, I wouldn't meet, I'd met.

Por favor respeten los otros huéspedes.
Yes, at two bucks a head
and free parking we could be quiet
but now at daybreak, the sign was gone,
a radio screeched, a noisy fog

embraced Quetzaltenango.
I watched you, still sleeping,
float like a bar of soap
towards the drain:
your awakening sent my nightmares reeling.

Translated by the author

ARMANDO F. VALLADARES (Cuba, 1937) is a celebrated Cuban poet who was imprisoned by the Castro régime in 1960, and only upon the intercession of leading writers and the personal intervention of French President Mitterand was released in 1983. His first book, *From My Wheel Chair (Desde mi silla de ruedas)*, achieved extraordinary success and was translated into French. His second collection, *The Heart I Live With (El corazón con que vivo)*, was smuggled out of prison and published in 1980.

Reality

Dedicated to Humberto Medrano, who
denounced this nightmare so many times
to the world.

A black, humid sun fell on those waiting for the bus. A car from the National Police moved slowly along the dirty, dusty road, leaving in its wake a terror which rose like some reddish mist. Everyone lowered their heads avoiding the looks of the patrol car's occupants, and hence did not see the cluster of eyes floating over the group as their phosphorescent pupils radiated a soft greenish light.

The man with the package had held his breath but did not make a single movement. The patrol car moved on, trying to avoid the potholes, and even the braced balconies of the buildings on the verge of collapse turned pale with fright.

"Stay in place, comrades," repeated mechanically a member of the Vigilance Committees whose task it was to keep order on line.

The last bus had passed by an hour and ten minutes before. The man with the package meditated: if he didn't catch the next one, he would have to go on foot. He was not carrying identification papers and that was an even greater risk because control searches were more frequent on the street than on buses.

Yes, it was risky, but his hours were running out on him. . . .

He had been walking for nine blocks. The narrow streets of old Havana were even more narrowed because of the accumulation of garbage and refuse spilling over from the sidewalks. In some spots, sewer drains formed dark fetid pools of water. This was the most run-down part of the city. Entire blocks stood leveled, and others, on the verge of collapsing, had been evacuated. Outbreaks of typhoid and other illnesses would start here and ravage the population on a large scale.

He was about to cross the intersection when he heard someone call him: he heard the bicycle stop beside him:

"Your papers, comrade."

The first thing he saw was the armband of the Vigilance Committee, and without hesitating a second he kicked the cyclist and ran away. From the ground the agent's whistle sounded shrilly.

With his package pressed firmly against his side, he hurriedly strode off, and this time he did not see the phosphorescent eyes blinking a few yards above his head.

Another whistle answered the first one, and another, and yet another: the hunt began. He realized that his possibilities of escaping were already remote now that the alarm had been sounded. Not a single door would open to offer him shelter even if the occupants had wanted to do so. They were closed by the insurmountable fear of the National Police and the terror of reprisals against their families.

The shrieks were joined by sirens, barks, shouts and howls, and a hate prickling and swift as an arrow.

Suddenly he came out upon a street that he had never seen before. It became lost on the horizon. Wide. Symmetrical, with buildings along both sides. All identical. Rectangular. Smooth. Gray. Windowless, doorless. They seemed like enormous concrete boxes. Sidewalks wide and clean, with some earth-filled receptacles where strange trees and extremely high palms grew. Others were empty.

His mind caught all this in a matter of seconds. The cries of his pursuers were approaching and he decided to get rid of the package quickly. He tore off the thick wrapping paper, and a beautiful gun appeared. Steel and wood. Holding it in his hands, he raced along the center of the empty street. A group was already in pursuit. They were drawing near, and he turned to face them. Those in front had empty eyes, and their skin—that of their faces was falling in flaps—. . . . They were forced, shoved to continue their hunt by others who held them by the neck on chain leashes and hide belts as though they were dogs.

He ran faster and faster. Trees fled in his path; he stopped, turned toward them, the gun aimed at their faces, and pressed the trigger tenderly, as a flash of flowers and brilliant butterflies shot through the clear blue air. He continued running down that long street, and palm trees sought to escape behind him.

He had been running for weeks, months, years. He felt crawling up his legs an atavistic, ancestral fatigue, that of a cornered animal, the shouts behind him, the street that suddenly ended in a granite wall; he drove his gun barrel into the earth of one of the receptacles, and his hands free he climbed the wall and could not see how, in contact with that earth, the grooving of the gun's soul came to life, became untwisted and took the form of roots and avidly plunged into the fertile soil, penetrating and drilling rocks and the strata of time, extending like a gigantic net; the wood handle awoke and palpitated, bulging, vibrated as though revitalized; shoots appeared, branches sprouted and grew toward the sky; leaves grew green filled with the juicy sap of life-eternity, and the tree became fronded in spite of the contradictions; on its top rested clouds and the unknown, as those branches extended miles and miles of yesterdays and tomorrows, and the tree resisted the wind's buffeting and the hurricanes of envy and the bitter saltpeter, flourishing in flashing galaxies; its ungraspable shining fruits ripened and fell to heaven, and he finally leaped to the other side of the granite wall, where he found himself before three vaulted galleries, causing him to hesitate. He again heard the shouts and saw the wall advancing towards him to crush him, and he leaped toward one of the doors, and the wall sealed it behind him flowing like gelatine, fusing with the door and then made them all disappear, erased, as it were, in the air.

He advanced, pressed against the wall of that vault, descended a staircase where a spark of yellowish light shone at the end of the passageway.

From outside there arose several voices that entered through an open window like a skylight, for the walls were six feet thick, and he had to squeeze himself into the opening of the window, and crawl on all fours to the grating.

Below, in the trenches, he heard orders and shouts and laughs, and saw tied to a post an enormous fish the height of a man, turning its head calmly, meekly toward both sides. Its whole presence exhaled an infinite sweetness. And like a monstrous thunderclap the order to "AIM" was given, and the speckled fan of men facing the post lifted their Soviet-made guns to their faces: "FIRE!" The discharge resounded and the echo leapt and ricocheted from tear to tear, from ant to ant, stone to stone, star to star, and for an instant the music of the spheres stopped.

The fish convulsed, and from its sweet, large, timid eyes sprouted trembling snow-white wings; they joined together in its mouth, and from there took flight in a dazzling white dove that fluttered above the spot and set off toward the infinite sky in a ray of love.

A group of respectable personalities of the Western world invited to the party applauded jubilantly. There were distinguished presidents and secretaries of international conglomerates and ambassadors and rulers.

And from the side of the slain fish sprung founts of blood and from those wounds were filled goblets as toasts were offered with the bubbling lymph.

An unfathomable sadness moved him. It was the sadness of all Humanity. He recognized that spectacle when all the roses were extinguished on the tip of a lance. And he continued along that gallery and he perceived an exit and passageways opening up left and right. He entered one that was lit, and with cells along the walls. In them one could see men and women shackled in irons. Orphans of the sun, they shone spectrally, as if the moon cast on them forever its pallid silence, as though there was no blood to be found in their flesh, or that they were filled with snow.

Their faces were pressed against the bars, and the flesh on their cheeks had leapt from their cheekbones. Like a climbing vine these faces rose up, grew, surrounded the bars, covering them with an unheard of grafting, already a doughlike substance, comprising faces and metal, the flesh of the iron, the dust of the years; lips cracked by the salt of all the sufferings, privations, lapses; the hoarse throats, lacking bread and articulated word; the eyes that had been devoured by saltpeter and gun powder, or gouged out by bayonets and the picks of the barbed wire fences; there only remained the dark, deep cavities of all the anguish that tortures, alienates and finally annihilates.

The hands that one day caressed roses and algae and an unperishing dream of liberty were now boney forms, covered by a yellowish flesh; and the iron bars glistened as though wanting to squeeze them with their coldness.

No one spoke. Words had remained in the past, and from there they leapt to the future. The present was merely silence.

And no stranger was perceived in that place. In his brain many doors opened, many dikes were lifted; he understood and remembered suddenly as though he were returning to a known place from generations past, as if an imperishable comprehension had continued to be transmuted within his spirit. And he felt a tremendous admiration toward those beings. . . .

He advanced, and at the end perceived an illuminated room, heard cries and drew near. A group of men armed with garrotes, bayonets and guns was beating, punching others who—defenseless—could not prevent it. Using gun butts they crushed skulls, faces, collarbones. Bayonets plunged into those skeletal, exhausted bodies, and everything was filled with a cry of blood.

One of those jailers turned around suddenly. Dressed in olive green like the others, from his chest hung a badge: a hammer and sickle, in gold, upon a background of blood.

He could not run. All the lead of the world was now contained in his feet, and anguish oppressed his chest. They leaped upon him rabidly, savagely, bayonets first. He felt the lethal coldness of steel. He fell on the floor, and it was then that he saw above his head those greenish phosphorescent pupils casting a soft glow; he no longer felt any fear.

10 July 1979

Translated by Wayne H. Finke

CARMEN VALLE (Puerto Rico, 1948) has collaborated in numerous magazines with her poems and short stories. She served as the coeditor of the Puerto Rican poetry journal *Ventana* and published *Stolen Diaries (Diarios robados)*, 1982, and *Glenn Miller and Several Lives After (Glenn Miller y varias vidas después)*, 1983.

With the Psychiatrist

Among other things—
    I drink to recall.
I ride on the emptiest
subway car.
I dance in the rain.
I'd take a lover
over having a husband.
I can listen to the same symphony
over and over
I am here
for being *persona non grata* and starting to believe
I should change
the story of my life.

Hide 'n' Seek

From my window,
the orange dress
was the stain
marking on the beach
the water's edge.
The wind
and rain photographed
her hips, as she kneeled
face to the sea.
Waves climbed her thighs
as she stood
to run from the water.
She returned, shy,
to stroke
the foam over the sand.
She began to walk into the water.
I ran. But,

in slow motion over the sand,
all that spread out before me
was the vast ashen blue.

Days

There are days when a pale, three-meal love
with its possibility of passion on turning off a night light
is worthless.
Days after you've arrived at your loneliness
by the short cut of trusted friends
and you fear becoming your own ventriloquist.
Days that from a single touch your apprehensive flesh will howl
and the indifferent floor cave in.
Bargain days,
when you'd sell yourself for any price.

When We Live

When we live
facing power on our knees
all the clocks' hands
point to only one place;
we stuff an owl into our eyes
and the biggest glass window
opens in our heart.
We make ourselves
tourists of life
and end up paying
the fare
in monthly installments
for all eternity.

Translated by Julio Marzán

Aníbal Yaryura-Tobías (Buenos Aires, Argentina, 1934) is a poet and short story writer who now resides in the United States. His book of poetry *Circular* was published in 1982. At present he is writing a nonfiction work titled *The Integral Being*, to be published by Holt, Rinehart and Winston. Recently he served as coeditor of the poetry magazine *Xanadu*.

The Voyeur

What a beautiful morning! he said to himself looking through his half-opened eyes beyond the window where the intensity of the blue sky enhanced the green of the old sycamore. At age nineteen, Georgi was beginning to put the pieces of his life into one single unit; walking toward manhood is not easy, primarily if there are not that many men around to imitate, he said to himself. He finally got up with an erected penis, and a lot of thinking from the night before. To see one's father dead is not a pleasant experience; to see one's father dying gives the most awful feeling of impotence and powerlessness that one remembers forever; but to see one's father jumping off a cliff, recording into one's retina the flying body, hearing and listening to his scream of repentance, it becomes a difficult memory to suppress.

Succinctly, it took Georgi seventeen years of his life to see his father do away with his job, his energy; a chronic suicidal who finally succeeded. When Georgi came downstairs, his mother was already gone. She had to be at the house of Mrs. Ibsen by seven o'clock. Mrs. Erika Ibsen was bedridden in her house at the top of the hill. A common house, in the Tudor style of yesterday, still surviving in this small town, along with its people and its past.

The pot of coffee was still hot; the bread was crusty and his appetite good. By the time he finished with his breakfast, the summer heat had begun to move into the house; but the day was magnificent, and the happiness of being alive today was enough to create a careless attitude about summers and heat waves.

He locked the door, and checked the knob twice to be sure that it really locked even if he used a double lock. It was nice to make mother jolly; a good reason to double-check. Little things like that were important for her, especially since his father's suicide. She still felt betrayed by him; a divorce could be talked over and then accepted, a natural death also; even if he walked off, she could take it, but a premeditated act of departure without previous notice? Never! He simply betrayed her; he broke the matrimonial contract, and he did it singlehanded! She was still angry at him, and why

302

shouldn't she be full of hate at that beast that left her a slave without a penny in the bank, a huge mortgage and a sycamore tree?—"Poor mother," Georgi said to himself, while checking the knob—if she knew what he knew of his father taking Mrs. Erika Ibsen from the wheelchair into the bed, slowly taking off her black lace dress to kiss her neck passionately; if she knew that Georgi saw his father's hands in continuous tremor removing all of Mrs. Erika Ibsen's clothes, and throwing them in a hurry on the carpeted floor, while he, Georgi, son, watched in ectasy how the limbs spoke silently in the evening, how the sweat invaded his own forehead while his imagination became his father's! Of course, it was not his fault if he looked through the window, because Georgi, then fifteen years old, was a chronic voyeur, a charming Peeping Tom who had ejaculated over the most important window sills that could be found in a town the size of his town.

When he crossed the threshold of the house, to his surprise he was able to see standing by the sycamore the figure of his father, with his tightened jaws, a piercing set of black eyes and his rocky body covered with a black overcoat. It was summer; it didn't matter; father was always in opposition to nature, to the ecological balance of life and death, so he had to wear an overcoat in the summer, as he did. He usually made the decisions, unfortunately, for others as well. Immediately, Georgi became frightened, and thought he was having visions. He closed his eyes; everyone closes his eyes to come back to reality, to check whether one is awake or not. So he did. But the sycamore and his father were still there; the intensity of the blue sky enhanced the green of the old sycamore that shaded his father's shade.

An irresistible impulse, maybe atavistic, forced him to move forward, towards his father, but no matter how many steps he took, the distance between his father and him remained the same. He turned his head to his right; the image blueskysycamorefather was still there; then he proceeded to turn to his left; the image was right in front of his eyes; he finally decided to turn completely around, because if he was still facing his father standing by the sycamore for sure he couldn't see all this blueskysycamorefather vision behind his back. And he did turn, and the image was there. The four cardinal points were a failure; either he was going crazy or a supernatural phenomenon was taking place. After that experience, reasoning became harder, for he was fearful, and later on, he became terrorized; he couldn't move and his bladder gave in; he cried softly. No matter where he turned, the same image of the blueskysycamorefather was there.

But Georgi was a teenager of logic, and finally he began to calm down, and he did so by sitting on the lawn. He arrived at the natural conclusion that everything was an illusion, a mirage, as in the desert, it was hot, so, why not? The best thing to do was to stand up and go back to the house to figure things out.

His eyelids were closed; therefore, it was a matter of opening them up to face whatever he was supposed to face. . . . The intensity of the blue sky enhanced the green of the old sycamore that shaded his father's shade, for the image as before was still in front of him. He tripped on the steps of the porch, and fell on his face; with a bloody nose and his heart beating fast, he managed to grab the keys from his coat pocket, and slowly, groping in the dark, he sought for the door.

August the third at 2 P.M., Georgi had an appointment with an oculist. He was blind, but it had to be confirmed by a professional. But Georgi did not want to go to an oculist; he couldn't believe that his sight was gone forever; he was a voyeur, the act of watching others, of secretly witnessing the loneliness of people, the way they eat when they are by themselves, the way they smell their armpits when they think no one can see them, what a pleasure to be there in the middle of the action without being there, to discover the shape of legs of people he knew, to find out about the color of their panties, that was fun; to omnipotently watch without being watched; like God, to be the witness of witnesses!

"Mother, I can't see, I can't open my eyes!", he would scream and moan over and over again the same pledge. But Georgi would open his eyes when he was alone in his bedroom and he could see the blue-skysycamorefather image in front of him. "Father? Would you talk to me?", but father wouldn't talk to him, as the sycamore did not move its branches and the sky did not change its color. For Georgi was not blind. Or was he?— He simply had that single image arrested in front of his eyes, stopped in the middle of time, a perpetual glance of one scene of his life.

The nurse told him to walk in; he did so accompanied by his mother, who held his arm. Formal questions were answered and finally the doctor began to examine Georgi's eyes. The eyes were examined with a powerful light, a pupil contraction would follow that, light was obviously registered. "Can you see the light, Georgi" the doctor would ask; "Yes, I see the sky brighter," he would respond.

"Do you mean the same image is still present?" the doctor would ask.

"Yes, doctor, it is present," Georgi's monotone voice would again affirm. His eyes were perfectly normal.

Doctor J. T. Morgan has been in the practice of ophthalmology for the last forty years; he was one of the best in his field, yet he never before had observed such a case. Late in the evening, he went home, and after supper, he went into his library to research the subject. . . . "The eye is the photo-receptive organ that although refined, only takes certain light information such as ultraviolet rays. The light receptors, called rods and cones, contain certain pigments that pick up an image; once the image is picked up, the pigments are destroyed, and that accounts for the absence of permanent images, which subsequently allows the formation of new ones in the retina." This is what Doctor Morgan read once again, for he obviously knew things like that, but for reassuring purposes, he wanted to read it again; he could not conceive that Georgi's rods and cones refused to destroy the image. He could not accept the apparent fact that Georgi has had the same image in front of him each time he opened his eyes; yet he had to admit evidence that no one could deny. The next step was to request a psychiatric examination of Georgi; maybe he was a hysterical personality. But Georgi's personality was not hysterical; he was a voyeur. But a voyeur is someone that obtains some form of sexual gratification by watching others perform a sexual act, or any other act related to sexuality. However, in addition, Georgi was a voyeur of people's intimacy; of people's lives, an activity not rare among people who become spectators rather than actors.

Georgi left the office. A hopeless case.

Days went by as usual, while Georgi became gradually accustomed to being blind without being blind, to use a white cane, to give primacy to his hearing, which became keen and helpful in this business of walking within one single image. He was condemned to the sight of the blue-skysycamorefather image, which remained undisturbed every time he opened his eyes. A month went by, and finally autumn arrived. To his wonder, the sycamore tree began to change colors; the sky was cloudy, and his father was wearing summer clothes, as usual, in opposition to nature. At first, he felt a shiver going through his spine, but it didn't last long; he was already used to the idea of his one-image life, although this change was stimulating, because for a voyeur the change of scenery is important. Thereafter, the image became seasonal. Furthermore, the image became old and his father interminably older.

Forty years later, things had changed considerably because after forty years, things do change a great deal; failures become excuses, hopes become faded memories; life is definitely shortened, and no one can do what wasn't done before. However, Georgi was there, older, but with his image, roaming the rooms of his house, while conceiving theater plays for his echoed monologues of every night of loneliness, frustration and sheer anger. By then, he was mute, since he had decided not to speak again, remaining silent, having only eyes and ears, although his eyes only tested the one vision: the blueskysycamorefather image.

A drought arrived, fields were scorched, animals were stripped of flesh, ribs became outstanding, drought and famine took a big share of lives, so many that common graves were rapidly dug. But Georgi couldn't see the dead, nor the living, yet he could feel the dryness of his throat, and understand his impotency to quench his thirst and placate his hunger.

In his image, the blue of the sky became gray, the tree began to shrink and all its leaves were gone, while his father, for the first time naked, had wrinkled as a dried fig. To his surprise, his father spoke, few words, but he spoke. Jacob spoke to his son Georgi, two words: "Free me," then he showed his wrists handcuffed and chained to a tree, while an almost featherless black bird was bringing a gigantic grape with a child's head inside, Georgi child, Georgi baby, Georgi to be born; and then his father swallowed the grape and the image became blurred and the rain poured down, and as expected, he didn't have a raincoat.

When the sun shone again, the blueskysycamorefather image was intact in front of his eyes, around his eyes, inside his breath, within his touch; he knew he had to kill the whole thing at once, without hesitation; an irrevocable act to be performed right there and then. He grabbed the shotgun, to become a parricide, to complete his blindness, to give away at last, his only image, sky, tree and resurrected father, and he aimed the gun with shaky hands and weakened knees.

Georgi lay widely spread by the door; his head was facing the sky, gushing blood was pouring from the place where his eyes used to be. Georgi's eyeballs, brown and intense, were looking at him from a distance. His own eyes were peeping at Georgi's death, but Georgi never knew about it, at least, for the time being.

Saúl Yurkievich (La Plata, Argentina, 1931) is a leading critic and poet who since 1969 has held the chair of literature at the University of Paris. As a critic he published *Founders of New Latin American Poetry*, 1973, and *Celebration of Modernism*, 1976. His verse collections include *Bodies (Cuerpos)*, 1965, among others.

Spaces

Cloistered in a room without windows,
suddenly, blindingly, it lights up.
And it is death.

A closed space. As one crosses it,
one stretches, without losing its mist.

Another, completely open. And one walks on
a floor that is not seen.

Of another one knows it is spherical, but its center is unknown,
as is the extension of its diameter.

Another is a cube without gravitation:
any face can be a floor, wall or ceiling.

In another, exclusively horizontal,
nothing nor anyone has depth.

Another where all is within.

Another where all is behind.

Another where all is descent.

Another where all is shrinkage.

Another revolves in another that revolves in another that
revolves in another that . . .

Another space is completely immobile: its distances
can only be established from a single point.

In another, nothing is a fragment. Points are inconceivable,
the same as an isolated line or any segment.

That space is where no straight line is possible.

That one where the curve does not exist.

The sinuous space where all straightness is only apparent
and where the shortest path is never found.

That one where concavity is unimaginable.

That one where immobility does not exist
or where the mobile cannot be differentiated from the immobile.

A space where all moves but nothing is displaced
or vice versa
or versa vice

A spiraled space where alternatively
rising is descending
or descending is rising
                    but one never knows when.
A space where everything is an edge.

An intermittent space.

A space where nothing is full
and where nothing is empty.

Or a space of uniform consistency.

A space where everything is one single body.

A space of completely homogeneous light.

A dark, empty, limitless space.

Perhaps Pursuit

Perhaps pursuit
or precipitously
                    you flee as the surprised lizard escapes
you crawl into the cracks of your walls
you flee
        as nails and hair grow on you tenaciously
        when I dream
                    my implication
                    my girding
you dream   hidden traps

where milked females ovulate
                        swelled they spawn
little animals   the beasts of the night
                   slippery
forays   cessations   incisions
mute mutation   shadowy mutation   mute
larval gestations   occur   concur
in the night of returns   of followings
between interstices   through interlinings
alternate intensity   groping
clotted corpuscles
    dissolved by aloes humors
    acid tides attack
    the consistency of signs
    the liquid liquidity   the rigid reserves
flotations
    misty vapor
steam of swamp ground
              spumes   your seguidilla
    roots grow thick and die implanted
    stir of auguring birds
    some sudden flash
                   lightning
in the heavens of your dream
through the treacherous air dreamed air is interned
the fugitive flow of your visible
time swims in your nothingness
a glance back   intermittent
when you rest   when there sets
on your bow dream that evanesces
that diffuses
             the pulsating gust
your firm dough unties its clusters
opens the mists   you open to chance   to pursuit
other nadirs   uncertain passages
another zenith   unexpected crossing   pulses
scattering of scintilla
                on errant paths
to remit you, to return you to the vertigo
to the recommencement   to the turbulent
eclipse of the marks   marks
you rig your sails   you cross
adrift   black lagoon   long passage of shadows
       river of lymphs   lactescent wakes
ebbs   eddies   whirlpools
             aerating you and burying you
             sinking you and inflaming you
the word is extinguished   it ceases   it is unheeded

lips move
hoarse throats   mute theater
a parade is perceived   a wheel
                              and you are seen
nebulous passage   every so often a certain neatness
flock of birds
                    the wind hisses between the leaves
                              its stupidity
the crickets make their castanets clack
furiously   the crickets
clack their castanets calling
faces of yore
hidden presences   scanned
figurations
the knots of destiny   madness
your abominations   world
larvae reaching their plenitude
                              they grow wings
they flutter   they pass   and are lost
carnivorous plants   silently
                    await you   watch you
soporiferous corollas
                    close and swallow
deep bells keep
                    absorbed covers
résumés
                    are lodged in your enclosure
                              in your sore
trunks of burned turpentine
the pith of fire rises
to inflame treetop
to inflame you
night grows quiet and falls into a lethargy
latitude dilating
                    under your eyelid
emanations   vague vapor
bodies melt and sink
the sockets of the eyes are hollowed and faces fall
in drops like melting food
the oozing blindness
                    heavy with imminences
great clouds of elytra
crumblings
caking together   drying out
fragile covers
the flow of serums   the watery swell
concentration and disbandment
fecund swamp and sterile dry land

the wind sweeps swirls
pollen is scattered through the vastness
occurrence   concurrence   incidence   coincidence
occur   you occur   cease   you cease   they repeat you
undetainable   uncontainable
    they go to their perdition

Translated by Wayne H. Finke

Raúl Zurita (Santiago, Chile, 1951) is one of the new generation poets whose collection *Purgatory (Purgatorio)* appeared in 1979. His latest endeavor is *Anteparadise (Anteparaíso)*, 1982, featuring poems of which some were spectacularly written in the skies over New York City by skywriting planes.

Pastorale

All of Chile is a desert
its plains have changed and its rivers
are drier than stones
There is not a soul walking through its streets
and only evil
seemed to be found everywhere.

Ah! if only you stretched your arms to me
the stones would dissolve on seeing you!*

Pastorale of Chile

Chile is covered with shadows
the valleys are burnt, the bramble has grown
and in place of newspapers and magazines
only black bands† are seen on the corners
All have left
or are asleep, even you yourself
who until yesterday were awake
today you are sleeping, in Universal Mourning.

Splendor in the Wind

The whole village
saw them, unrecountable, splendor in the wind

Swept by light the feet of that crowd hardly seemed to brush the ground

---

*These three poems appear with kind authorization: Raúl Zurita, *Anteparadise* (Berkeley and Los Angeles: University of California Press, 1982).
†The wearing of a black armband on one sleeve is a traditional symbol of mourning.

Approaching in small groups as though the wind
were pushing them from behind like leaves
touched on the mouth till they erupted in a single voice
singing to their blood pulsating within them

pricking the hollows of their eyes to see if it was
not a dream carrying them   looking higher
from where the crowd of their brothers emerged
to greet them   with open arms as if a
brief flight of light dragged them along singing towards them

But listen   if you do not come from a poor section of Santiago
it is difficult for you to understand me   You would know nothing of
     the life
we lead   Look it is without breath   It is madness   It is ripping
     oneself to shreds for
     but a minute of happiness

Utopias

   i. The whole desert could have been Notre Dame but it was Chile's
      desert
  ii. All the beaches could have been Chartres but they were only Chile's
      beaches
 iii. All of Chile could have been Our Lady of Santiago
      but arid, these landscapes were only the
      evanescent Chilean landscapes

Where the inhabitants of Chile could not be Chile's inhabitants but a Plea
        that was lifting them to touch the sky that they looked at
        sweet   blushing   showing through as though no one had fixed
        them in their stares
  iv. For the sky could not be the sky but they
      themselves   celestial   covering so easily the arid landscapes
      they saw
   v. Those must have been the sweet inhabitants of Chile
      silent   squatting   peopling themselves are
      the chapels of their Plea
  vi. They themselves could then have been the populated chapels of
      Chile

Where Chile could not be the landscapes of Chile but, yes, the blue sky
they looked at and the landscapes would have been then a Plea unending
that escapes from their lips like a breath of all
the homeland making a type of love that would people their heights
 vii. Chile will be then a love peopling our heights
viii. Even the blind will see there the jubilant ascent of their Plea

ix. All silent   we will then see the whole
    firmament rise   limpid   illuminated   like a
    beach extending to us the starry love of the homeland

Translated by Wayne H. Finke

TRANSLATORS

MAUREEN AHERN is a professor of Latin American Literature in the Department of Spanish at Arizona State University. She has translated the poetry of Rosario Castellanos into English, as well as Peruvian poets—among others, Antonio Cisneros.

JANET BROF lives in Mexico City, where she writes short stories and poetry. Her verse has appeared in *Aphra* and *The New York Quarterly;* her stories were published in the *Kansas Quarterly* and *El Cuento, Mexico.* She coedited *Doors and Mirrors: An Anthology of Spanish American Fiction and Poetry, 1972–1973.*

PAMELA CARMEL has an M.F.A. degree from the University of Arkansas' creative writing program. Some of Ms. Carmell's translations have appeared in *Nimrod, Intro-14* and *International Poetry Review.*

JOHN CHANDO was graduated from Fordham University with a major in French and Spanish. After completing his M.B.A. at Hofstra University, he entered banking and is currently a Vice President in the International Division of Manufacturers Hanover Trust Company, New York. He has traveled to Mexico, Argentina, Panama and Venezuela.

JEANNE COOK was born in Burke, South Dakota, and raised in North Platte, Nebraska. She was educated at the University of Nebraska and the University of Massachusetts. Her current studies at Indiana University and Notre Dame concentrate on medieval literature, particularly Old English. Her own poetry has appeared in the *Malahat Review* (University of Victoria, British Columbia, Canada) and *december* (Chicago, Illinois).

WAYNE H. FINKE is an Assistant Professor of Spanish at Baruch College (CUNY). His Ph.D. dissertation at New York University provided the first study of the pioneering medieval criticism of the Catalonian critic Manuel Milá y Fontanals and is due to appear shortly. He has written extensively on this important XIX century critic, and has done work on García Lorca and on onomastics. He was recently elected Executive Secretary-Treasurer of the American Name Society. He coedited the Winter 1980 issue of *The Literary Review:*"Latin American Literature, the 60's and 70's."

DIANE J. FORBES is a graduate student in Spanish at Pennsylvania State University, where she is preparing her Ph.D. thesis on the poetry of the

Mexican writer Manuel Maples Arce. She has published studies on Arce's work in *Rimas y Palabras, Hispanófila* and *Los escritores y la experiencia de la ciudad moderna.* She is currently on the faculty of Penn State.

KIM GEROULD is a writer, translator, and teacher of adult education in the Boston area.

JENNIE IBARRA was born in La Serena, Chile, in 1960, of Basque descent, but has lived in New York for the past nineteen years. A graduate of Queens College in 1984, she is at present with the law firm of Stroock, Stroock and Levan in Manhattan. She is preparing a prologue titled "On Cuban Poetry" to be included in an anthology of cross-cultural poetry.

ANTHONY KERRIGAN was born in Boston and raised in Cuba. He has taught at the University of Illinois and SUNY Buffalo and is currently at Notre Dame University, where he is Senior Guest Scholar in the Kellogg Institute for International Studies. He won the National Book Award in 1975 for his work on the Spanish writer Miguel de Unamuno, and was editor, translator and annotator for the seven-volume edition of *The Selected Works of Miguel de Unamuno* (Princeton: 1967–1984). Having translated over fifty books, he recently published a new edition of Ortega y Gassett's *The Revolt of the Masses,* 1984, with his new translation, annotations and introduction.

BARRY J. LUBY, a Professor of Spanish at John Jay College (CUNY), received his Ph.D. at New York University. He is the author of *Unamuno a la luz del empirismo lógico contemporáneo* and *Maimonides and Spinoza: Their Sources, Cosmological Metaphysics and Impact on Modern Thought and Literature.* His published works also include several anthologies and articles on Spanish and Latin American literature as well as articles on Sephardic philosophy and culture. He edited *The Literary Review's* Spanish issue and coedited the Latin American issue. He is currently writing a book titled *Unamuno in the Light of XX Century Thought.*

JULIO MARZÁN was born in Puerto Rico in 1946. A poet and translator he has published *Inventing a Word: An Anthology of XXth Century Puerto Rican Poetry* with Columbia University Press; his book of verse, *Translations with Originals,* appeared in 1985.

RAIMUNDO MORA was born in Colombia, South America, and studied at New York University. He is currently an administrator and teacher at Solidaridad Hispana where he coordinates the Advanced Education Program. His translations have appeared in the volume *Guatemala in Rebellion: Unfinished History,* 1983.

MARC NASDOR was born in 1958 in Baltimore, Maryland. A poet and graphic artist, he has served as Program Director of the Committee for International Poetry, and Coordinator of the Monday Night Reading and Performance Series at The Poetry Project (St. Mark's Church). His poems have appeared in many East Coast literary magazines, and translations have been published in *The World* and in *The Festival of International Poetry:*"Latinoamerica" (May, 1983).

JOHN NEYENESCH was born in southern California and did his undergraduate work at Stanford. After serving in the Peace Corps in Colombia for two years, he came to New York and, in 1975, received a doctorate in Latin American literature from New York University. In addition to translating the poems of Roberto Echavarren, he has published an article on Julio Cortázar and an interview with Colombian artist José Urbach. He lives in New York and teaches at the Fashion Institute of Technology.

ROBERTO-SELIM PICCIOTTO was born in Argentina in 1939 but resides in New York City. He is a novelist and translator and teaches Spanish at Queens College.

MARÍA PITA is a young American poet and translator, the daughter of the writer Juana Rosa Pita. She is a student of Egyptology and has recently published a book of prose poetry titled *Fragments for a Papyrus*.

GREGORY RABASSA was born in New York and grew up in New Hampshire. After graduation from Dartmouth College, he earned a Ph.D. in Portuguese at Columbia University. He is currently on the faculty of Queens College and the Graduate School of CUNY. His many translations of novels by Julio Cortázar, Gabriel García Márquez and Luis Rafael Sánchez, among others, have earned him universal prestige and national honors, such as the National Book Award, the PEN Translation Award and the PEN-Gulbenkian Prize.

EUGENE RICHIE holds an M.F.A. in poetry and translation from Columbia University and an M.A. in Comparative Literature from New York University. His poems and translations from the Spanish have appeared in literary magazines and books in the United States. At present, he teaches English at Pace University in New York City.

ELIAS L. RIVERS was born in Charleston, South Carolina, and completed graduate studies at Yale University with a Ph.D. on Spanish Golden Age poetry. One of the world's leading Hispanists, he has been on the faculties of Ohio State University, The Johns Hopkins University and the University of California at Berkeley. He is currently Chairman of Hispanic Studies at SUNY at Stony Brook. Among his principal publications are his editions of the poetry of Garcilaso de la Vega and Dámaso Alonso, as well as studies on Renaissance and Baroque poetry of Spain and on Don Quixote.

CATHERINE ROVIRA was born in New York City of Puerto Rican and Dominican parents, and at present teaches at John Jay College. She has published short stories of her own, *The Stroll (El paseo)* and *A Vacation (Unas vacaciones)*, and has translated the poetry of Dominican women writers for Brooklyn College Press.

HARDIE ST. MARTIN is a professional translator and editor whose publications include *Roots and Wings,* an anthology of contemporary Spanish poetry, and Pablo Neruda's *Memoirs.*

LINDA SCHEER was born in Brooklyn, New York. Her translations have appeared in literary magazines and newspapers in the United States and Mexico. She is cotranslator and coeditor of *Poetry of Transition: Mexican Poetry of the 70's* (Ardis, 1984), as well as cotranslator of *Rome, Danger to Pedestrians* by Rafael Alberti(*Quarterly Review of Literature,* 1984).

AMALIA SIMPSON is a Ph.D. candidate in the Department of Spanish and Portuguese at the University of Texas at Austin. She is at present writing her dissertation on the Latin American detective novel, and she also writes poetry.

JOAN L. SMUCKER was educated at Grinnell College and Harvard University. She is a professor of English, freelance writer and translator, currently on the staff of the University of the District of Columbia.

EDWARD J. SULLIVAN received his Ph.D. from New York University, where he teaches fine arts. At present he is working on a study of the interrelationship between Spanish painters and writers in the nineteenth century.

BRIAN SWANN is a graduate of Queens' College, Cambridge, England, and holds a Ph.D. from Princeton University. At present he is on the faculty of The Cooper Union, New York City. His poetry and fiction have appeared in many anthologies and journals, including *The New Yorker, Poetry, Paris Review, Yale Review, Antioch Review* and *Kenyon Review.* He has recently published *The Middle of the Journey* (University of Alabama Press, 1982).

DONALD WALSH was born in Providence, Rhode Island. A graduate from Harvard University, he taught for many years at the Choate School in Wallingford, Connecticut. Editor of the journal *Hispania* from 1949 until 1957, he became one of the most respected translators of Spanish and Spanish American poetry. Among his translations are *Residence on Earth* of Pablo Neruda (New Directions, 1973) and *Poems in Correspondence (from Jail)* by Angel Cuadra (Ediciones Solar, 1979). Juana Rosa Pita's *Sea Behind Bars* and *Manual of Magic* are his posthumous works.

Index of Authors